MAFIA AND MAFIOSI: THE STRUCTURE OF POWER

Mafia and Mafiosi:
The Structure of Power

HENNER HESS

Translated from the German by
EWALD OSERS

SAXON  HOUSE | LEXINGTON BOOKS

First published in 1970 as Mafia: Zentrale Herrschaft und lokale Gegenmacht
© Henner Hess
J. C. B. Mohr (Paul Siebeck) Tübingen 1970

Published by
SAXON HOUSE, D. C. Heath Ltd.
Westmead, Farnborough, Hants, England

Jointly with
LEXINGTON BOOKS, D. C. Heath & Co.
Lexington, Mass. U.S.A.

ISBN 0 347 01008 3
LC No. 73–3960
Printed in The Netherlands by D. Reidel Book Manufacturers, Dordrecht

Contents

Foreword

In the behavioural sciences, as in historical and classical studies, there are few final answers. Facts are not 'out there' to be unearthed, found, discovered, stumbled upon. Rather, what is fact depends upon context. Facts in one time, place or setting are not facts in another. It is not only that changing social contexts produce new interpretations of old data. More basically, social facts are always a fusion of data, context and interpretation.

This means, among other things, that in sociology there always is room for improvement. No important issue is settled once and for all. No riddles of theory are unravelled to the satisfaction of all theoreticians. No problem has a final solution. There are no technological inventions that change the course of history, and no Nobel Prize 'breakthroughs' that change the course of science.

But where there is room for improvement there is room for creativity. Occasionally—perhaps once in a decade—there comes a sociological book that makes a difference because it lets the reader know that a new set of facts has been negotiated out. It is more a matter of beauty than of science. After you have read the book, the patterns of the social world or some part of it seem clearer, the colours brighter, the smells and tastes and sounds sharper.

Those rare volumes that truly make new sense of a broad range of social patterns become sociological classics—the works of Durkheim, Marx, Weber. Other books, ordering a narrower range, become benchmarks for certain sociological specialties—William F. Whyte's *Street Corner Society*. And still others, attacking more particular problems of social order, become 'classics in their field'. *The Mafia: Central Rule Against Local Power* is one of these.

I struggled through the German edition of this book, published in 1970. Books dealing with its subject matter abound. Some are whole-cloth fabrications. Some are biographies or autobiographies of involved criminals. Some are policemen's or prosecutors' gang buster stories. Some are carefully documented historical or sociological monographs. Most are mixtures of all these. It was a pleasant surprise, therefore, to find a 'Mafia book' that made the patterns clear, the colours sharp. In a little book on criminal organisation published in London a year ago, I pronounced Henner Hess' book 'among the best of some two hundred books on the Sicilian Mafia'.

In truth, however, my limited knowledge of the German language restricted my perception. I really was not positive that I had read what I thought I had read. It was a delight, therefore, to learn from this English-language edition that I was not mistaken. This is truly a magnificent piece of work.

There are many things that make the book a significant one. It is well written. It is beautifully documented. There are many good stories and reasonable accounts. It casts new light on what American criminals call 'right guys', 'stand-up guys', 'wiseguys'. No 'real man' is going to have a fly dancing on his nose.

The book lets us clearly see that criminal behaviour springs in part from the very efforts of political authorities and others to prevent it, control it, repress it. Moreover, official hearings and enquiries produce both pride and respect when they identify Mafia Dons as Dons: 'Make yourself famous and lie back and relax.'

Dr. Hess demonstrates the disastrous consequences to the poor and powerless of the historic shift from status to 'free contract' in economic and legal affairs, so long ago discussed by Sir Henry Maine. He lets us witness the advantages to lawyers and others of the ability to claim 'connections' even if none exist. However, he also reminds us that every criminal corrupter has a counterpart in a political corruptee. He makes us understand that the world of organised crime is not so different from the weird world of legitimate government and business after all.

Most importantly, I think, the book teaches us to distinguish between *an* organisation and organisation. Dr. Hess does not use these words, but he makes the distinction nevertheless. 'An organisation' (*e.g.*, the Mafia) implies membership, offices, a hierarchy of authority. 'Organisation' (*e.g., mafia), on the other hand, implies understandings, common methods, parallelisms.

Organisation often is obvious even when there is no evidence of *an* organisation. But in discussing organisation we often go wrong because we find it necessary to use 'the' in phrases such as 'the establishment', 'the military-industrial complex', 'the police'. By using 'the' we create more structure than we know exists. We transform organisation into an organisation.

This book most beautifully documents how mafia organisation in Sicily developed, persisted and gathered power despite the absence of a Mafia. Each mafioso personage operates in specifiable ways and maintains a network of relationships. Violence, threat of violence, and fear of violence are the cement that holds the network together. In a village or territory, the location of deference, respect, honour, fear, and other manifestations of power has become predictable. This is organisation. But a way of life neither reflects nor anticipates the existence of a Mafia apparatus with inducted members, a division of labour and a hierarchical pattern of authority.

DONALD R. CRESSEY
Santa Barbara, California
15 February, 1973

Preface to the English Edition

Presidente: Non facevate parte della mafia?
Imputato Mini: Non so che significa.
(Processo Amoroso)

Unlike the defendant Mini most people have a fairly accurate idea of what Mafia means—a secret society with criminal aims, centralised, strictly directed, with initiation rites and statutes. After all, they have been fully informed on the subject by the specialised literature as well as by the daily press, in 'who-dunits' and sensational novels, and by thriller series on television.

But anyone taking the trouble to examine the facts and trace back the string of secondary and tertiary sources will arrive at a totally different picture. He will reach the conclusion, as I have done in the course of my work, that the defendant Mini probably was not lying when, in reply to the question whether he was a member of the Mafia, he replied: *Non so che significa*—'I don't know what that means'. True, he knew individuals whom he called 'mafiosi'; not because they were members of a secret society but because they acted in a certain way, a *mafioso* way.

This thesis is based mainly on my most important source material, the archives of police reports and trial transcripts which contain nothing about 'the mafia' but a great deal about individual *mafiosi*. Unfortunately the only documents accessible in Sicilian archives are those deposited at least seventy years ago, but even so the period examined, from 1880 to 1890, provided all the vital information on this most interesting classical period of the *mafiosi*. These documents had not then been considered by any author. They served me as a criterion for judging the subsequent literature and as the basis of the description I have given in this book of the person of the *mafioso,* the structure of *mafioso* groupings and the functions of *mafioso* behaviour.

The word *mafia* itself should be used with care, since the mere use of the concept suggests the idea of a big organisation behind it. Most of the wrong interpretations of *mafioso* behaviour have their origin in this false premise. Wherever I have used the word *mafia* it stands merely as an alternative for 'mafioso behaviour' and is designed solely to characterise a certain type of action.

The juxtaposition, which I have emphasized in my book, of *mafioso* groupings on the one hand and the organs of the State on the other, has run into some criticism. I do in fact now believe that I have spoken too often of 'the State' as an abstract entity above party groupings. This applies mainly to the final chapter. To avoid misunderstanding I would therefore like to emphasise that every State obviously has a certain class content; i.e. that the State machinery is operated in the interest of a definite class. Where this State machinery is too weak as a governmental instrument or where conflict exists within the ruling class—both these conditions applied to Sicily—part of the ruling class can seek support from extra-State means of power, illegal ones in the juridical sense, such as *mafioso cosche*. This does not mean that there must be a conflict in the sociological sense between State and *mafia*; the two may supplement each other in their objectives and in fact have done so often enough.

I should also like to offer a warning against an undifferentiated view of a strong State as a cure for *mafioso* crimes. True, the Fascist dictatorship succeeded in breaking the power of the *mafiosi* but in doing so it most brutally practised itself all those forms of extra-economic coercion which accompany the system of class rule and exploitation. Thus the Fascist State offered to the ruling class of Sicily an alternative to *mafioso* methods, one which might be superior to it in effectiveness, for instance, in suppressing the organised peasant movement.

Similarly the increasingly fascist methods of the American police in their struggle against crime syndicates must not, without further discussion, be excused by the increasing violence and power of its opponent. The truth is that the struggle between the two sides is only a pseudo-conflict, to be seen as thesis and antithesis within one comprehensive entity—they are both determined by the same pattern of a social system based on exploitation and the pursuit of profit.

A strong State therefore is meaningful only if it combines the struggle against crime with a struggle against its social causes, if it becomes an instrument of consistent social reform. The heroin trade, for instance, cannot be successfully suppressed by the use of ever more cunning or brutal methods against the crime syndicates but only by the removal of those conditions which drive the consumers to escape into drug addiction. The same applies, *mutatis mutandis,* to Sicilian society.

It is a great pleasure to me that my book now also appears in English translation. I hope that it will prove a useful contribution to scholarly discussion.

HENNER HESS
Heidelberg, 1972

1 Etymological Note

The word *mafia* exists in the Florentine dialect in the sense of 'povertà' or 'miseria'. A cognate word is the Piedmontese 'mafiun', meaning an 'uomo piccino', a little or petty person.[1]

The meaning of the word as used in Sicily is very different from the two meanings above. It is first found in a document of 1658, in a list of heretics who re-embraced the faith at a solemn ceremony in Palermo (elenco dei riconciliati dall'Atto di Fede). The word is used as a nickname after the name of a witch: 'Catarina la Licatisa, Nomata ancor Maffia', and here has the meaning of boldness, ambition and arrogance.[2] Pitré and Capuana record the word in a similar meaning in the Palermo dialect 250 years later. Especially in the suburb of Borgo, which until 1880 was separated from the city proper, *mafia* meant as much as 'bellezza, baldanza, orgoglio, graziosità, perfezione, eccellenza'. A pretty girl, for example, 'ha della mafia'; she is 'mafiusa' or 'mafiusedda'. A neat little house can be 'una casa mafiusa' or also 'una casa ammafiata'. Fruit and pottery were advertised by street vendors as 'mafiusi' and brooms were sold with the cry of 'Haju scupi d'a mafia! Haju chiddi mafiusi veru!'. Used in connection with a man, these attributes referred chiefly to his superiority, to his manliness; the word was synonymous with 'superiorità, sicurtà d'animo, coscienza di esser uomo'.[3]

> A *mafioso* is simply a courageous, brave fellow who won't stand any nonsense from anyone.[4]

The origin of the Palermo word, however, remains uncertain. Several authors derive it from the Arabic—either from 'mahias', meaning a bold man or a braggart, or from 'Ma afir', the name of the Saracen tribe that ruled Palermo. A third theory of Arab origin relates *mafia* to 'maha', a quarry or a cave in a rock. The 'mafie', the tuff caves in the Marsala region, served the persecuted Saracens as hiding places and later provided hide-outs for other fugitives.[5] A slightly far-fetched variant of this theory is put forward by Loschiavo: prior to Garibaldi's landing, he suggests, the rebellious Sicilians had hidden out in the *mafie* near Marsala and had therefore subsequently, during their successful advance on Palermo, been called *mafiosi*, the people from the *mafie*. In the course of time the word had come to be used as an adjective, meaning 'outstanding, manly, handsome' and had kept this meaning in popular speech.[6]

Some Arabic origin at least seems plausible. Until the second half of the nineteenth century the word was then used in the meaning of 'eccellenza' and 'perfezione' and 'baldanza'—meanings which continue to echo in the word *mafia* to this day. Of more recent origin is its other colouring, suggesting 'malavita' and 'associazione a delinquere'. When Pietro Ulloa, the Procuratore Generale of Trapani, in his report to the Naples Ministry of Justice refers to typical *mafioso* behaviour and undeniable *mafioso* groupings, he still did not use the word *mafia* but spoke of 'unioni o fratellanze, specie di sette, che dicono partiti'.[7] Thirty years later the word *mafia* was in common use to describe these phenomena. Its spread is attributed to a comedy by Rizzotti and Mosca, which had its première in the Palermo dialect in 1862 and scored a sensational success throughout Italy during the next few years. This *dramma folcloristico* 'I mafiusi della Vicaria' describes scenes from the prison of Palermo; the principal characters enjoy a particular respect among their fellow prisoners and are in a position to impose on them norms of behaviour because they are members of an association with definite usages (among others, initiation rites) and a graded hierarchy. They are the 'camorristi' for whom here the term *mafiusi* is used as an alternative name for the first time. It is claimed that the titles were suggested by Mosca, a Sicilian schoolmaster, after he had heard in Palermo the exclamation: 'Chi vurrissi fari u mafiusu cu mía?' (Are you trying to play the boss with me?).[8]

It is of some importance to note that reference in the play is invariably to *mafiosi* but not to any *mafia*. The organisation exists only in vague hints and then—as in the comedy just mentioned—is used for the 'camorra', the organisation that was known from Naples, and there mainly in the prisons.

Nevertheless, the term gained currency and first appeared in official language in 1865. In a letter of 10 August, 1865, the *delegato di Pubblica Sicurezza* in Carini justifies an arrest by the charge that the arrested man had committed the 'delitto di mafia'. Filippo Gualterio, the Prefect of Palermo at the time, then likewise used the word in his report to the Minister of the Interior.[9]

Gradually the 'delitto di mafia' came to mean more the offence of 'manutengolo', of being a fence or planner of crimes, and not so much the offence of 'malandrino', of banditry, of being an executant criminal. Eventually the word *mafia* was used, above all, for organised crime, until sensation-hungry journalists, confused North Italian jurists and foreign authors interpreted it as the name of an organisation. The emergence of the word was linked with the emergence of a secret society and thus gave rise to fantastic speculations.

The theory which assigns the greatest antiquity to this society suggests that *mafia* is a corruption of the Arabic word 'mu afah', in which 'mu' means something like 'inviolability, strength, vigour' and 'afah' something like 'to secure, to protect'. 'Mu afah' had therefore been an association which provided security for its members.[10]

Other authors date the origin of the *mafia* back to the days of the Sicilian

Vespers (1282). It had been an association of nationally minded men, and its name was an acronym of its slogan 'Morte alla Francia, Italia anela!'[11] (Death to France, Italy groans.)

Others, applying the same principles, see *mafia* as the name of a secret sect whose head is said to have been Mazzini. The name is seen as an acronym of the slogan: 'Mazzini autorizza furti, incendi, avvelenamenti'[12] (Mazzini authorises theft, arson, poisoning.) And finally the *mafia* was seen as a secret masonic society, said to have been founded by five men in Mazara del Vallo in 1799.[13]

About 1875 the concept of *mafia* penetrated also into German, French and English. At that time the public was absorbed and excited by a parliamentary debate of special measures designed to restore public safety in Sicily, measures proposed by the Minghetti government. In 1891 came the murder of the police lieutenant Hennesy and the lynching of a group of Sicilian convicts in New Orleans jail; in 1899 the Notarbartolo trial took place; in 1912 the assassination of the American police agent Petrosino in Palermo; in 1927 Mori's activities; about 1950 the bandit Giuliano; in 1951 the Kefauver Report; and in 1957 the arrest of sixty-five Italian-American gangsters at Appalachin in New York State, to name but a few highlights. Fantastic as some theories about 'the mafia' may be, their continued currency is readily explained by the powerful need to find explanations for all the incidents listed and for many others. Ignorance of Sicilian conditions then leads to the transposition of familiar patterns. (Cf. ch. 5, §4.)

Notes

[1] Cf. Novacco 1959, p. 207

[2] Cf. Sciascia 1964 (Appunti), p. 3

[3] Cf. Capuana 1902, pp. 89–90

[4] Pitré 1889, p. 287. The original quotations will be found in the Appendix under the same number as these notes

[5] Cf. Lestingi 1884, p. 362

[6] Cf. Loschiavo 1964, pp. 30–1 and 170–1. The report of an actual participant, however, contains not a single word in support of this hypothesis. Cf. Dumas n.d.

[7] Cf. Pietro Ulloa's letter (3 August, 1838) in Pontieri 1945, pp. 190 ss.

[8] Cf. Novacco 1959, p. 208. The text of the comedy is printed in Loschiavo 1964, pp. 242–389. An adaptation (libero adattamento) by Leonardo Sciascia, which puts greater emphasis on the relations between *mafiosi* and politicians and which concludes with a satire on the *mafioso*'s view of himself, has been traced by the author as an acting manuscript only of the Piccolo Teatro of Milan

[9] Cf. Novacco: *Bibliografia della mafia* in *Nuovi quaderni del meridione* 1964, p. 201 and Novacco 1963, pp. 147–8

[10] Cf. Candida 1960, p. 56

[11] Cf. Reid 1952, p. 12

[12] Cf. *Enciclopedia Universale Illustrata*, Milan 1954, vol. xiii p. 532. The interpretation of a word as an acronym was natural at a time when the walls of houses in Austrian-dominated Venetia frequently carried the inscription *Verdi* as an abbreviation for *Vittorio Emanuele Re d'Italia*. Cf. Hofstätter 1963, p. 244

[13] Cf. Petrai 1900

2 Brigantaggia-Ladrismo-Mafia

Both in everyday language and in historical and journalistic literature 'mafiosi' are distinguished from 'banditi', 'briganti' or 'malandrini' and both these groups are set apart from the 'ladri'. A close examination of the facts shows that this classification is also necessary for the sociologist. It is important, above all, not to confuse *mafioso* groupings with groups of bandits. Some authors have used these terms indiscriminately, rendering the consequent understanding of these two phenomena more difficult.

Banditry illustrates a criminological theory which does not confine itself to explaining, by its own definition, a criminal course of action in terms of biological, psychological and sociological categories, but which includes in its examination also the definition and those who do the defining. A social action may be described as a crime by the ruling stratum of a society because it is directed against its rule. Positive law as an instrument of government and as an expression of the norms defined by the ruling stratum label such action as banditry. The same course of action, however, may be seen in a totally different light from the norms of another social stratum; e.g. the peasantry or of a colonially overlaid sub-culture. The so-called bandit may be acting in complete conformity with these norms and, for that very reason, clash with the overlying legal system. From this point of view, life as a bandit and being on the run are then the logical consequences of such a clash. The bandit, therefore, can be reintegrated in his old group because for this group he is not morally an outsider and can therefore lead the life of an ordinary citizen[1]—provided, of course, he has not first fallen victim, as is usually the case, to the ruling group's machinery of sanctions.

In every brigand there is a revolutionary. Admittedly, in the historical bandit of peasant origin the revolutionary intention usually remains unconscious or, at best, is articulated by the ideas of traditional revolt, by a subjective understanding directed not against the system but against persons who merely seem to have corrupted a system regarded as good. Conversely, movements which lead an entirely deliberate struggle against the established order, justifying this struggle rationally on grounds of natural or historical law, are customarily defined as bandits by the ruling power. To the organs of justice in the Latin American countries the *guerilleros* are bandits. Analagous cases would be the Sinn Fein, the maquis, the Haganah, the Mau Mau, etc.

Our analysis will presently show that *mafia* and *brigantaggio* must be seen, in principle, as antagonistic phenomena since *mafia* is a special method for the consolidation of ruling positions. True, *mafiosi* and bandits may enter into

5

symbiotic relationships. Between 1944 and 1950, when the largely unculti-vated feudal estates of inland Western Sicily were threatened with seizure by the peasants and when numerous well-known *mafiosi* were appointed *gabellotti* by the owners, five bandit gangs in the provinces of Palermo, Agrigento and Caltanissetta were in the service of this alliance. Their task was to deter the peasants, by violence, from seizing those lands. Giuliano, the most famous Sicilian bandit of this most recent post-war era, also temporarily worked for Conservative Party groupings; for instance at Portella delle Ginestre, where he turned a peasant May Day rally into a bloodbath. (Incidentally, when Giuliano felt disillusioned by his employers he later turned against them.) [2]

There are, in consequence, instances of such a crossing-over from 'peasant bandit' to 'landlord's bandit', as Hobsbawn would call it.[3] But it hardly seems helpful to describe the so-called 'landlord's bandits' as bandits at all. Perhaps they should be counted as belonging to the 'bassa mafia' in view of their functional relations with the holders of positions of power.

The classic bandit of the Robin Hood pattern, as found in Sicily, requires some further characterisation:

(1)   The reasons for his embarking on his career are numerous. They may be sub-divided into:

(a)   the need to excape capture by the State's enforcement machinery follow-ing the commission of deeds in accordance with his sub-cultural norms. This includes men who have restored their family honour by drastic means, who have committed murder from passion, who have shot a policeman or killed someone in the course of blood vengeance, but it also includes less serious offenders, such as smugglers or persons sentenced to a fine for some offence or other and unable to pay it. An important part in the choice of this solution to the conflict of norms is played by family tradition and the possible exis-tence of blood relations in bandit groups;

(b)   escaped convicts on the run;

(c)   fear of persecution threatening casual participants after one of the many revolts;

(d)   the desire to avenge injustices suffered; these may have been inflicted on the fugitive by the State (sentence in a trial, excessive taxes, etc.) or perhaps by the employer (with holding of wages);

(e)   after 1860 the disillusionment of former Garibaldi followers and also dissatisfaction of former Bourbon soldiers, or the inability of either to return to civilian life. This cause became important again after 1918 and 1943;

(f)   the wish to avoid military service; this resulted in mass flight chiefly in 1818, in 1862–3 and during the First World War.

(2)   The bandit must conform as closely as possible to the Robin Hood pattern. He is a victim of the enemies of the peasant; he fights these enemies and protects the peasants, he robs the rich to give to the poor. He is a good man in the sense of peasant morality, chivalrous, a 'cavaliere', and kills only in self-defence.[3a]

> The legend of the beneficent brigand is handed down from generation to generation. There is no gang leader of any importance who has not used the opportunity of equipping some poor girl with a dowry or of paying a peasant's debts, or of publicly reproving one of his subordinates for having robbed a poor muleteer and forcing him to return what he had stolen.[4]

He will frequently maintain close contact with his family and usually therefore operates in the vicinity of his native village. The framework of his life is the dual morality which will be discussed more closely in the following chapter. The regions of strictest *omertà* are also those of greatest bandit activity; reports as early as 1838 chiefly name the Provinces of Palermo, Trapani and Girgenti, and matters remained much the same until Giuliano. An important part is also played by the mistress, or the mistresses, of the bandit. In winter, when the gangs are temporarily dissolved, but when life with one's own family would be too dangerous, the brigands find asylum with these women. The *Giornale di Sicilia* had this to say of Salvatore Salpietra on 10 September 1878:

> The armed gangs invariably move into winter quarters in the following manner: the gang leader dismisses his subordinates who disperse, each man to his region and to his hideout. The gang leader does not disclose to anyone the place to which he is retiring, and he honours with his presence, in turn, one of his fair ones at Alia, Ciminna and Montemaggiore.[4a]

Very often a bandit finds further support from corrupt elements of the State enforcement machine itself. The 'compagnie d'armi' set up by the Bourbons were each responsible for law and order within their own territory, but they co-operated with the bandits whenever it was a case of cattle-rustling or theft within the territory of other *compagnie*. As recently as the Giuliano case some sections of the police played an equivocal part. Furthermore, the bandit usually does business with field guards, *gabellotti* and other *mafioso* persons and temporarily enjoys their protection. In this way he mostly succeeds in holding out for quite a while, on average two to four years; Giuliano pursued his activities for as long as six years. Not only in Sicily but elsewhere too, bandits of this kind cannot be tracked down by the police and normally end up through betrayal by individual members of their gang. The judicial machinery then tries to gloss over its incompetence and, by means of threadbare manoeuvres, claims credit for the death of the bandit. (In Corsica there even exists a saying: Killed after death, as a bandit by the police.)[5]

(3) Lone-wolf bandits are rare. The organization of a group of bandits, a gang or—as it is usually called in Sicily—a 'comitativa armata' is determined chiefly by its economic form of existence and also by its command structure. Membership usually fluctuates between three and ten; a larger group would have difficulties in supporting itself without arousing the dislike of broad sections of the population. The cohesion of a gang is guaranteed only by the personal prestige of a charismatic leader; this is another reason for the generally small size. Surprisingly, its structure is often stabilised also by natural kinship relations,[6] alongside the customary 'ritual kinship relations... in the form of blood brotherhood, godfather relationships and other ceremonial forms of patronage'.[7]

(4) The financing of these gangs (financing 'in the widest sense of the word, including the provision of food supplies'[8]) is irregular. It rests, apart from purely voluntary services from relatives, upon extorted services, i.e. the collection of booty and tributes. Cattle stealing (*abigeato*) is the classic form of meeting requirements in Sicily and is universal both in time and geographically. Raids on lonely settlements (*assalti alle case campestri*), theft (*furti*) and highway robbery (*grassazione*) are recorded offences even in the pre-Bourbon period. Abduction and extortion of ransom (*sequestro di persona*)—an ancient practice and described in full detail even in Apuleius's *Golden Ass* but so far recorded in Sicily only from the Saracens—were introduced as a new method only after 1860 as a result of the successes of the bandit Angelo Pugliese, known as Don Peppino il Lombardo. Francesco Paolo Varsalona, the last great bandit of the pre-fascist era, who operated in the Cammarata region between 1891 and 1902, probably survived so long only because he dispensed with such rather conspicuous methods and almost exclusively lived on tribute payments in return for guaranteed safety.[9] Naturally, all these listed activities may occasionally make murders (*omicidi*) necessary.

Nothing much need be said about *ladrismo*, mainly because this phenomenon is generally widespread and therefore not nearly so often identified with *mafia* as is *brigantaggio*. In contrast to the bandits, the *ladri* are an urban phenomenon; whereas the bandits are almost exclusively recruited from the peasant class and spend their life on the run in the mountains, or at least invariably in a rural environment, the *ladri* are typical products of the urban proletariat. Bandit activity is felt to be an exceptional behaviour while the activity of the *ladri* is of professional character. The Sicilian *ladri* are thieves, burglars, petty crooks, pimps, persons who in criminological language are comprised in the term 'blue-collar criminals'.

To define *mafia* itself is more difficult. All we have seen so far is that we must be careful not to confuse *mafia* with either of the above-named phenomena. Pitré was the first to criticise the wrong identification of the word *mafia* with fundamentally different phenomena:

> It becomes synonymous with brigandage, *camorra*, highway robbery, without being any of these three, since brigandage is open struggle against the law, *camorra* an illegal profiteering from economic transactions, and highway robbery relates to the most vulgar and common people, indulging in vice, and has power only over people of little importance.[10]

We must begin with an elucidation of the psychological attitude covered by the word *mafia*, an attitude to which the term is exclusively applied by some authors. This may be defined as a proud awareness of one's own personality, of independence in every respect, the ability to look after oneself and to defend one's own dignity at any price, and as an awareness of chivalrous ties with the members of one's own group.

> (... *mafia* is a trait of character, a philosophy of life, a concept of society, a moral code, a particular sensibility predominant among all Sicilians. They are taught in their cradle, or perhaps know even when they are born, that they must help one another, stand by their friends and fight their common enemies, even when the friends are in the wrong and enemies are in the right. Every man must defend his dignity under all circumstances and must not let the slightest disrespect or affront go unavenged. They must not divulge secrets and always keep clear of official authority and laws.) ... In this sense any man conspicuously displaying his pride is a *mafioso*.[11]

Mafia is the awareness of a man's nature, an exaggerated idea of the power of the individual, the sole power of decision in each conflict and in each clash of interests; hence the inability to tolerate the superiority

9

or, worse, the arrogance of others. The *mafioso* wants to be respected and almost invariably shows respect himself. When offended he does not turn to the judiciary and does not rely on the law. If he did so he would be displaying weakness and offending against *omertà* which brands as distasteful and despicable any man who turns to an official in order to get his rights.[12]

The decisive point, however, the crux of this attitude of mind and moral code, is the fact that a man of honour, a *mafioso*, 'che sa farsi rispettare', must avenge any violation of the integrity of his person (and of his property, theft representing disrespect and affront) by his own efforts, which mostly means resorting to violence. Admittedly, this rule applies to certain things in any society. Even in a social system within which individual recourse to sanctions has very largely lost all legitimacy—both in law and, more important, in public morality—a great number of affronts, quarrels within the family, traffic disputes, arguments within special groups, etc., are regulated without recourse to the State's enforcement machinery. Norms relating to such cases are sanctioned by disapproval, boycott, duel, etc. Within the Sicilian sub-culture this range of conventional sanctions, however, is extraordinarily wide and reaches far into the sphere for which other cultures apply the sanctions of the law.

The term *mafia*, however, is generally used in the literature to cover also another aspect—the totality of *mafioso* associations, the groupings of *mafiosi* for the purpose of joined action.

> The *mafia* is the instinctive, brutal and interest-conditioned solidarity which, to the detriment of the State, the law and regular organisations, unites all those individuals and social strata which prefer to derive their means of existence and comfort not from work but from violent action, from fraud and intimidation.[13]

Although this formulation is still a little imprecise, it suggests that men in whom the *mafioso* attitude is particularly strong come together in a kind of instinctive solidarity in order to support one another mutually in the pursuit of their aims. A somewhat clearer formulation is offered by Cutrera, who has this to say about the *mafioso*:

> He knows how to achieve his rights by his own efforts, and if he lacks the power he will do so with the help of others who think and feel the same way.[14]

The whole process still seems a little indefinite and lacking in structure, but closer inspection soon shows that the persons somewhat vaguely described as 'altri di medesimi pensamenti' are for those seeking support not just from any people but invariably the same individuals, that within a village social system they are found to hold institutionalised positions and that the relationship of mutual aid is structured in a very precise form.

> In those cases when a man needed the help of others and could not turn to the law, either in order to assert his right or a presumed right, or to resolve a dispute, he would turn to the authority of persons known for their influence or their presumption or those who, through their energetic and violent action, had previously achieved recognition for their arbitration.[15]

> From this *mafia* mentality there emerged not an association—no such association ever existed—but small groups of malefactors, more or less organised, who obeyed local leaders. Their totality constituted that which is normally described by the name of *mafia*.[16]

> ... The same word (*mafia*) describes in Sicily not a special association but the complex of many small groupings which have set themselves a variety of objectives. These objectives, however, are mostly of a kind that makes the members of the association come hard up against the limits of the criminal law and sometimes in fact fall foul of it.[17]

These small clique-like associations which are independent of each other but maintain relations with one another, which support each other, make arrangements with each other, at times take joint action, but on occasion can be at daggers drawn, are to be designated in this book as 'cosche' ('cosca' is the name used for such an association in the Sicilian dialect). To describe the totality of these *cosche* as 'the *mafia*' holds certain dangers to which reference has already been made in the Introduction. If the term is used these dangers must not be lost sight of.

A *mafioso* therefore is a man whose actions are determined by *mafioso* behaviour and who operates within the framework of a *cosca*. To this must be added a few further pecularities which will be described in detail in the following chapters. But a brief outline of them will now be given in order to differentiate the subject under investigation from the two types described above: Although by this actions, by the private use of force, he offends against the codified law, the *mafioso* is an 'uomo di rispetto', a respectable citizen of his village; he does not, like the bandit, live in a precarious or abnormal situation. His position is legitimated in popular morality, and its peculiar consolidation is due to the fact that his activity serves not only the satisfaction of his own needs but performs a function (a protective and intermediary function) for the entire sub-cultural system. In spite of this he does not, as the bandit does, get into increasingly sharp conflict with the powers of the superimposed State but throughout his career successfully strives to legalise his position. In this he succeeds mainly because he commands a 'partito', a network of relationships with holders of institutionalised power, a network maintained by continuous reciprocal services.

Notes

[1] Cf. Pitt-Rivers 1961, p. 183

[2] Cf. Pantaleone 1962, pp. 117–30, also Chapter 6 of the same work. On Giuliano cf. Pantaleone 1962, pp. 155–82, Maxwell 1963 *passim*, and Gaja 1962 *passim*

[3] Cf. Hobsbawm 1959, p. 13

[3a] Cf. Hobsbawm 1969, especially Chapter 3 about the 'noble' robbers

[4] Franchetti 1925, p. 146

[4a] Cf. the original text in the Appendix

[5] Hobsbawm 1959, p. 15. Cf. the above-listed literature on the Giuliano case and on other cases in D'Alessandro 1959 *passim*

[6] D'Alessandro's material contains data on ten such relationships: the three Marinello brothers (p. 60), the Aleimo and Madonia brothers (p. 61), the Buzetta brothers (p. 62), the Mangione brothers (p. 71), the Pizzolanti brothers (p. 73), the Belucci brothers (p. 87), the Valvo brothers (p. 89), the Bofalino cousins (p. 105) and uncle and nephew Ferrarello (p. 111). More recent examples can be found in Giuliano's gang: Salvatore Giuliano and his two brothers-in-law Pisciotta and Sciortino, the three Misuraca brothers, the Genovese brothers and the Pianelli brothers, cf. Gaja 1962, pp. 291 and 347

[7] Robert Redfield: *The 'Folk' Society* in Mühlmann and Müller (Ed.) 1966, p. 341

[8] Weber 1964, p. 146

[9] Cf. Cutrera 1904, pp. 7–9

[10] Pitré 1889, p. 288

[11] Barzini 1965, pp. 263–4

[12] Pitré 1889, p. 289

[13] Relazioni della Giunta per l'inchiesta sulle condizioni della Sicilia (Relazione Bonfadini), Rome 1876, p. 114, quoted from Alongi 1887, p. 65

[14] Cutrera 1900, p. 41

[15] Ibid., p. 38

[16] Ciasca in *Enciclopedia Italiana*, vol. xxi, Rome 1934–42, p. 863

[17] Mosca in Russo (Ed.) 1964, p. 438

3 Characteristics of the Sicilian Social Structure

Pubblico Ministero: Statia per sciabola è parola di mafia.
Avvocato Gargano: È semplicemente dialetto siciliano, signori ...
(Processo Amoroso)

In dealing with a social phenomenon it is indispensable to examine the structure of the society in which it is embedded. Not only are certain features of the phenomenon moulded by the prevailing social structure, but frequently the phenomenon as a whole can only be understood from the function which it has to perform within the structure of the society. One of the starting points of a critical examination of a structural-functional theory is the difficulty, when applying such a theory, of defining the limits of the system for which a structural element can be seen as structure-supporting, i.e. functional, or structure-changing or structure-destroying; that is, dysfunctional.

In an investigation of *mafioso* attitudes, for instance, one is instantly faced with the temptation of accepting Italian society with its values, norms and sanctions as an all-embracing social system, that is as a society whose claim to a monopoly of legitimate physical coercion by the State is matched by its ability to use its official coercive machinery for enforcing its norms in accordance with a codified law by means of a staff of persons available for this purpose.[1]

To a way of thinking moulded by Central European conditions such a state of affairs may easily seem normal, or may offer itself as an ideal type, so that divergent phenomena are classified as pathological cases. Such a prejudiced theoretical approach will tend to treat *mafioso* behaviour as a criminal phenomenon and ascribe to it a dysfunctional character. There is a special need, therefore, to practise the caution called for above in the development of structural-functional theories. The sociologist will have to define his own values and try to detach himself from them. He will find that far more profitable possibilities of description and elucidation will emerge once the concept of a sub-culture is introduced and once the Sicilian social system is recognised as one such specific sub-culture.

It is from the conflict of the norms of the bureaucratic State with the sub-cultural attitudes, i.e. chiefly the jurisdiction and application of physical coercion by non-State holders of power, that the emergence of the *mafioso* type must be understood—with all the shades of meaning covered by this concept, including the criminal one.

As an exponent of power the *mafioso* lacks the matter-of-course legitimacy which still attached to the 'bravi' of the feudal barons (even in popular morality) and his attitudes are condemned as criminal by the State morality. He is neither a legitimate ruler nor has legitimate power been delegated to him; he is neither feudal lord nor *bravo* nor official. His type is inconceivable without the collapse of the feudal order on the one hand and, on the other, the failure of the bureaucratic State to make its monopoly of legitimate physical coercion truly effective. The rôle of the *mafioso* in this situation is a self-help institution. But only when the feudal order has lost its legitimacy and the modern State is not (yet) in a position to enforce its norms can one speak of self-help in this sense. And then only in this situation with its dual morality—on the one hand that of the State's claims and on the other the sub-culture morality of actual conditions. Once the State has asserted its norms and popular morality coincides with State morality the *mafioso* becomes a criminal.[2]

The history of the type must therefore always be seen against the background of the conflict between State and non-State powers, and, later, as the conflict between such a non-State power (with its always somewhat problematical legitimation through popular morality) and the actual State power with its claim to the monopoly of legitimate physical coercion.

1 The political structure. The weakness of the state and the tradition of dual morality

Sicily's political structure has always been marked by a very definite situation—an extraordinary weakness of the formal Government machinery, popular mistrust and even hostility towards all State organs and a withdrawal into an informal system of self-help institutions, chiefly the family and clientage. This lack of loyalty towards formal organisations is not, in the historical perspective, some irrational factor, but must be understood as an entirely purposive, rationally motivated behaviour pattern. It is a product of Sicilian history. Even a cursory glance at historical facts permits two important conclusions—first, Sicily never was the subject of its own history but invariably a colonially ruled territory, and secondly this rule was subject to frequent changes. Both these factors—remoteness and change of the centre of government—made it difficult for the population to identify with the exponents of government, quite apart from their usual impotence. Most of the time Sicily stood in a kind of tutelage relationship to its masters, i.e. it neither possessed its own functioning government (we shall refer later to the rôle played by the Sicilian Parliament) nor was it a totally subjected, ruthlessly exploited colonial country. Either would have resulted in a certain power of the formal government machine. Some of these forms of alien rule gave rise to social phenomena which undoubtedly had an important effect on the moulding of the national character. At the time of Roman domination the island was predominantly a supplier of grain and the labourers on the big estates were slaves, 'strumenti vocali', accounting for a large part of the island's population. Beloch estimates the population of Sicily in classical antiquity at about 600,000, of whom 200,000 to 300,000 were slaves.[3] A number of common names in Sicily testify to this past, such as Schiavo, Loschiavo, Nigro, Lo Nigro. Slaves live in permanent conflict with the established power, and where there are slaves there are also fugitives and men seeking asylum.

Bandit-type groups of fugitives on a major scale were represented also by the Saracens, i.e. Arab–Berber elements, forced back by the Normans and Hohenstaufens towards the central part of Western Sicily. Their area of retreat is described as 'Marca dei Saraceni' in a document of 1224, but this refers not so much to an official territorial delimitation as to the actual distribution of the Islamic population. This territory roughly corresponds to what are today the Provinces of Palermo, Trapani and Agrigento, its centre being a triangle bounded by Giardinello, Alcamo and the forests of Ficuzza. It is estimated that 60,000 Moslems lived in this triangle alone, with further large groups living in the regions of Cinisi and Misilmeri.[4] For the most part they lived as bandits in the mountains or in other inaccessible areas and offered a possibility of asylum also for numerous Christian Sicilians, fugitive slaves, criminals, vagabonds, etc. Their importance for the formation of the character of the region which they inhabited should not be underestimated. They handed down certain norms and values which stemmed from the fugitive and asylum character of their political existence and from the impermanent and haphazard character of their economic existence; a major feature is a strong anarchist dislike of any State system of law or coercion and of any hierarchically or centrally organised governmental structure.

More important still and more decisive were three other institutions which were never in quite such open conflict with the State and, for that very reason, were less easily overcome by the State. The behaviour patterns moulded by these institutions continued to survive even when the institutions themselves had been abolished—a sense of being exempt from the State's judiciary thanks to one's belonging to a privileged clientage, and a sense of being therefore legitimately entitled to practise private violence. The first of these institutions were the 'familiari dell'Inquisizione'. In 1487 Ferdinand the Catholic of Spain sent Fra Antonio della Penna to Sicily; within a short time he covered the entire island with a network of 'familiari', 'collaboratori' or 'coadiutori' of the Inquisition. These included several thousand people from all walks of life whose task it was to supervise the faithful and fight heresy.

On 15 January 1535, the Viceroy decreed (i.e. the Viceroy had to concede) that all 'officiali e familiari dell'Inquisizione' were subject to a special court of their own both in civil and criminal matters, and were exempt from all other jurisdiction ('ab omni alia jurisdictione exempti'[5]) and that, contrary to the general prohibition, they were allowed to bear arms. Palermo, moreover, was exempt from the payment of taxes. These exceptional rulings, which at first only applied to the *familiari* in person, were later extended to those serving under them.

Protected by these privileges the *familiari* as well as the members of their clientage committed numerous crimes. Murder, theft and extortion by the threat of denunciation were the order of the day.[6]

The second institution was the 'maestranze', as the craftsmen's guilds were called in Sicily. Such associations according to trades and quarters since the members of the same trade lived close together, as can still be seen in Palermo to-day—have existed ever since Roman days ('collegia opificum et artificum'[7]). In 1786 there were seventy-four *maestranze* in Palermo. Their purpose was the avoidance of clashes from competition and the regulation of all working relationships within a trade. The collegium of registered members elected a 'console' who exercised jurisdiction within the craft and who, together with two advisers, decided on the admission of new members. The members of a *maestranza* usually lived in a solid block around the church of their patron saint and observed a joint saint's feastday. The functions of the association included support for those incapable of work, for the sick, the aged and the poor, provision for widows and orphans, guarantee of a decent funeral and help for those in prison. At certain times, principally after the revolt of 1773, the craft associations also raised armed men to protect law and order in the city, the so-called 'ronde delle maestranze'. This military power, and altogether the existence of a co-operative structure rendering joint procedure possible, made these associations into permanent rivals of the barons in the urban struggle for power. Moreover, there were some open conflicts with the State as represented by the Viceroys, in particular in 1647, 1773 and 1820; at least the *maestranze* invariably tried to exempt their members from the reach of the State's jurisdiction. This is illustrated by a passage from the 'Capitoli ed Istruzioni da osservarsi dalle Maestranze d'arti mechaniche', decreed in 1785 by the Giunta dei Presidenti e Consultore in Naples. Article XIV expressly forbids the granting of asylum to fugitive criminals:

> It is forbidden, however, to grant asylum in the church or adjoining houses to delinquents or debtors even when these are members of the *maestranza*.[8]

Probably the most important result of remote and weak governments was the evolution of a great measure of independence of the most important local powers, the barons. The Sicilian nobility cared little about the politics of whoever happened to be their sovereign at the time; it was neither a military nor a court nobility—a state of affairs which likewise emerged from Sicily's special position of tutelage under the Spanish Crown which did not require the Sicilian nobility to participate in military service or life at court. The barons lived on their possessions virtually in the world of an *oikos*, a medieval *oikos* until late into the modern age, with all the privileges and immunities ever possessed by feudal lords. In the seventeenth century, when in the rest of Europe feudal independence was beginning to yield to national centralisation, Philip III granted the Sicilian barons the 'maerum et mixtum imperium', i.e. the right to administer penal justice.[9]

The Sicilian Parliament, consisting of the deputies of three estates—the clergy, the nobility and the bourgeoisie of the domanial territories—was an instrument of the barons. About the middle of the eighteenth century the first estate provided 63 deputies, the second 228 and the third 43.[10]

To protect their estates and their town and country houses, to conduct private feuds and to enforce their rights *vis-à-vis* the dependent population, the barons each surrounded themselves with a group of armed men, a small private army, the so-called *bravi*. Like other institutions which discharged the same functions at a later date (*compagnie d'armi, campieri*), these groups of *bravi* enlisted above all violent, fearless and criminal elements, frequently bandits who had proved by their previous actions that they were capable of discharging such military and police tasks. Even when penal justice passed from the feudal lords to the officials of the State, the barons ensured that these subjects of theirs, who were frequently 'facinorosi', criminals, remained outside the State's jurisdiction. We can observe here the same process which also in other cases (e.g. with the Saracens and later with the *gabellotti*, the great *capi banda* and *mafiosi*) led to the emergence of clientages, i.e. a situation when somebody, 'thanks to his ability to admit an original stranger as his guest . . . and if necessary protect him, could, from being a provider of asylum, become a crystallisation point of accumulating power'.[11]

In the case of a baron's *bravi* there was the element both of protection (asylum for the 'latitante') and of economic support, both of them ensuring personal ties.

A baron was able to apply economic pressure not only on the peasants dependent on him but also on formally free peasants, he could conclude contracts to his own advantage or at any time break any contract concluded since he alone possessed the power to guarantee a contract. The peasants were subjected both to economic exploitation and to personal arbitrary jurisdiction. As a result of the prolonged duration of this state of affairs a sense of equality in the eyes of the law—as expressed in the judicial principle of the legal-bureaucratic State 'la legge è uguale per tutti'—has not been able to develop in their minds to this day, any more than it has among the heirs to positions of privilege.

Many authors keep emphasising the militant reaction shown by the Sicilian peasantry to this state of affairs, i.e. violent revolt. But it is more important to emphasise the more usual passive reaction of resigned submission. For it is this submission that provides the historical background to the acceptance of the arrogation of power by individuals, viz. the *mafiosi*, by the rest of the population.

The progressive assertion of the bureaucratic State against the described powers can be observed clearly since the end of the eighteenth century. The State deprived these powers of their judiciary privileges and of their privileges in the application of physical force; the persons until then subject only to these powers were brought within the sphere of competence of the State. As one of the reforms of the Viceroy Caracciolo the 'tribunale del Sant'Ufficio' in Sicily was suppressed;[12] in 1812 feudalism was abolished under the decisive influence of the British occupying power; and in 1822 the *maestranze* were banned in Palermo. The retreat and weakening of the Church and its loss of privileges began in 1782; a further important step was the sequestration of the monasteries in 1860.

A problem which we shall touch upon repeatedly in this book is the guarantee of public safety. Originally this task, too, was in the hands of the barons. But as early as the sixteenth century the Crown was trying to withdraw the *bravi* at least partially from the exclusive influence of the feudal lords and to use them under their own discretion against the brigands. (Similar attempts can be noted at a later date with the *ronde delle maestranze*.) The so-called 'compagnie d'armi' were set up in 1543, consisting of one *capitano* and 10 men in each of Sicily's three districts (Valle del Mazaro, Val di Noto, Val Demone). This is a phenomenon which survived for a long time (e.g. for tax collection, and, to this day, for refuse collection), i.e. the farming out of public tasks to private individuals. The *capitano d'armi*, to whom it was left to choose his men, would, in order to ensure their effectiveness, pick them from among the same elements of which the guards of the barons were composed. A decree of 16 December 1813 reorganised these armed companies. Their number was laid down at 23, each consisting of 12 men and each assigned to the *circondario* of the seven administrative districts now set up (Valle di Palermo, Messina, Catania, Trapani, Girgenti, Caltanissetta and Noto). In theory they now came under the 'immediata dipendenza del Segretario di Stato dell'Interno'.[13] Their competence now no longer included crimes against the person but only crimes against property. Each *compagnia* was responsible for all thefts and damage to property within its district, and the *capitano* was held liable by means of a surety payment.

18

The *compagnie* were abolished in 1860 but replaced on 30 September 1863 by the similarly organised 'militi a cavallo' who were in turn replaced in 1877 by the 'guardie di Pubblica Sicurezza a cavallo'. This period of semi-private protection of public order only came to an end in 1892. Many authors of that period expressed the feeling that this institution was no longer in line with the 'civiltà dei tempi'[14] and that 'è questo compito dello Stato, nè può essere lasciato all'iniziativa privata....'[15] The advantage of the *compagno* or *milito* had been that he was not a member of the hated mainland police, that he did not wear a uniform or live in barracks, but lived in his own house, with his own family, in his own rural system of relationships and that information was therefore much more easily accessible to him. In speed of reaction and effectiveness he was, in consequence, superior to any policeman or *carabiniere*. But these very circumstances also prevented a business-like, task-orientated behaviour morality developing in him. He remained entangled in the network of friendships, hostilities, 'favoreggiamenti' and clientage relations, and his office frequently became just a means of private enrichment. Since every *capitano* was responsible for the solving of crimes committed in his district and since, on the other hand, there was no legal or moral cohesion between the separate *compagnie* as yet, each *capitano* tried to keep his own district free from the worst offences, and to favour the crossing over of culprits into other territories. Frequently he would come to an arrangement with the criminals, an 'accordo fra amici', also known by the name of 'componenda'. The robbed person had part of his loss restored to him but undertook not to report it; the thief escaped prosecution; the *capitano* did not have to make restitution from his surety deposit but in fact shared in the proceeds of the theft. Complaints about this state of affairs began as early as 1563 when the *compagni* were even accused of direct criminal activity;[16] they continued later, and were eventually summed up in Pagano's wry sentence:

> The corporation of the *militi a cavallo* was dissolved by simple royal decree and about a hundred of its members were sentenced on the spot to deportation to prescribed places of residence.[17]

It is useful to discuss at this point the field guards, employed by the communes, the 'campieri comunali'. In addition to the private field guards there were, and still are, in Sicily some who are paid by the community and some under the mayor. This means that they also discharge a public order function but, like the *compagni* and *militi*, they do not wear uniform—a symbolical aspect (an external one, admittedly, but interesting nevertheless) of the dubious value which they represent as instruments of the State. Frequently they are totally ineffective, often they represent factors in the private struggle for power among local parties, they are themselves *mafiosi* or else in the service of *mafiosi* elements. If their function, the protection of fields and grazing cattle, were really successfully discharged by a public security organ, there would not be the power vacuum which this book attempts to adduce in explanation of *mafioso* attitudes.

Among the files in the office of the Prefect of Palermo there are some depositions throwing light on these conditions. In a letter of the commune of Collesano to the Prefect of Palermo (of 20 September 1893) we read:

> The incidence of crime in Sicily and of brigandage is increasing more and more, the main cause being economic misery. The harm which this does to the normal development of productive forces is unfortunately plain and known to everybody.[18]

This letter gave rise to a general census of the *guardie campestri* throughout the Province. The officials of the Pubblica Sicurezza (P.S.) or the mayors reported on conditions in their locality.

The following statistics are compiled from this material:

Table 1

	circ. Palermo	circ. Termini	circ. Cefalu	circ. Corleone	Whole Province
Communes	32	19	16	9	76
guardie camp. a piedi	291	126	26	42	485
guardie camp. a cavallo	10	30	–	7	47

Source: ASP, 1893, busta 133, cat. 20, fasc. 23 bis.

Of 76 communes 19 had no communal field guards at all; of the remaining 57 communes, 42 had no mounted field guards. Of 76 communes, therefore, only 15 had *guardie campestri a cavallo*!

Here are a few illuminating passages from letters:

> The royal police station of Monreale to the most illustrious Prefect of the Province of Palermo, 5 November 1893 ...
> I have the honour to inform Your Excellency that the field guards of this community are in no way helpful to the government authority in

the protection of public security. If a crime is committed they appear for a moment, but presently with great skill and cunning they evade the task of any investigation whatever and no hope can be placed in their pursuing any kind of service in the interests of public security. They supply no evidence of any kind, nothing that could enlighten the judiciary, just as one cannot expect them to take any preventive measure or to watch persons under police surveillance, persons with previous convictions, or the hostelries. They perform no patrolling services of any kind....This office has at its disposal only a single field guard who appears at nine o'clock in the morning, leaves at noon and turns up again at six in the evening but only to bring the mail. And it has not been possible to improve this state of affairs.

With most humble respects ...

Royal police station of Piana dei Greci, 6 November 1893.

... If the field guards of this jurisdiction are called up for some service or other they will, now and again, make themselves available to this office. They have, however, shown that they are extremely unwilling to help the government authority in protecting public order and security. They have just become useless and indeed sometimes harmful forces as far as this office is concerned.

Royal police station, Villabate, 5 November 1893.

In reply to Your Excellency's letter I hasten to inform you that there are no field guards in this community.

Most respectfully, ...

Community administration of Bolognetta, 4 November 1893.

This community has eight field guards in addition to the leader; none of these, not even the leader, is mounted. With the exception of the leader they receive no wages but private rewards from the proprietors, in proportion to the land these possess. They draw no other income.

The last quotation reveals an aspect found quite frequently—the *guardie campestri*, though properly organs of public security, are under the influence of private holders of power. In a letter of the Municipio di Borgetto, Gabineto del Sindaco, of 15 January 1884 we read:

... The old *mafia* system predominated on all occasions and the total lack of discipline among some guards progressively weakened the sense of personal duty and that esprit de corps which makes even the incapable capable of service. This led inevitably to mistrust and demoralisation which I attempted to contain by rigorous action. However, I had failed to consider that to some community councils and to some deputies the restoration of discipline and service would seem a disaster. What happened was that exhortations and special measures for the regulation of the service were understood as personal prejudice. And the guards, far from obeying their leaders, received their cue from whoever happened to be their protectors ...[19]

In addition to these institutions there was, of course, also a group of persons directly dependent on the State—the Bourbon police, after 1860 the Pubblica Sicurezza, the *carabinieri*, and military units for special operations —which frequently met all requirements of effectiveness (in training, equipment and resolute action)[20] but which nevertheless did not succeed in guaranteeing public safety. Among all the categories of offences listed in the statistics it is above all the incidence of murder and of robbery and extortion which, in Sicily, lay very considerably above the average for Italy:

Table 2

Province	Murder	Robbery and Extortion
	1890–3	
	annual average per 100,000 inhabitants	
Genoa	8.63	11.09
Milan	2.56	7.04
Bologna	4.96	10.95
Treviso	0.75	1.00
Rome	20.79	17.95
Naples	27.97	16.75
Caltanissetta	42.76	26.24
Catania	26.21	21.22
Girgenti	66.87	47.04
Messina	19.80	8.51
Palermo	32.07	22.22
Syracuse	11.87	10.11
Trapani	22.05	21.41

Source: Direzione Generale della Statistica. Statistica Giudiziaria Penale per l'anno 1893. Roma 1895, S. LXXXIV–XCII.

The annual average for the rural provinces in the North is only about half that for the great cities listed (see Treviso); this should be borne in mind in considering the Sicilian figures, since here one is likewise dealing with rural provinces. For the whole of Italy (Regno) we find an average rate of murder of 13.44; top of the list are the Provinces of Girgenti, Caltanissetta, Palermo and Sassari (Sardinia). There is a striking increase in the crime rate south of Rome.

For robbery we find an annual average of 8.59, with the Provinces of Girgenti, Sassari, Caltanissetta and Palermo heading the list.[21]

Marked differences between Sicily and mainland Italy are attested also for the years 1902–6. The annual average for 'omicidi volontari di ogni specie' in the Regno is 8.94 per 100,000 inhabitants, as against 22.35 for Sicily; that for 'rapine, estorsioni, ricatti' is 11.83 for Italy as a whole and 31.46 for Sicily. The figures for the various Sicilian provinces are as follows:

Table 3

Province	Murder	Robbery and Extortion
	1902–6	
	annual average per 100,000 inhabitants	
Caltanissetta	44.52	41.41
Catania	13.87	24.76
Girgenti	38.75	46.80
Messina	8.13	7.19
Palermo	29.06	33.65
Syracuse	8.20	10.30
Trapani	26.12	76.84

Source: Inchiesta parlamentare sulle condizioni dei contadini delle province meridionali (Inchiesta Lorenzoni), vol. VII, Roma 1909, S. 853.

It is worth noting—and we shall return to this point—that there are very marked differences within Sicily. As against the Provinces of Caltanissetta, Girgenti, Palermo and Trapani the remaining three provinces show considerably lower rates of incidents; indeed Messina and Syracuse lie below the Italian average.

Whereas the figures for the crimes listed in Sicily are almost three times the Regno average, those for the other categories of offences are only slightly higher. Under the heading 'furti' (thefts), for instance, the all-Italian annual average of 416.75 is, most interestingly, matched by a Sicilian figure of 439.72 per 100,000 inhabitants.[22]

The above figures show that the State organs did not succeed in guaranteeing public security as they understood it. But this does not mean that there was anarchy in Sicily; the murders and even the extortions must largely be seen as sanctions of a different sub-cultural system of norms (cf. ch. 5 §5), i.e. mostly as vengeance (by an interested party) as distinct from punishment (through an impartial body) in Vierkandt's terms.[23]

What, then, were the reasons for this failure? Chiefly the fact that policemen, *carabinieri* and jurists, in contrast to the *compagni* and *militi* were confronted as totally alien bodies by the population. Naturally, without the continuous co-operation of the citizenry, without complaints, reports, depositions by witnesses, verdicts by jurors, etc., their effectiveness was severely restricted. The chances of any State authority of enforcing such co-operation are slight, and after 1860 were even slighter than at the time of the Bourbons when it was still possible to punish the 'testimonio reticente', whereas nowadays only false testimony is punishable.[24] Whenever statements were obtained after an arrest, under physical or psychological pressure, these were revoked before the investigating magistrate or in court.[25] Anonymous letters or the so-called 'confidenze' (confidential information), of which there is frequent mention by the *delegati di P. S.*, admittedly result in the authorities knowing the crime and the criminal, but do not yield effective results under criminal law. Franchetti writes:

> ... In other countries the difficulty consists in finding somebody who knows anything useful to the investigation; in Sicily, by way of contrast, the difficulty consists in finding someone who will speak up.[26]

For the moment we shall record the fact that the public very largely refuses to co-operate; the positive and negative sanctions of this attitude will be discussed in Chapter 5, §5.

Further reasons for the difficulties of the police and *carabinieri* were their inadequate knowledge of the local geography (footpaths, forests, mountains, caves, remote barns) and of the language of the people, the Sicilian dialect. Quite apart from overlapping areas of competence between *carabinieri* and *militi a cavallo* and between *carabinieri* and *Pubblica Sicurezza*, which continuously led to friction, an additional reason for failure was the splitting up of the command of the security forces. Not only did *militi, carabinieri, guardie di Pubblica Sicurezza, guardie campestri* and army units receive their orders from totally different and mutually independent persons, but collaboration within the separate formations across provincial boundaries was also problematical:

24

When these rural criminals have associated with one another they operate by preference in the boundary zones between districts and provinces because they know full well that there the attention of the powers of law and order is weaker. If it exists at all in these zones then it does so only sporadically and temporarily.[27]

The Province of Syracuse which, as we have pointed out, had a particularly low incidence of delinquency, possessed, according to Taiani, 'quasi una completa rete stradale'.[28] As for the rest of the island, according to Pontieri,

> ... there is a total inadequacy of roads, as a result of which the country not only remains cut off from the populated centres, but also makes an impression of strange solitude.[29]

The lack of adequate facilities of communication thus also prevented the State governmental machine from permeating Sicily.

Not only the effectiveness of the security organs but that of the bureaucratic administration suffered, and suffers to this day, from widespread illiteracy.[30] The functioning of major formal structures, after all, depends largely on written communications. The fact that a large number of Sicilians can neither read nor write (and the fact that many who were able to do so at one time have rapidly forgotten it) is both a consequence and in turn an important cause of the unilateral emphasis on informal structures.

It should be remembered that we are never dealing with simple causal relationships but invariably with inter-dependencies. Thus the chronic weakness of the State resulted in the emergence of self-help institutions, and the exclusive power position of informal groups subsequently made it impossible for the State to win the loyalty of the public, while its resultant weakness again strengthened the family, the clientage and *mafioso* positions.

As we have said, the State, even after 1860, was far from winning the loyalty of the population with its measures. Incorporation in the national kingdom of Italy was felt, just as all previous occupations, as an invasion by a foreign power. Apathy and indifference (at best) towards the government and pure hatred towards the policeman, the '*birro*', were feelings which united all Sicilians.[31] This hatred was further fed by the measures which were to have served the State's penetration of the island. The first call-up decreed by the new government gave rise to particular indignation: thousands of young people were called up but a great number preferred to go to the mountains as bandits rather than as soldiers to the North where—according to rumour —the young men were threatened even with castration.[32] Moreover, the Bourbon taxation system, which had been based on landed property and land rent, was more favourable to the poor than the new system, which taxed also the income from work.[33] Another factor was the sequestration of Church and monastery property, the 'mano morte'; the hereditary lease-holders of these lands, as well as the recipients of alms from the monasteries, thousands of them, lost the basis of their subsistence. A further factor was the disillusionment of the landless peasants whose hopes of a plot of land of their own were not satisfied since the expropriated land swiftly went to finan-cially more competitive landowners, principally *gabellotti* and *civili*.

The backward and fanatical clergy, who exercised considerable influence on the peasants in the interior of the island, gave the Church's blessings to this hatred of the new, liberal Italian government. Alongi writes:

> It is convinced, and repeats, that the government is a usurper, excom-municated and Protestant, and it fights it, persistently and in large num-bers, with all means and all weapons which superstition, the pulpit and the confessional offer. To this day, one frequently hears priests publicly repeating (naturally in front of peasants): But how can good and justice be done by governments which do not believe in purgatory or the Holy Virgin? And the peasants believe them and feel their own mistrust of the government officials growing. The priests authorise them to lie to them and to display to them an only outward respect while hating them from the bottom of their hearts.[34]

Incidentally, the endeavours of the Church to work towards a dual moral-ity, claiming of course for itself inclusion in the in-group, has a long tradition. We have already mentioned the Inquisition. We can now also mention the 'Taxae cancellariae et poenitentiariae romanae', printed in Palermo in ten editions between 1477 and 1533, published by Giovanni Battista dei Conti Naselli, Archbishop of Palermo. Article 6 forgives false testimony in court, even when this is punishable, and Article 10 describes any other kind of obstruction of legal proceedings and bribery of judges as morally justified in certain cases provided it leads to the acquittal of the accused.

> The action becomes legitimate through the purchase of the Bull and by the payment of alms to the Church: Two *tari*, 12 *grana* and five *piccioli* for every 77 *tari* and seven *grana* of the value of the stolen property. The culprit thereby obtains forgiveness, his conscience remains clear and he remains in possession of the money as if it were his own and lawfully earned or acquired.[35]

Certainly all these listed circumstances led to a situation, after 1860, when the organs of the State were seen as the tentacles of an alien monster. The Pretor of Partinico in 1885 expressed the views of the peasants as follows:

The law is regarded as a conventional pact, as something imposed on the people to its detriment; the government is a huge personified monster, from the office servant all the way up to that privileged being who calls himself King. It desires everything, steals undisguisedly, disposes over property and persons for the benefit of a few because it is supported by henchmen and bayonets.[36]

The moral absorption of the State norms was no more successful than the actual organisational one. On the contrary, a dual morality emerged whose positive side was directed towards personal ties and the negative side against the prototype of formal order, the State. But the broad masses never displayed much enthusiasm even for political movements led by Sicilians for Sicily— neither for the revolutions of 1849, 1860 or 1866, nor for the separatism after the Second World War.[37] The Sicilian feels no loyalty to any such abstract ideas; they are none of his business.

The norms of the in-group relationships, on the other hand, the relationships with family, relatives, ritual relatives, friends, patrons or clients, and also the relations within an extensive solidarity framework constituted by *omertà*, are observed with conscious conviction, even at the cost of sacrifices and sometimes self-sacrifice. This is a key factor in the life of brigands and *mafiosi*; the protection which they enjoy on the part of the population stems from the dual system of State morality and popular morality. They are protected against the State police organs because, from the point of view of local morality, these are acting illegitimately, persecuting people whose actions were in entire conformity with the demands of their in-group. Nothing could more clearly illustrate this lack of social identification with the State morality (and indeed all that has been said in this chapter) than the following episode from the trial of the five Amoroso brothers in Palermo in October 1883:

E. A.: Make him swear on the soul of his father that I was not in his house.
Public Prosecutor: Yes, this could be sworn.
Lawyer M.: But sworn in the manner stated by the defendant.
Presiding Judge: There is only one formula for an oath, the one prescribed by the law.
Lawyer M.: This is not applicable here.
Presiding Judge: Oh, why not?
Lawyer M.: Because the mob does not believe in it.
Presiding Judge: The mob believes in it too.
After some further argument it was decided that the witness should swear upon the soul of his father.

Presiding Judge: Giuseppe Amoroso, do you swear this?
G. A.: Yes.[38]

'D'altra parte però, la magistratura non è sempre all'altezza del proprio ufficio.'[39] A further characteristic of the period in which we must seek the phylogenesis of the *mafioso* is the fact that, while a specific ethic was by then being demanded from a State functionary, this functionary was still far from being equal to this requirement. The ties which bound him to the business of his office were not nearly as strong as those felt for individuals, mostly individuals outside the State institution; the central feature of modern public service ethics was therefore lacking. His ties with the in-group—ties to his family, to his 'amici', 'sentimental' friends as well as instrumental ones whose 'favori' had to be returned, ties with his clientage which cut across the official hierarchy—all these also governed the way in which he discharged his official business. The loyalty demanded by these ties cut across that towards the State. The characteristic feature of the feudal official, a directly felt personal dependence on one's employer, is exceedingly important in Sicily—except that one must differentiate here between an official and an unofficial employer and that one must remember that the latter may also stand outside the bureaucracy. This phenomenon is crucial to an understanding of the *mafioso's partito*.

Max Weber says of the modern civil servant that he does 'not regard tenure of an office... either in law or in fact as possession of a source of revenue or advantage'.[40] By contrast Novacco says of the Sicilian official that he fairly frequently confuses the law applying to everybody with the privilege of exercising authority.[41] His office becomes a source of income, i.e. alongside his remuneration from the State it provides him with other, illegal, revenue. Above all, it gives him power—not only the clearly defined power of authority within the bureaucratic stratification but power in social relationships outside the bureaucracy—in that it enables him, in view of the above-described inadequate (from the State's point of view inadequate) social identification of the office-holder, to rule over a public ignorant and helpless because of the actual non-excistence, or because of its unawareness of, the possibility of appeal or control, and to exact the performance of all kinds of *favori*.

Naturally this 'treason' is most striking in the security organs. Thus we read in the Relazione Bonfadini: '... The difficulties of public order are a question of personnel rather that a question of the laws'.[42] The machinery exists and the laws regulating its function are no worse than in other parts of Italy; what is lacking is the professional ethics of the office-holder. Thus, if official secrets are not kept, the whole machinery is bound to fail:

Between the police stations, the guardians of the law themselves, on the one hand, and the population on the other, there is a continuous and mysterious current of relationships. ... Persons who are to be arrested are notified even before the warrant for their arrest has been signed; and when the forces of the law arrive in order to arrest the person they discover that he has disappeared for the past three, four or more days. [43]

An important rôle is played in Sicily by the Pretor, whose office combines police and judicial functions. He can receive complaints, he inspects the spot where a crime has been committed, he institutes investigations, he functions as examining magistrate and he can, as the lowest judicial instance, pronounce sentence in certain cases of civil and criminal law. Most important of all, he is able, without any weight of evidence and without resorting to jurors, to impose the 'ammonizione' upon a suspected person. This *ammonizione* places the person concerned under police surveillance and restricts his freedom of movement to the commune where he is domiciled and its immediate neighbourhood. In the event of repeated infringement it leads automatically to the punishment of 'domicilio coatto', i.e. to forced residence at a place of deportation. With these two penalties the State power has at its disposal two tools developed specifically for the suppression of *mafioso* attitudes and criminal action in a pattern of society in which one cannot count on civilian complainants, witnesses, jurors or the co-operation of the public. In its application the Pretor therefore enjoys a great deal of freedom, hence a great responsibility—and also numerous possibilities of abuse. And as the Pretors are often Sicilians one finds, not infrequently, an attitude which stems from the dual morality described above. Thus the Sotto-Prefetto of Cefalù had this to report about the Vice-Pretor of Gangi, avv. Antonio Milletari:

Indifferent in political matters, but with a tendency towards certain principles. Moral leadership very poor. Cunning and intelligent in office, but only in the interests of the *partito* and even more so in the interests of the *mafia*. In his hands the trials develop in accordance with favouritism and intrigue, and he thus degrades the office to an ordinary occupation. As a private citizen public opinion believes him to be a *camorrista*, a *capo-mafia*, a speculator in cattle thefts. Last year he was caught redhanded cattle stealing; a protocol was drawn up and nothing more was heard of it. As an official he is dishonest beyond description, he is not to be trusted at all. [44]

It is hardly surprising therefore to find the following remarks in a report of the *delegato di P. S.* about the leaders of one of the clientage parties of Gangi, Antonio Li Destri and Alessandro Milletari:

To all this must be added that these influential gentlemen, as soon as anyone is arrested for a crime or information laid against him, the minutest details of the crime in question become known to them, which helps them very considerably in preparing the defence of the accused.[45]

So much about the Sicilian-born official. The ethics of the Northern Italian were subject to a different threat: he came to the island with the prejudice of superiority and regarded the Sicilians as 'barbari' or 'semi-barbari', as not yet on a level of civilisation which would have required their correct treatment in accordance with administrative regulations or orders of procedure.[46] His discharge of official duties, in consequence, was not conducive to promoting the development of the Sicilian into a citizen of the State.

The jurors in criminal trials were subject not only to the moral norms of their own in-group with its hostility to the judiciary, but also to direct pressure and intimidation of every kind from the group of the defendant, and were thus an obstacle to an objective dispensation of justice. Typical of the imperfections of business contacts between State apparatus and citizen, typical indeed of a phenomenon governing all social relations, of the personalisation of all relationships including those which most require a business-like character, are the 'spicciafaccende'. They represent in effect an informal extension and enlargement of the formal bureaucracy. There were, and still are, the small *spicciafaccende* who make it their business to arrange the affairs of other people with the authorities; they accept rewards in proportion to the matter being dealt with. Their clients are, on the one hand, people who do not wish to waste time hanging about public offices and who can afford to let other people do their business for them, and, on the other hand, illiterates who are unable to complete the 'carta bollata', the stamped paper prescribed for all official transactions, and who cannot make their own way through the bureaucratic jungle. The *spicciafaccende* wait for their clients at the offices, but they also, quite frequently, make contact outside the office with the officials with whom they are acquainted from a large number of cases. To the student of the ideal type of bureaucracy the mere locale of their encounter, the café, speaks for itself.[47]

Alongside these small *spicciafaccende* there are the big ones who are socially superior to their clients, or, in this case, those who seek their help. They are *civili* and *signori*, who accept no money for their activity which they practise not as a profession but only occasionally. They create the impression of doing their clients a favour, but the illiterate peasants, from that moment onward, belong to their clientage and offer their patrons the advantages arising therefrom. Not infrequently a *spicciafaccende* also derives benefits for his own business from his knowledge of the papers he has read or written.

Like the 'avvocatucolo',[48] the *spicciafaccende* gives his client the impression that he maintains friendly relations with the official (if such relations do not in fact exist), and these are then represented as the decisive reason for the successful conclusion of some official transaction. Conversely the official, when granting the applicant some right to which he has a legal title, tries whenever possible to represent this as a 'favore' granted of his personal free will.

Our examination, in the early part of this chapter, of the inadequate spread of a modern legal-bureaucratic order of government has shown that the political life of Sicily, during the period of the last century here examined, reveals numerous feudal survivals. One such survival is the position of the *mafioso*. In order to understand this type it must always be remembered that his attitude, which in many respects corresponds to that of the feudal holder of power, no longer possesses the latter's unquestioned legitimacy. According to the need which, within the social structure, exists for his position, this position receives its ideological justification and acknowledgement in popular morality (the *mafioso* is an *uomo di rispetto*). As the need for it diminishes so its legitimacy disappears; as for the official norms, the codified law, the State morality—it has been in conflict with these from the very outset. The *mafioso* must be understood as a phenomenon between the power-holder authorised to apply physical violence and the criminal. The feudal baron, even if felt to be a tyrant, the corrupt official, the politician who abuses his position, the organised drug pedlar—none of these must be confused with the *mafioso*. It has become customary to describe the last two in particular as *mafiosi*, but in this way the concept loses its specific meaning.

The conditions described explain the decisive rôle played by the clientage as a structuring factor in Sicilian society in the past and, up to a point, to this day. Thus we read in Franchetti:

> ... Matters naturally reached a point where the instinct of self-preservation made everyone make sure of the help of someone stronger; since no such social strength in fact existed it fell to the clientage to provide the force which held society together. In this way Sicilian society, immediately upon the abolition of feudal rule, possessed all those features which the other States of Europe had possessed in the Middle Ages.[49]

And Alongi has this to say:

> ... It thus became necessary, I would almost say indispensable, to belong to a clientage from conviction or from fear or, as they are called here, a *partito*. Private and public life can be understood not only as a life led within the realm of the laws but invariably also as one lived within the *partito*. The honest man, even if he is rich but isolated, is exposed to

31

the arrogance and chicanery of the first person who comes along, while the common crook finds help in the *partito* and champions in the struggle against rival groups.[50]

The clientage was maintained by its instrumental character, its actual necessity, but its form of social organisation was supported also by a frame of mind which was specifically feudal and appealed to 'honour and loyalty freely given and kept as constituent motivations of action'.[51] We need only refer to the central meaning of the word 'uomo d'onore', which will be discussed in greater detail in the next chapter. A significant symptom among many is the popularity of the legends linked with the Paladins of Charlemagne and other mediaeval heroes, a subject which almost exclusively governs the plots in the 'teatro di pupi' and is the principal theme of the decorations on the 'carretto siciliano'. Another unmistakably feudal survival is the phenomenon, of considerable importance to the present examination, of submission to a person but never to an impersonal order.[51a]

On the basis of what we have said we can now modify the thesis of the 'fondamentale asocialità del siciliano'.[52] Danilo Dolci in his book published in 1966 [53] supported this thesis with numerous interviews but it soon becomes clear that the 'difficoltà della vita associativa' relates only to an inability to form formal groups with subject-orientated objectives. The questions 'Have you ever taken part in an organisation of any kind?', 'Did you ever feel a wish to join a political party?' and 'Did you never feel a wish to share in a religious group?' have invariably been answered with a variation of 'No, mai.' However, as soon as the interviewer asks: 'Could one say that your party is your family?' he receives a different reply. It is: 'Esatto, questo.'[54]

Because of the weakness of the coercive machine of the State there is an absence of a legal order and of the sanctions which lend dependability and durability to relationships in heteronomous groups. But this lack has no bearing on the possibility or stability of relationships in autonomous groups whose norms are not sanctioned by public law. *Famiglia, parentela, comparaggio, amicizia, clientela, cricca, partito, setta, fratellanza, banda*—these are meaningful words to the Sicilian. The bonds within these primary groups or informal groupings are felt clearly and as an obligation.

> Cumpari semu, cumpari ristamu,
> Veni la morti e nni spartemu,[55]

runs a popular saying: We are kinsmen, we remain kinsmen, only when death comes shall we part. Banfield, in his theory of the exclusive family orientation of the Southern Italian (amoral familism), described this state of affairs [56] but formulated his theory too narrowly through disregarding ritual relationship, friendship, clientage, bandit group and all kinds of clique relationships. In a society of 'amoral familists' *mafiosi* and banditry would not be possible.

2 Social stratification and economic situation

The social layering of a small Sicilian community about 1860 is characterised as follows in an article by Alongi:

> ... One or two baronial, ducal or similar families; a more or less numerous clergy; about 50 bourgeois families, about the same number or rather more workers, and finally the large mass of the peasants.[57]

The aristocratic families for the most part lived not at their place of origin but in Palermo, in mainland Italy, or abroad. The clergy came from the class of small leaseholders and small landowners (*burgisi, contadini agiati*):

> ... Perverted by smug pride at having risen from the mass of the peasantry they eagerly attach themselves to the class of *galantuomini* or *cappeddi*.[58]

The next stratum, the middle stratum, consisted of the bigger leaseholders, above all the 'gabellotti', and of the 'massari', the richer peasants who did not subdivide their own land, or any land they might in addition be leasing, into smaller leasehold plots, as customary, but worked it themselves with servants and hired hands. They were chiefly cattle breeders.[59] The upper levels of the middle stratum were formed by the 'cappeddi' (from Italian *cappelli* = hats), that is *civili, borghesi, professionisti*: landowners who did not themselves work, but followed the profession of lawyers, doctors, pharmacists, teachers and traders.

Between the middle and lower strate were the 'maestri', the 'artigiani', i.e. all types of artisans (Alongi's 'operai'). They were followed by the small share-croppers (mezzadri) and finally by the landless peasants who frequently did not own even the means of production necessary for the *mezzadro*, such as a mule and a plough, and who had to hire themselves out as day-wage labourers (*braccianti, salariati, giornalieri*). The lowest proletariat of this agrarian society was represented by the goatherds and shepherds (*caprai* and *pecorai*).

U   nobili

UM	civili professionisti, gabellotti	} cappeddi, gente di paese
LM	artigiani, massari	

33

UL	burgisi, mezzadri
LL	braccianti (vilici), caprai, pecorai

biritti, gente di campagna

Needless to say, the criteria for assignment to a category are here, as elsewhere, specific cultural or sub-cultural values. And the criteria which led to the emergence of the above stratification model characterise not only a class situation, but also a caste structure, i.e. they refer also to such things as honour, the prestige of an occupation, parentage, one's way of life, and education. And, last but not least, power:

> The private objective of Southern Italians and Northern Italians are, of course, more or less identical. However, the Northern Italian believes that in practice there is but one sure way of obtaining them—the acquisition of wealth, *la ricchezza*. Only the rich man, he believes, can in the long run guarantee security and prosperity for his family. The Southern Italian, on the other hand, knows that he can achieve this only by way of acquiring power, prestige, authority and fame. The Northern Italian of any class, therefore, is perpetually busy accumulating wealth. ... The Southern Italian ... above all wants to be obeyed, admired, respected, feared and envied.[60]

In addition to power, the decisive alternative criterion is manual labour—more precisely agricultural manual labour, work with the 'zappa', the hoe. Gaetano Mosca sees the difference between the small landowners of Piedmont and the small landowners of Sicily as follows:

> ... Whereas these [the Piedmontese] usually live in the country, in houses standing on their own land, dress like better-off peasants and, even if they employ a day-wage labourer, are not averse to working their fields themselves, the Sicilian *galantuomo* has a fundamentally different attitude to life even though as a rule he is the descendant of a peasant who, three or four generations earlier, succeeded, thanks to a lively intelligence, good work, rigorous saving and sometimes also usury, in accumulating a small fortune. He spends his life in continual hard and sometimes desperate efforts to keep up the customs, the rank and the outward appearance of the *civile*, the bourgeois who does not live by the work of his hands.[61]

The Sicilians nourish an ideal of human existence which is far removed from the real existence of most of them. Alongside the somewhat sombre and mysterious type of the *uomo di rispetto*, who exacts respect by a glance, a gesture or a word, who can settle problems and who in his own way matches up to the power criterion, there is the largely related type of the old-time *civile* and the Spanish *gentiluomo*, a man who leads a life free from continuous economic threat and from any connection with manual labour, let alone agricultural labour, a man who is educated, intelligent and superior, without everyday worries, and hence in a position to devote himself to nobler things. This is the life-style to which the peasant pays tribute whenever he addresses landowners, especially aristocratic ones, lawyers, priests and, last but not least, *mafiosi* as 'Don'.

Physical labour is generally despised as inferior. The life of the Sicilian *contadino* has never enjoyed the kind of positive interpretation which the German countryman has received through the ideas of the romantic movement or the American farmer through the glorification of the pioneer settlers. Contact with the soil and with animals is felt to be humiliating and unclean.[62]

This clash between ideal and reality was usually solved by escape into resignation. The world of *miseria*, an existence which differed so greatly from the ideal, was accepted as being imposed by fate. Changes had to come from outside or had to be sought outside Sicily. Towards the end of the century the United States became a symbol of a different world.

A second solution was rebellion. And the classical forms of rebellion against psychological *miseria*, the classical forms of realisation of this ideal, are brigandage and *mafioso* attitudes. Since the economic road and the educational road were both barred the solution was *violenza*; and, since power is a commodity in short supply, it was always only a solution for some individuals. More so than any criterion of possessions, it was the criteria of power and physical labour which gave rise to a dichotomous structure of society.[63] And in the absence of the nobility it was the *cappeddi*, the *gabellotti* and the *civili* who formed the real contrast to the peasants. In respect of them the feudal relationships between the castes have survived.[64] It is above all the *gabellotto* who takes the place of the baron, both in terms of economics and of power of command.

The centre of a big estate, a *feudo*, was the so-called *casamento*, the administrative and storage buildings and the stalls for the livestock. Attached to this, as a rule, was an olive grove (*uliveto*) or a vineyard (*vigneto*) which the owner himself worked with paid labour. He likewise grazed his livestock at his own expense, i.e. he did not hand it over into *gabella*, a form of lease. By far the greater part of the *feudo*, however, was planted to grain and it was here that the rural population chiefly found employment. This part of the estate was subdivided into a large number of small and very small plots which were leased to the peasants for one, two or three years. A rare form of lease was *enfiteusi*, a form of hereditary feudal concession which, however, greatly encouraged private initiative in meliorating the land. When feudal rule was abolished in Europe the land frequently was in effect in the hands of hereditary tenant families and was treated by them as if it were their own property. In Sicily there was no continuity of ownership nor any resultant investment of capital in houses, plantations, improvement of the soil, etc. [65] The customary form of leasehold in Sicily was a time-limited sharecropping (*mezzadria*). This in fact was a joint enterprise by owner and tenant: the owner provided the land and bore 50 per cent of the costs of seed stock, fertilisers and water, whereas the tenant was responsible for labour (his own, that of his family and, if necessary, *braccianti*) and for the means of production, i.e. livestock and tools. Of his yield the peasant then delivered to the owner either a certain proportion fixed in advance (in the case of *teratico*) or a percentage of the harvest (in the case of *metateria*). [66]

As the landowner did not originally have to compete with anyone for the labour of the peasant, and only later with the pull of emigration, he was able to keep him in total dependence. In view of the preponderance of a landless population and, in consequence, a surplus of labour there was exceedingly fierce competition among the peasants for tenancies, and his ability to grant or refuse a *mezzadria* made the landowner the master over the life of the share-cropper and also, by the provision of work, the life of the day-wage labourer. It is important to remember that the struggle for a livelihood was waged not in an impersonal market but for the favour of definite persons. The effects of this circumstance went far beyond the purely economic relations between landlords and those dependent on them.

It followed from the ruling position of the *padrone* and from his need to guard his fields, forests and pastures, to guarantee contracts verbally concluded and to collect the lease dues that the main rôle among the personnel even of the post-feudal estates was played by the *bravi*, the *campieri*, both of whom were field guards, and the bodyguards (*guarda spalle*) of the landowner. [67] The *campieri*, headed by a *soprastante*, mounted and armed, became for the *braccianti* and *burgisi* the embodiment of arbitrariness and arrogance. This sentiment is expressed in numerous laments and complaints in Sicilian popular poetry. [68] In order to 'enjoy' the 'protection' of the *campiere*, a share-cropper had to concede to his landlord the 'diritto di guardia', the right of protection, while conceding to the *campiere* himself the 'diritto di cuccia' or the 'diritto del maccherone', i.e. he undertook to make to him payments in kind of varying magnitude. [69] These feudal rights, which survived into the twentieth century, are the prototypes of the *mafioso* 'u pizzu' (*fari vagnari u pizzu* = to wet one's beak), [70] of tribute payment in return for guarantees of protection; they are the origin of the method and at the same time its rationalised justification.

More and more often a mediator, the above-mentioned *gabellotto*, interposed himself between the aristocratic landowner and the share-cropper. Because of their absence the landlords were increasingly compelled to give up managing their estates themselves and therefore they placed them in the hands of others. These others in Sicily were not agents but large-scale tenants; in this way the landowner avoided the drawbacks of bad or dishonest management and the trouble of continuous supervision. The large-scale tenant accepted the land in *gabella*, i.e. a form of tenancy; he hardly ever paid for it in kind but almost invariably in money; and moreover in advance. In formal legal terms he was no more than a tenant but in fact he assumed all the rights of the feudal landlord and in the eyes of the peasantry he stepped fully and entirely into the baron's place. By his origin the *gabellotto* was a small landowner, a trader or a cattle dealer, a cattle raiser, a *borghese*, or frequently a *soprastante* or *campiere* who had acquired some money through extortion—in short, he came from the group of people who had succeeded, in some way or other, in raising themselves above the mass of the peasantry and acquiring money. This new class of *gabellotti*, which is of vital importance to the understanding of *mafioso* attitudes, then realised its profits by the extreme exploitation of sub-tenants and day-wage labourers on the one hand and by a continuous reduction of obligations towards the landowner on the other.[71]

Since 1812 another process has been increasing noticeably—the transfer of the land from the hands of the aristocracy into those of this new bourgeois class.[72] It is estimated that between 1860 and the end of the century bourgeois-owned landed property increased from 250,000 ha. (about 670,000 acres) to about 650,000 ha. (1,620,000 acres)—an increase of roughly 400,000 ha. (1,000,000 acres). Up to a point this increase is due to the usurping of common land, and partly to the purchase of sequestrated Church lands. It is nevertheless estimated that something between 150,000 and 200,000 ha. (375,000 to 500,000 acres) had come from aristocratic landed property.[73] The feudal estates which their owners had not been allowed to sell—because they were fiefs—became private and hence saleable property after 1812, when parts of them had been added to the common community property in order to compensate the peasants for the loss of *usi civici*, the various small rights which they had enjoyed on the feudal property.

In the course of time the *gabellotti* exerted increasing pressure on the old landowners and the rent paid by them became smaller and smaller; frequently payment was withheld altogether under a variety of pretexts. This trend was in the nature of the economic relations between the two partners; even if the *gabellotto* did not always intend to force the owner to sell, he at least tried in this way to increase his profit. Frequently, however, this was in fact a means of getting possession of the land. The landlord, who needed a great deal of money for his life in the city (and moreover was often in debt to his principal tenant, who had become a money-lender both to the *contadino* and to the *nobile*), often had no other choice than to sell off part of his property. It must be remembered that the proprietor had hardly any power of enforcement available to him which might have guaranteed observance of the contract; the *gabellotto* represented the real power in the countryside. Since the State discharged its economy-regulating function only very inadequately the only law applying to such contracts (most of which were only verbal anyway) for all rent payments, duration of tenancy and anything else was the law of the stronger. And it is obvious that this stronger party need not necessarily have been the landowner. As soon as the State assumed its economy-regulating function (and in this particular historical situation this meant protecting property) conditions changed greatly. Thus a landowner wrote to Mori, the Fascist Prefect of Palermo, as follows:

> C., a former feudal estate of 120 *salme*, situated in the territory of S. M., used to yield us an annual profit of 4,000 lire and did so for more than 30 years. Since the arrival of Your Excellency and the magnificent offensive against the evil-doers of the other side we have leased it for an annual sum of 60,000 lire payable in advance.[74]

Mori himself, most instructively to us, summed up the result of his measures as follows:

> Within a short period 320 estates were liberated from the *mafia* in the Province of Palermo alone and 28,000 ha. of land for which the *mafia* had been paying rents kept low through extortion, again yielded profit in accordance with its value. The difference between the old and the new rents amounted to a good 18 million.[75]

If financial pressure proved unsuccessful there were other ways of making a landowner tire of his property or at least of preventing him from visiting and inspecting his property regularly—the methods of terror, threatening letters, attempted abduction, warning shots. In the event of a sale the *gabellotto* usually succeeded in keeping competition down or indeed in making an auction sale a fiction by presenting himself as the only buyer and thus dictating the price.[76]

Frequently this playing with violence was not necessary for the unrolling of this economic process but in some form or other it almost invariably served to speed it up. The factor of 'physical violence' has been running through the whole of this chapter; it is time, in conclusion, to highlight it once more.

At the time of feudal rule the use of legitimate physical violence was not a prerogative of the organs of the Monarchy only but also of the barons or indeed the *bravi* to whom the barons delegated this right. It might happen that the *bravi* abused this right and acquired personal advantages by means of violence and arbitrary action. Nevertheless physical violence until 1812 was the legal instrument of the ruling caste by which it maintained its status. The law, actual conditions and popular morality were in agreement. After the end of feudalism, however, and even more so after 1860, a gap opened between the law on the one hand and real conditions and popular morality on the other. The codified law now regarded violent action of any kind as an offence, and the State tried to suppress it also in practice. However, actual conditions did not change and physical power continued to be the decisive element in the creation and monopolisation of opportunities of economic gain and in the assignment of social status. But, in parallel with the changes in ownership conditions, this instrument became accessible now to a larger number of persons.[77] The open bourgeois society broke the ancient monopoly (also for popular morality) and made a redistribution possible, a continuous process of redistribution with a new kind of only temporary monopolisation, invariably confined to a certain person and not hereditary, and hence neither caste nor class determined. In this manner it produced the type of the *mafioso*.

By no means rare prior to 1860[78] and to be found in all strata of the population, he gained his typical form in the person of the *gabellotto*. The *gabellotto*'s economic position, his two-fronted position against peasant and landowner, and the fact of his social rise which, as a new man, gave him less moral authority than was enjoyed by the *padrone antico*, if only by tradition —all these required of him, if he was to assert himself, at least the ability to apply force, the threat of violence. The *gabellotto* is the typical *mafioso*, or, conversely, since his position requires *mafioso* qualities, the *mafioso* frequently succeeds in becoming a large-scale tenant. He brings these qualities to the position, or his position teaches him these qualities—we are faced here with an interdependency.

Intimidating threats and violence, however, began to appear also in all other kinds of economic transactions and eventually became attributes of positions of power. The officials of the new Italian State had their hands tied to a far greater extent than their Bourbon predecessors; they were no longer able to dismiss arbitrarily an elected mayor or dissolve a municipal administration. Moreover, they depended on Ministers who in turn had to keep the goodwill of the Deputies. And these had to keep sight of their major electors and could not refuse to return favours if favours were demanded of them. Thus the real power, which in the countryside also commanded the votes of the electors, exerted an influence on the machinery of municipal and provincial administrations and upon the State's judiciary organs. And this arrangement with the holders of office prevented those private acts of violence, which had been declared offences by the codified law, from being in fact suppressed.

Notes

1 Cf. Weber 1964, pp. 658, 24 and 39

2 'Self-help thus pressupposes a higher, more comprehensive, authority than the party helping itself...'; i.e. there must be at least the claim of a superior authority—in this case the Bourbon or the Italian State—but also no more than the claim. 'As soon as self-help is condemned not only by the law but also by custom and popular conscience it becomes a crime.' Both quotations from S. R. Steinmetz, article *Selbsthilfe* in Vierkandt (Ed.) 1931, p. 518

3 Cf. Titone 1964, p. 176

4 Cf. Amati 1939, vol. iv, pp. 558–60, 602–4, and 626 ss.

5 La Mantia 1886, p. 8

6 Cf. Cosentino 1885, pp. 7–10, Garufi 1920, pp. 230 ss., and La Mantia 1886 *passim*

7 Cf. Scherma 1896, p. 38

8 Quoted in Lionti 1886, p. 52

9 In 1610; cf. Titone 1964, p. 219

10 Cf. Franchetti 1925, p. 73

11 Mühlmann 1962, pp. 304–5

12 For the history of the conflict between State and Inquisition cf. Pontieri 1945, pp. 123–88

13 The Decree is quoted in D'Alessandro 1959, p. 30

14 Parliamentary Debate of 11 June 1875, quoted in Russo (Ed.) 1964, p. 121

15 Ramistella n.d.

16 Cf. D'Alessandro 1959, p. 162

17 Pagano 1877, p. 42; further on this subject cf. Franchetti 1925, pp. 50–1, Novacco 1963, pp. 69–71, D'Alessandro 1959, pp. 29–32, Briatico 1963, p. 55, Titone 1964, p. 46, Romano 1966, pp. 97–102 and Colajanni 1900, pp. 66–7.

Novacco 1963 on p. 193 quotes the statement of the captured English banker John Rose (1876) to the effect that the bandits who were keeping him captive one day encountered a police force: '... queste furono salutate dalla banda Leone con dei fischi e segni convenzionali.'

18 *Archivio di Stato di Palermo, Gabinetto di Prefettura* (hereinafter abridged as ASP) 1893, busta 133, cat. 20, fasc. 23 bis. The following quotations ibid.

19 ASP 1884, busta 77, cat. 20, fasc. 20

20 Cf. Cutrera 1900, pp. 23

21 *Direzione Generale della Statistica. Statistica Giudiziaria Penale per l'anno 1893*. Rome 1895, pp. LXXXIV–XCII

22 *Inchiesta parlamentare sulle condizioni dei contadini delle province meridionali (Inchiesta Lorenzoni)*, vol. vii, Rome 1909, p. 854

23 Cf. Vierkandt 1928, pp. 79–80

[24] Cf. Franchetti 1925, pp. 12–14 and p. 55, *Relazione della Giunta per l'inchiesta sulle condizioni della Sicilia (Relazione Bonfadini)*, Rome 1876, partly reproduced in Russo (Ed.) 1964, cf. especially pp. 234–7, and Loschiavo 1962 *passim*

[25] Cf. Loschiavo 1956, pp. 201–11 for a good example

[26] Franchetti 1925, p. 177

[27] Alongi 1899, p. 17

[28] Diego Taiani in the Chamber of Deputies on 11 June 1875, published in Russo (Ed.) 1964, p. 139

[29] Pontieri 1943, p. 58

[30] Colajanni first drew attention to this fact in 1899

[31] Cf. Smith 1959, pp. 31–2

[32] Cf. Candida 1960, p. 88, also D'Alessandro 1959, pp. 87–8, Alongi 1887, pp. 42–3 and Novacco 1963, pp. 145–6

[33] Cf. Hammer 1965, p. 26

[34] Alongi 1887, pp. 45–6, cf. also Novacco 1963, pp. 138–9 and Wermert 1905, p. 452

[35] *Atti della Giunta per la Inchiesta Agraria...* 1885, vol. xiii, 2, p. 430

[36] Ibid., p. 488

[37] Even the fame of Garibaldi's *picciotti* is probably partly due to a romantic legend. Cf. the account of an eye-witness (Dumas): '... with the *picciotti* of Sant' Anna and of Coppolo who linked up at Salemi with the volunteers; about 450 men (p. 69). ... At the very first shots some of the *picciotti* disappeared. About 150 held out (p. 70) ... abandoned by the *picciotti*, whom they saw fleeing down the road, the *carabinieri* were forced to withdraw to the mountain ridges (p. 84).'

[38] Processo Amoroso 1883

[39] Franchetti 1925, p. 58

[40] Weber 1964, p. 705

[41] Novacco 1963, p. 89

[42] In Russo (Ed.) 1964, pp. 215–16

[43] Franchetti 1925, p. 19

[44] ASP, busta 85, cat. 20, fasc. 91

[45] Ibid., letter of 19 July 1885

[46] Romano 1966, p. 148

[47] Cf. the self-portrait of the *spicciafaccende* 'Uncle Andrea' in Dolci 1961, pp. 78–81

[48] Cf. Franchetti 1925, p. 244

[49] Franchetti 1925, p. 91

[50] Alongi 1887, p. 135

[51] Weber 1964, p. 826

[51a] Cf. also Mühlmann and Llaryora 1968

[52] Titone 1964, p. 308

[53] *Chi gioca solo*. Turin 1966

[54] Ibid., p. 17

[55] Briatico 1963, p. 105

[56] Banfield 1958

[57] Alongi 1894, pp. 229–55, quotation p. 230

[58] Ibid., p. 232

[59] Cf. Sereni 1947, p. 324

[60] Barzini 1965, p. 246

[61] Moscow 1949, p. 189

[62] Cf. Alongi 1887, pp. 31–3, Friedman 1960 *passim* and Friedman 1963 *passim* (on p. 223: 'exemption from labor... becomes the only true criterion of distinction...') as well as Lepsius 1965, p. 332

[63] Cf. Franchetti 1925, p. 83, Wermert 1905, p. 452, and Lepsius 1965, p. 332

[64] Cf. Gatto 1950 and Alongi 1887, p. 32

[65] Cf. Ghino Valenti: *Il latifondo—proprietari, gabelotti e contadini*, first published 1895, reprinted in Romano 1945, pp. 383–8

[66] Cf. Sereni 1947, pp. 176–7, and Hammer 1965, pp. 7–10

[67] Cf. Alongi 1887, p. 30, and Sereni 1947, p. 178

[68] Cf. the poems of the illiterate day-wage labourer Andrea Albano in Sereni 1947, pp. 178–9, 181 and 191–3

[69] Cf. Sereni 1947, p. 179

[70] Cf. Pantaleone 1962, p. 43

[71] Cf. Pontieri 1943, pp. 55–7 and pp. 65–74, Sereni 1947, pp. 183–6, Franchetti 1925, pp. 86–7, Hammer 1965, pp. 8–9 and Giuseppe Montalbano: *La mafia siciliana* in Tocco 1950, pp. 86–102, especially p. 100

[72] This rise of a new class has found its literary reflection in the works of Giuseppe Tomasi di Lampedusa, cf. in particular *The Rise of a Tenant* and *The Leopard*

[73] Cf. Sereni 1947, p. 291

[74] In Cesare Mori 1932, p. 354

[75] Ibid., p. 351

[76] Cf. Alongi 1887, pp. 21–2, Hammer 1965, pp. 16–17, Romano 1966, pp. 174–5, Novacco 1963, pp. 21 and 99–100, Pantaleone 1962, pp. 28–9, 49–50 and 100, as well as Sereni 1947, pp. 164 and 291–2

[77] Cf. the same idea in Franchetti 1925, p. 90

[78] Cf. also the examples quoted in this book from the letter of the Procuratore Generale of Trapani, Pietro C. Ulloa (1838—Chapter 5) and from the letter of the Commandant of Castellammare del Golfo to the Prince of Satriano (1849—Chapter 6). Cf. also Costanza 1966 and Roberto Llaryora, *The Sicilian Mafia: Early Structures and Social Dynamics in the Period of Spanish Rule (16th and 17th centuries)*, to be published shortly

4 The Mafioso

Having discussed the historical and socio-structural conditions which gave rise to the *mafioso* boss type, its phylogenesis, we shall now attempt to show how the personal career of a *mafioso* took shape against this background— his ontogenesis, as it were:

1 Origin

Let us look first of all at the social stratum from which the *mafioso* comes. It is difficult to generalise on this point as the available material is exceedingly limited. The scant sociological interest of authors on the subject has meant that no importance has been attached to this question. As, moreover, many of the authors have, or had, a highly critical attitude to the ruling strata and to the social order as a whole, they were only too ready in a polemical manner to assign the 'great criminals' to the middle and upper strata. (Admittedly with a certain justification, since a successful *mafioso* usually belongs to the middle class both in economic status and way of life—but this of course does not state anything about his origins.) Thus even such an objective author as Cutrera writes:

> ... The leaders of the *mafia* can always be found among the big tenants and landowners, i.e. among persons who by comparison with the rest live in better economic circumstances. The poor peasant, the real victim of the feudal estates and of the present-day economic and social situation, on the other hand, is rarely a *mafioso*.[1]

Hobsbawm accepts this view from him:

> ... All the heads of the local *mafias* were (and are) men of wealth, some ex-feudalists in the inland areas, but overwhelmingly men of the middle class, capitalist farmers and contractors, lawyers and the like.[2]

Unfortunately a *mafioso* usually does not draw attention to himself until his position is consolidated and turned into a monopoly, i.e. when he has become a true *mafioso*, and not during his career. Police reports and records of trials frequently deal only with the circumstances of the crime and pay little attention to the life story of the criminal.

Nevertheless, there are certain data which permit a very interesting and hitherto largely disregarded conclusion about the origins of the *mafioso*: many (probably the majority) come not from the middle, but from the lower, stratum. Often these facts are mentioned only in order to demonstrate the particular greed, ruthlessness and shiftlessness of the 'criminal': once so poor, and now done so well for himself thanks to his evil-doings!

Thus three of the most famous *mafiosi* of the century came from very modest beginnings. Vito Cascio Ferro, who, up to the era of Mori, enjoyed the greatest respect in Palermo, was the son of poor, illiterate peasants from Bisacquino. Calogero Vizzini's father was a small 'coltivatore diretto', i.e. he owned a small patch of land which he worked himself but in addition had to hire himself out as a day-wage labourer. Giuseppe Genco Russo, after the Second World War the unchallenged master of Mussomeli and a man of far-reaching influence, did not own a penny in his youth and was forced to work as a goatherd on the Polizello estate whose *gabellotto* he subsequently became. Thus he was on the very lowest step of Sicilian agrarian society: 'Un tempo era scarso preciso'[3], at one time he was just a beggar, a fellow-villager said of him.

Nitto Minasola, *capo mafia* of Monreale in the 'forties, likewise began his career as a shepherd. '... Minasola's father had left him two scrawny goats' is how Lewis picturesquely if not accurately sums up his situation.[4] Vincenzo Lauria, after the Second World War a wealthy wine merchant of Alcamo, had begun his career as a *carrettiere*: though poor he at least did not belong to the *gente di campagna*. Vincenzo Rimi, on the other hand, also from Alcamo, a rich cattle dealer and proprietor of the Motel Beach at Alcamo Marina, was the son of a shepherd and was himself *bracciante* and *vaccaro*, a cowherd.

An anonymous letter of 1885 reports:

> One of the many dangerous and mysterious members of the *alta mafia* is the despicable Filippo Battaglia from Alia, who within 20 years managed to work his way up from a simple ceramics worker to a social position which seems enviable. He bought land and he bought houses, built new ones and now indulges in immoderate luxury. ... And moreover he has for the past few years kept his son Angelo at the University of Naples, which must involve him in not inconsiderable expense.[5]

A man who can let his son study in Naples (and whose *mafioso* attitudes will be mentioned later) had thus started as a ceramics worker; he is described not as a craftsman (*artigiano*) but as a manual worker (*manovale*). Examples can also be found in literature: Lampedusa in *The Leopard* does not actually mention Calogero Sedara's father but everything points to the fact that Sedara has risen only in the course of his own life; his father-in-law, a poor share-cropper, 'was so dirty and uncouth that everyone called him Peppe 'Mmerda'.[6] And in Loschiavo's novel *Gli inesorabili* we read this about the *mafioso* Luparello:

> You, bailiff of the Baron Ochipinti, have created for yourself an economic position often at the risk of your life, through the work of your own hands, and have made a name for yourself in the Madonie region. You are the bailiff and superintendent of the estate. ... My father told me that you began your career by grazing sheep and cattle.[7]

Frequently even rich *mafiosi* are illiterate and thereby betray their low origin. Vito Cascio Ferro could neither read nor write; Nitto Minasola had never been to school; Calogero Vizzini had been to school for only three years and was always regarded as illiterate.

A few others possessed an inherited fortune, such as Giuseppe Valenza from Prizzi, whose activity between 1860 and 1890 will be repeatedly mentioned later. Likewise in the case of a *mafioso* doctor or lawyer the social rise must have taken place at least in the preceding generation. Nevertheless, in the great majority of cases on which no data are available, one would be justified in assuming an origin from the lower stratum.

It is an interesting fact that frequently not only the *mafioso* son but the whole family from which he comes is engaged in vertical mobility. The motivation of achievement appears to be higher for such a family than the Silician average, and different members use different vehicles of social enhancement. Thus priests are not infrequently found among the relatives of *mafiosi*.

There is no doubt that horizontal mobility also plays an important part in the shaping of the personality of some *mafiosi*. A time spent in another environment certainly contributes to ridding them of the sense of impotent dependence which is traditional for their stratum of origin. Thus Vito Casio Ferro, Genco Russo, Vincenzo Collura from Corleone and others spent some of their earlier years as emigrants in the U.S.A. and Lauria in France. (For a more recent phenomenon, the more far-reaching cultural exchange and the type of the 'nuovo mafioso' see Chapter 7.)

2   Career

A specific *mafioso* career leads to the attainment of a position of power and to a step up the social ladder. The two processes are not independent of each other but the rise to power is the condition for economic advancement. (It should be mentioned, of course, that a better economic position can in turn strengthen a person's power.) We must therefore, first of all, examine those selection criteria which are effective in a person's power career. Needless to say, the Sicilian sub-culture (at least in this process of distribution of power) did not operate its selection in accordance with values reformulated into norms by formal institutions. The assignment of status in the power hierarchy was conditioned not by codified norms but, in line with the importance of informal structures, by some criteria specifically excluded by the legal institutions—a man's ability to use force, a successfully survived clash with the judicial organs of the State, recognition by other informal holders of power, the ability to instil fear, and recognition by the subjected.

2.1. *Act of violence*

All power is ultimately based on the ability to use force. If a power holder's position is supported by codified law then this ultimate possibility of enforcement may gradually be forgotten in the conscious mind of the subordinate; in the case of the *mafioso* the relationship always remains much more direct. An act of force opens a man's road to power; without having applied physical force at least once he would find it impossible to meet the other requirements necessary for the exercise of *mafioso* functions. He could not gain recognition, instil fear, or successfully confront *mafioso* rivals.

> Frequently a field guard enjoys the reputation of having one or two 'cuio al sole', i.e. of having already committed one or two murders. Once he is surrounded by this aura his career is made and he has become a person who must be feared, a person 'chi duna suggizioni', who demands subjection—a necessary and therefore better paid person.[8]

> ... His sole prestige stems from his past and from the crimes committed in his youth, from his potential ability to apply force, as confirmed by his youthful deed. He is a man who can kill without further ado because he has killed before.[9]

The authority of the *mafioso* is based on this act of physical violence. An ordinary goatherd or shepherd has become a man to be reckoned with, a man who has demonstrated 'c'avi sangu 'ntra li vini, c'avi ficatu, ch'è uomo', that he has blood in his veins, and that he is a man, and that he will not 'na musca supra lu nasu', have a fly dancing on his nose.[10]

In 1926 Vito Cascio Ferro was accused in his indictment of participation in twenty murders, eight attempted murders and five robberies with violence —not to mention the thirty-seven acts of extortion and fifty-three other offences which were accompanied merely by threats of physical violence. This

46

participation, moreover, was not always confined to instigation; he himself boasted of murdering the American F.B.I. agent Petrosino. Vizzini and Russo started their careers as 'giovani malandrini', juvenile highway robbers. Acts of violence are known of Malta, Liggio, Collura, Sacco and many others; Filippo Battaglia was accused in the anonymous letter quoted above of having ambushed a mail coach and killing the accompanying 'uomini della Forza'. Domenico Militello from Montemaggiore, *'possidente, consigliere comunale, ammonito quale scroccone, camorrista, mafioso, manutengolo di briganti'*[11], had been sentenced to *domicilio coatto* for an abduction (*sequestro di persona*) in his youth.[12]

In his report 'Biografie riferibili ai Signori Li Destri Antonino di Antonio e Milletari Alessandro di Michelangelo da Gangi' the Pubblica Sicurezza official in Gangi writes to the Questor of Palermo as follows:

> Li Destri Antonino, son of Antonio, 45, landowner from Gangi, is regarded as a *mafioso* and, moreover, is one. He is arrogant and hides fugitive criminals of all orders of magnitude. Because hereabouts he is considered a capable swordsman he believes he can intimidate anybody....[13]

We observe here that an exalted social or economic status does not automatically result in a good position in the power hierarchy. Li Destri was an impoverished baron. Like him, Giuseppe Valenza from Prizzi, a rich landowner mentioned earlier, founded his power not so much on economic circumstances as on performed or threatened acts of physical violence. In 1866 he participated in several raids of Don Peppino Il Lombardo's gang, 'as an amateur, i.e. solely in order to be present when these misdeeds were committed, without sharing in the booty which he did not need'.[14] He used violence not to enrich himself but to gain a reputation; or else to avenge himself, as in the gang's notorious raid on Cammarata which Valenza used for raping Baron Cassaro's daughter whose hand he had asked for in vain.[15] (Documents to be quoted later will show that he was not always disinterested in material profit.) Even afterwards he never hesitated to regulate his affairs if need be by force:

> Together with Murò Francesco, who is already under arrest, and his brother Murò Salvatore, Valenza personally took part in the murderous attack on Fucurino Sebastiana and Macaluso Vincenzo in September 1882.[16]

The great importance of violence sometimes resulted in the *mafia* being exclusively defined through it:

> I recognise the *mafioso* by his *mafioso* behaviour, no matter what it is,

and I believe that *mafia* in all its forms means the commission of an act of violence against another person.[17]

This 'sopruso', this act of violence, leads to the discovery of power, the discovery that it is possible to manipulate other people and gain not only outward advantages but a deep psychological satisfaction from the imposition of one's own will. And the wish to hold and multiply what has been once discovered, enjoyed or exploited requires recourse to violent action also in the future.

2.2. *Clash with the State's judiciary system and acquittal*

To say that every *mafioso* must have used force at some time or other does not, of course, mean that everybody who uses force becomes a *mafioso*. In fact, it is in the events following the violent act that the career of the *mafioso* differs from that of the bandit. By their actions both, *mafioso* and bandit, clash with the legal norms of the State. The bandit has to evade the arm of the State by escape; the typical end of his clash is his taking to the mountains, the *latitanza*. The *mafioso*, on the other hand, remains the stronger—or rather, the inability of the judiciary machine to touch a culprit for a violation of the law proves that he is made of *mafioso* stuff. The typical end of his clash with the law is acquittal for lack of proof, 'per insufficienza di prove'. A great many—indeed nearly all—*mafiosi* (including Ferro, Vizzini, Russo, Sacco, Liggio, Collura) had indeed been to prison, but nearly always only under detention pending investigation. Vito Casio Ferro was charged sixty-nine times and sixty-nine times he was acquitted—until in 1926 Mori succeeded in getting him sentenced. Valenza, whom we mentioned earlier, was caught together with the entire Don Peppino gang and charged with several felonies.

> For this deed he was arrested and spent three years in detention pending investigation. Then he was released for lack of evidence.[18]

And this in contrast to all other defendants. The following report may be found in the 'Copia dei cenni biografici di Giuseppe Valenza da Prizzi trasmessi al Giudice Istruttore ed inseriti nel processo d'assassinio in persona di Anzaldi Nicolò'.

Delegato di P.S.   Corleone 14 Giugno 1883

1868:   The Palermo Assize Court acquitted him of the above-mentioned charge. It was universally said that he achieved this result through *mafia* intrigues and with the help of a few thousand *onze*.[19]

The same 'Copia dei cenni biografici' contains yet another illustration of the present argument:

1877: In an anonymous letter to the Royal Prefecture of Palermo he was denounced in March as the principal receiver of the Capraro and Di Pasquale gang and as the organiser of the abduction of Francesco Mancuso from Palazzo Abriano.

1877 (June): The Pretor of Prizzi put him under police surveillance, *in absentia*, as he had escaped and gone into hiding in Rome under the protection of a highly-placed and greatly respected personage.

1877 (August): The police official of Prizzi reported him for infringing the regulations of police surveillance by continuing to be a fugitive.

1877 (August): The Court of Palermo acquitted him of the above-mentioned charge.

1878 (April): The Pretor of Prizzi discontinued his police surveillance.[20]

The trial to which the above biographical notes refer marked the conclusion of an investigation which had been running from 1883 to 1885: Valenza had been accused of instigating the murder of the peasant Nicolò Anzaldi. The outcome of the trial is commented on in the following letter:

Office of the Questor of Palermo.

To the Most Illustrious Prefect of Palermo

Palermo, November 12, 1885.

Re: Indictment of Valenza Giuseppe from Prizzi.

The Assize Court today heard the case of the notorious Valenza Giuseppe, charged with instigating the murder of Anzaldi Nicolò. Following the negative finding of the jury he was acquitted and released.

The task of the Defence, represented by the honourable Attorneys Crispi and Cuccia, was greatly facilitated by the evidence of the police official Farini who withdrew his earlier reports, stating that he had been the victim of a deception and confirming that Valenza was a man of unblemished character.

In point of fact I am not surprised as I have always regarded Farini as a not entirely reliable employee.

So much for Your Excellency's better understanding of the matter.

Respectfully,
The Questor [21]

There are two reasons why acquittal—not acquittal for proved innocence but acquittal for lack of evidence—becomes the second vital selection criterion. It proves, on the one hand, a man's ability to silence witnesses and, on the other hand, the existence of influential friends and protectors. The former might just be due to the rules of *omertà* and be enjoyed also by the bandit, but the second factor as a rule is absent in the case of the bandit and becomes the fundamental feature of *mafioso* authority. The first acquittal after the first trial strengthens a young *mafioso*'s sense of power and consolidates his position towards the outside world. He begins to be respected and feared.

2.3. *Recognition by other mafiosi*

Naturally, as the quoted texts show, acquittal continues to be important for the regular renewal of *mafioso* authority; nevertheless it is the first acquittal that is vital for a man's career and opens up future possibilities. The most important of these is recognition of the novice by other *mafiosi*. He becomes an 'amico degli amici', a friend of the friends, when a *uomo di rispetto* mentions him with commendation or respect and tries to draw him into his own *cosca*, into the group which he has built up around himself, into his *mafioso* clientage, by demanding services from him (or rather giving him the chance of discharging such services) and offering him his protection. This process, which is entirely informal, without any rigid rules, and may take different forms in detail, has frequently been simplified into admission to a secret society. Combined with this process, or sometimes independently of it, a second occurs—the assignment of *mafioso* functions. A landowner or a *gabellotto* employs the novice who has proved himself by the successful use of force as a *campiere* or *guardiano* and entrusts him with the protection of his fields, his herd or his orange groves. Since he has proved his abilities people turn to him. A robbed person will seek his mediation in the recovery of stolen cattle. Two others will ask him to settle a dispute between them. A candidate in a local election will appeal for his support in the hope of getting more votes.

2.4. Qualities ascribed to the mafioso by his social environment [21a]

The act of violence and subsequent acquittal form the nucleus around which the rest crystallises—they are the reality. Around this reality the *mafioso*'s halo of reputation now begins to form, a halo of attributes which the *mafioso* is credited with.[21a]

> A *mafioso* is not the man who regards himself as one, but he who is regarded as one. It is the public that makes a *mafioso*.[22]

In his first trial the defendant must be believed to possess the ability to silence witnesses—then the witnesses will in fact keep silent. The first acquittal may well be the result of a formal legal impossibility of bringing in a verdict of guilty, due to the fact that the court has to stick to the penal law procedure. Nevertheless the Sicilians invariably ascribe it to the intervention of influential protectors, even though, as a result of this success, the culprit only creates his *partito* subsequently.

To start with, *mafioso* action is not possible without certain complementary action by others. In 1960 there was a strike of *braccianti* on the estate of Baron Bupillo near Vittoria, in the Province of Ragusa. *Campieri* brought from another estate in Agrigento Province were intended to break the strike by their threatening behaviour. However, the peasants refused to be intimidated and the *mafioso* means proved totally ineffective.[23]

> The point is that the people in this village are cowards.[24]

> We hold back from fear because we are afraid they might do harm to us and our families.[25]

> If a lot of us young people are timid and keep quiet I don't think that this is really timidity, because there are quite a few here who would like to speak out—it is simply fear because many a person thinks that tomorrow, or tonight, or whenever he goes out to the fields to work, a hail of bullets from a *lupara* might get him.[26]

A *mafioso* must be in a position to instil fear, and this must be matched by fear on the part of the subjected—otherwise he cannot succeed in exerting an influence on others, in discharging the functions which constitute his part, without having continually to apply physical coercion—and this would not be practicable.

> *Mafia* can be objectively defined as the mysterious sense of fear which a

man notorious for his crimes or brutal use of force arouses in the weak, the meek and the cowardly.[27]

This objective is served, above all, by the peculiar technique of terrorisation which is discussed in greater detail in the next chapter. But even the everyday behaviour of the man of power is designed to work in that direction.

> What most creates the impression of awe in the charismatic personality is an icy impenetrability or a mysterious lurking, cunning or uncertain element. The power technique of those inspiring awe operates with the creation of this kind of impression—e.g. with deliberate pauses in propagandistic persuasions, mysterious silences. ... All this is designed to create directly a sense of insecurity.[28]

Thus Alongi writes:

> It is strange that in that hot and colourful country, where ordinary speech is so honey-sweet, hyperbolic and picturesque, that of the *mafiosi* is curt, restrained and decisive.[29]

And Vaccaro has this to say:

> The true, authentic *mafioso* almost invariably behaves modestly, speaks with restraint and similarly listens with restraint, and displays great patience; if he is offended in public he does not react at all but he kills afterwards.[30]

The pressure which is exerted by such a personality, or which the subordinates feel to issue from such a personality, is described by the Pubblica Sicurezza official of Prizzi:

> Following the arrest of the above-named according to warrant, public opinion has picked up a little and many are regaining confidence and courage to talk about matters which hitherto have been secrets. On the other hand, it is true that everything is still kept within the bounds of utmost confidence, inasmuch as many of those who might submit convincing evidence about these facts continue to be irresolute and cautious from fear that Valenza, in view of all the influence he enjoys, might find himself very quickly released from the grasp of the judiciary.[31]

Moreover, the exercise of certain functions soon develops a momentum of its own. Once the rising *mafioso* has succeeded in successfully playing the part of protector, mediator and collector of tribute, he is soon regarded as competent in these things. The smooth progress of his enterprises is guaranteed less and less by actual physical force and increasingly by this competance attributed to him. The more persons believe him capable of discharging that function the more new persons will submit to him without contradiction and in this way render possible his success. This interdependence, this continuous reciprocal inflation of being and appearing must never be lost sight of in the characterisation of the *mafioso*.

Giuseppe Genco Russo sees this process as follows:

> Because of a certain way of life matters simply happen one after another, they follow each other. When someone came to me and I did him a favour, when a second person came to me and I did him a favour too, things just continued and became a kind of habit. In this way the circle of people where my name was well known grew larger.[32]

One can hardly improve on this way of putting it.

Denti di Pirajno throws some light on a further small piece of the mosaic of informal acclamation:

> Puddu saw the *maresciallo* toying with a cigarette, nervously rolling it this way and that between his fingers, and gave him a light. Don Calogero was restlessly fidgeting on his chair. Well, well—how inquisitive Don Puddu has suddenly become. ... A surge of pride flooded Puddu's heart: for the first time the *maresciallo* had addressed him as 'Don' and thereby recognised the rank which he had gained for himself among the people who counted in the district.[33]

The prestige of the *mafioso* is determined by three factors—his own actions, the attribution to him of further qualities (*'La gente immagina di più di quello che è'* a peasant from Mussomeli said about Genco Russo[34], and the authority and respect enjoyed by the *mafioso* type and now transferred to the individual.

The indispensable social background of the processes described is the face-to-face group or at least a society in which oral communication renders possible this particular kind of prestige formation and dissemination. We therefore invariably find an emphasis on rumour in connection with *mafioso* attitudes. Thus in the Cannizzo trial: *'correva già la voce ... per voce pubblica si disse ... era la voce pubblica che dicea essere persone mandate dagli Scalia ... e poi in un piccolo paese tutto si sa presto ...'.*[35] Or in the Amoroso trial: *'pri bucca di populazioni si dissi'.*[36] Or in the documents concerning Giuseppe Valenza: *'una sorda voce chiamasse responsabile ... qualche giorno dopo corse voce in paese che attribuiva ... fu voce generale ... giunta all' orecchio del Valenza la voce pubblica ... per come si vocifera ...'.*[37] *'Fatti la fame e curcati'*,[38] make yourself famous and lie back and relax—this Sicilian proverb sums up this important aspect in the career of a *mafioso*.

3 Consolidation and defence of position

3.1. *Occupations*

Mafiosi on totally different steps of their career naturally exist alongside each other in Sicilian agricultural society. It is therefore almost impossible to generalise about 'the' occupation of a *mafioso*: after all 'mafioso' is not an occupational designation. The *mafioso* is not, as is sometimes assumed, an inactive parasite; he does not live by his *mafioso* activity but merely uses it in order to render more profitable another occupation practised by him. *Mafioso* novices are found amoung the shepherds and those who have 'arrived' are among the rich landlords. One general statement can be made: in accordance with their high social mobility we time and again encounter *mafiosi* in those very occupations which, in an otherwise so immobile agrarian society, are mobile and flexible, in occupations which combine a high risk with a chance of rapid advancement. The *gabellotto*, since he pays his rent in advance, could be ruined by two poor harvests or a single cattle plague; on the other hand his two-way exploitation may raise him to wealth in a short time. The *campiere* risks his life every day but the extorted dues he collects offer him profits far beyond the reach of a *mezzadro*. It is in entrepreneur occupations, as mediators, in positions between the peasants and the wealthy landlords that we find *mafiosi* named again and again—as *curatoli* and *guardani* of markets gardens and water in intensive cultivation zones, as produce dealers, as *campieri, soprastanti* and *gabellotti* in the zone of the big estates, as corn merchants, cattle dealers, as dealers of all kinds, and as butchers who play an important rôle as receivers of stolen livestock. The *carrettieri* also are frequently *mafiosi*. In a Sicilian village—frequently right up to the period after the Second World War—they provided the only carrier service and represented the most important medium of news communication. The advantage which being thought a *mafioso* brings to one of these lonely travellers is obvious. Among the *professionisti* they are lawyers, pharmacists and doctors. The doctor in a Sicilian village invariably has a large clientele but this profession deserves mention chiefly because of its importance in the *partito*, i.e. in the faction of the *mafioso*.

3.2. *Monopolisation*

All these occupations are open and there is no formal restriction to access to any of them except the last three, in the shape of educational diplomas or other formalised proof of ability. The functions of the *mafioso* can likewise, in principle, be exercised by anyone inclined and able to do so; the *mafiosi* therefore do not represent a closed caste or some secret society conspiring to debar non-members from access to power. Nevertheless each *mafioso* endeavours to consolidate his own position and to exclude others from it, so that one may speak of a temporarily limited monopoly, limited to an individual rather than a caste or a stratum of diploma-holders, a monopoly of the function of (real or fictitious) protection and of mediation in certain types of social relationships, as well as the exacting of tribute payments connected with these activities. Because of his illegal position *vis-à-vis* the State government machine the *mafioso* cannot appropriate these opportunities of exercising power, and hence legally entrench or formally buttress his position. Its defence is left to himself. From this state of affairs emerges the typical pattern of continuous struggle, of often bloody clashes, and of repeated repulsion of ever new attacks. The *mafioso* is frequently compelled to resort to physical violence in order to dictate his law to his subordinates; but physical violence is a vital criterion also in the second type of conflict, the one we are now concerned with, i.e. the confrontation with the holders of or candidates to positions of power. The young man of violence, the *giovane mafioso*, who is still on one of the rungs of his career described under (2) above, has always existed. (The concept of the 'nuova mafia' and the phenomenon nowadays understood by this term are a new feature and will be discussed later.) He has always been anxious to displace the established *vecchio mafioso* from his position since otherwise, in view of the inevitable shortage of positions of power, no advancement is possible for him. And the holder of such a position has always been obliged to take counter-measures.

On 24 March 1897 the body of the 18-year-old Antonino Comparetto was found in the *contrada* Santa Barbara, about one kilometre from Prizzi. He had his throat cut. Since no traces of blood were found the crime had evidently been committed elsewhere and the body subsequently transported to the place where it was found. The most intensive investigations yielded nothing. A few days later a rumour went about which attributed the deed to Giuseppe Valenza but this was soon stifled by the widespread fear of this man. When Valenza was arrested in 1883 the official of the P. S. succeeded in compiling the following picture from confidential reports: At the beginning of March 1879 Valenza received a letter which, with menaces of grave damage, tried to extort a sum of money from him. Valenza, on the one hand, was unwilling to pay the sum demanded and, on the other, for reasons of *omertà* did not wish to turn to the police. As he was fairly certain that the author of the letter was the young Antonino Comparetto, who had behaved arrogantly towards him several times before, and as he was afraid of the threats against him, he decided to get the blackmailer removed forcibly and instructed Salvatore Rizzutto, 24, Filippo Greco, 48, and Salvatore Giordano to kill Comparetto. In the evening of 23 March Comparetto left his father's house towards seven o'clock and went to a café to play billiards. There he was approached by a certain Giuseppe Campagna, a *contadino*, whose task it was to lure the victim to the spot chosen for the deed. He played billiards with him and subsequently, in darkness, succeeded in leading the unsuspecting Comparetto to a barn which belonged to Valenza. There he was first beaten up by the three assassins who had been waiting for him and subsequently killed. The body was wrapped in a *scapolare* (the Sicilian shoulder cloak) and taken into the *contrada* Santa Barbara on a donkey.[39]

Another instance from the material on Valenza, about his confrontation with a hostile *mafioso* group, will illustrate what we have stated theoretically above.

On the evening of 2 December 1881 two shots rang out near his house. Shortly afterwards a rumour sprang up that a servant of Valenza's, at the latter's command, had wounded an as yet unknown person who had then been hidden and silenced by bribery. This spontaneous explanation of the facts is characteristic of the reputation Valenza enjoyed in Prizzi. Police investigations, as usual, remained unproductive. A few days later a servant of Valenza's appeared at the P. S. station and declared himself to have been the target of the shots. However, he disclosed no further details. Not until 1883 did the whole circumstances of the case and its connection with other events become clear to the *Delegato—per confidenziali notizie avute*.

A certain Giuseppe Collura, 35, who had been employed by Valenza as a *campiere*, had been dismissed by him some time prior to December 1881—*per varie quistioni*, as the report states. The dismissed man's indignation was heightened by a sense of having been unfairly rewarded: Valenza had refused to hand over to the *campieri* 12 *pumoli* of beans which had been his due. Collura, who had meanwhile entered the services of someone else, joined with his brother Giovanni, with Paolo Sparacio and his brother Giuseppe, as well as with Vincenzo Macaluso 'per formarse un partito averso al Valenza'.

Shortly afterwards Valenza had eight head of cattle and a little later a mule stolen from him. He suspected Collura but resisted from reporting him and instead began to take counter-measures himself—'*pensò di opporsi colla forza e colla mafia, e farsi rispettare col farsi temere*'. In order to get rid of the Collura brothers he got two men from Mezzojuso and one from Campofelice to come to Prizzi. [Such hired assassins were either financially rewarded or else they belonged to the clientage of the employer and had to render services for *favori* received. But even in the case of financial reward the tie is not simply one of business. It should be noted that these men are never encountered singly but always in twos or threes, and that they frequently come from other localities. Further details in the next chapter.] The opposition, however, got wind of the plan and tried to defend itself by attack. The bullet missed Valenza and injured a servant in the shoulder since master and servant had exchanged their *scapolari* that evening.

During the night of 5 February 1882 three individuals who claimed to be police officers knocked at the door of the above-named Paolo Sparacio. Being under police surveillance he opened in the belief that this was just the usual surveillance routine. He was gravely wounded by a pistol shot. *'Lo Sparacio d'indole mafiosa, osservando l'onestà, non volle mai declinare i nomi dei suoi assassini quantunque si sappia che furono da lui conosciuti perfettamente. ...'* The men had been Francesco and Giacomo Rizzutto and Francesco Grisaffi, acting on behalf of Valenza.

Valenza, however, personally participated in another counter-move. While Vincenzo Macaluso, 38, a *sensale* from Prizzi, *'persona pregiudicatissima, mafiosa, dedita a qualunque reato'*, spent the night of 25 July 1882 with his mistress Sebastiana Fucarino, 25, sleeping in a barn, the two were attacked by three persons and very seriously wounded. But since Macaluso, nevertheless, defended himself with a weapon the attackers made off. Sebastiana subsequently stated during interrogation at the hospital that she had recognised two of them—Giuseppe Valenza and Francesco Marò, 34, a former lover. Later she withdrew her first deposition and identified only Marò whom (as the reporter adds) Valenza had picked as an accomplice because he knew him to be jealous of Macaluso.[40]

Closely linked with the monopolisation of power is the monopolisation of profitable operations within a certain occupation. As practice of the occupations typical of *mafiosi* is not in any way formally restricted, competitors are eliminated by means of violence or the threat of violence in a manner illegal under the laws of the State. Thus *mafioso* power, which in itself can offer satisfaction to its holder, as a rule also serves his economic interests. That is why rivalries between individual *mafiosi* are often fought out within individual occupations.

It is worth looking in detail at the dispute between Michele Navarra and Luciano Liggio because it not only represents a good illustration of many of the abstract points made above but also resulted directly from the clash of economic interests.

In 1943 Don Calogero Lo Bue, *gabellotto* of the Donna Beatrice estate, died in Corleone. According to rumour he said on his deathbed: When my eyes close I shall see with those of Michele Navarra. Even if this was not in fact true the rumour nevertheless picturesquely illustrates the process of recognition by a successful prestige-holder, as described under (2.3) above. Navarra was a doctor, director of the Corleone hospital (ospedale dei Bianchi), and in the course of time assumed several further functions—he became chairman of the Association of *coltivatori diretti*, inspector of the Cassa Mutua Malattia for Corleone and the neighbouring villages (Mezzojuso, Campofelice, Roccamena, Misilmeri, Bolognetta, Lercara Friddi, Godrano and Marineo) and official medical adviser to the State Railways. This last office was offered him when, in public competition, he proved to be the only candidate. The part played by him in elections as the chairman of the Christian Democratic Party will be discussed later.

Navarra also exerted a great deal of influence on the Consorzio di Bonifica dell'Alto e Medio Belice, an association of all landowners along the upper reaches of the Belice, whose elected chairman, together with the *consiglieri*, was able to dispose over an invested capital of 37,854 million lire for various improvement projects, principally roads. An old plan of the Consorzio to dam the Belice at the Piano della Scala near Corleone was taken up again in the 'fifties and supported by the then chairman, Prince Giardinelli, a Liberal. Naturally such a plan was bound to be resented by those who controlled the water supply throughout the neighbourhood of Corleone. Springs in Sicily are private property, their exploitation, yielding large profits, is traditionally associated with *mafioso* affairs, i.e. they are an economic monopoly guaranteed by *mafioso* power.

The proprietors of vegetable monopolies, needless to say, likewise opposed the project which promised an abundance of vegetables. In alliance with Navarra they got people close to them to gain control of the Consorzio. By amending the voting rules they deprived the small landowners of the right to appoint proxies for their votes, so that on the day of election only the votes of those present, chiefly medium-sized and big landowners, were counted, and instead of the Prince of Giardinelli the lawyer Alberto Genzardi was made chairman. Genzardi was the son-in-law of Vanni Sacco, the well-known *uomo di rispetto* from Comporeale. The twenty-five *consiglieri* moreover included a son of Sacco, the father of Sacco's daughter-in-law, and two further relatives of well-known *mafiosi* from San Giuseppe Jato and San Cipirello.

Giardinelli had enjoyed the support of a now defeated *mafioso* clique which, in contrast to the first grouping, favoured the construction of the dam. The man at the centre of this clique was Luciano Liggio.

Liggio had started his career as one of a gang of cattle thieves headed by a certain Francesco Barbaccia. Young Liggio was famous for his particular cold-bloodedness and hardness, and was known in Corleone as 'cocciu di tacca' which is only inadequately translated as 'fire bean'. In 1944, shortly before Liggio began to participate in the gang's activities, some of its older members were shot and Barbaccia disappeared. That same year Liggio succeeded in obtaining the Strasetto estate in *gabella* by threatening its owner. At 20 he was the youngest *gabellotto* in Sicily. In 1948 he was accused of the murder of the Socialist trades unionist Rizzotto but had to be acquitted for lack of evidence. He switched his activity to Palermo, bought a number of lorries and, together with some others, founded a haulage company. As he was still exerting considerable influence in the theft and secret slaughter of cattle in Corleone, it may be assumed that he used these lorries also for illegally smuggling meat into Palermo. More importantly, he foresaw a great opportunity for gaining a monopoly of haulage work in connection with the building of the dam. In the summer of 1958 he was invited by Michele Navarra to meet him at an estate but instead of Navarra he found 15 armed men there; however, after an exchange of fire, he managed to escape from them. Shortly afterwards, on 10 August 1958, as Navarra was driving home from Lercara Friddi, his car was blocked on the open road by two other vehicles and Navarra, together with Dr. Russo who accompanied him, was shot dead by submachine-guns. A few weeks later, on 6 September three men known as friends of Navarra's were killed in a raid at Corleone. One of these, Pietro Maiuri, had been a cowherd for some time; at the time of his death he owned the only motor repair shop in the village. He and another man killed on the same day were the sole proprietors of a concession for the sale of petrol.

A large modern hospital had been standing empty in Corleone from 1952 to 1958 and was only put into service after the death of Navarra, the director of the old *ospedale dei Bianchi*.

The old abattoir had long failed to meet technical and hygienic regulations. The commune had built a new one but for five years this was not used because—unlike the old one—it offered fewer opportunities for illegal slaughtering. Only when Liggio had become a fugitive, after his action against Navarra, was the new abattoir put into use.[41]

The above examples are illustrations of attempts to monopolise opportunities of profitable livelihood and the clashes resulting from these attempts.

3.3. *Legalisation*

Physical violence is not only the most important means of rising to power but it also remains the most important means of defending that power. This statement, however, must be qualified by three separate developments:

(1) The *mafioso* creates a *cosca* for himself. This term describes the closest clientage dependent on him, consisting chiefly of a number of men of violence who thus relieve the *mafioso* of the need to practise violence himself. The established *mafioso*, in consequence, has a fundamentally ambivalent attitude to the 'nuvidduna', the novice: he must fear him as a rising rival but at the same time tries to use him for his own purposes.

(2) The *mafioso* creates a *partito* for himself. This term describes a network of relationships with socially and economically higher placed persons (barons, landlords, priests) and—either directly or sometimes indirectly through the mediation of the above-named—to holders of institutionalised, legal rule.

Cosca and *partito*, together with a few other sympathisers, represent the faction grouped around the *mafioso*, and this group is frequently very closely intertwined with a communal-political power group or a political party. Kinship, ritual kinship, friendship and clientage relationships create a kind of community bond alongside purely business and purpose-orientated associations. Two rival factions can polarise large parts of the population of a village, and a dispute between two *mafiosi* in consequence usually develops into a dispute between two such groupings; this, incidentally, may facilitate the rise of a novice. The phenomena listed under (1) and (2) are important enough to be discussed once more in the next chapter.

(3) The *mafioso* tries to achieve a far-reaching legalisation of his position.

(a) To begin with, even the *partito* may be described as a step in this direction, at least inasmuch as it consists of officials. The conservative *mafioso* tries to sever compromising links with open lawbreakers and instead to get well in with policemen, mayors, judges, medical officers of health, administrative officials and parliamentary deputies. Even mere acquaintance, which may subsequently develop into *partito*, is of advantage to him.

> He is constantly in contact with priests, the priests come to him, he goes to the bank which is always managed by priests; since the director of the bank is a priest the bank has always been in the hands of the priests. And as he meets these people socially, things have now reached a point where the police show him a great deal of respect, saluting him and

showing him many such marks of honour. Nowadays he is better dressed; the police sergeant will walk up to him and shake hands with him: *cavaliere*. ... Towards the end of May, in connection with the election campaign, he dined together with the Minister Zacagnini and the Deputy Lanza, and they then walked out together arm in arm.[42]

(b) Quite often older *mafiosi* themselves bear official titles of respect or hold public office. Vizzini, Russo, Santo Flores from Partinico, for example, were *Cavalieri della Corona d'Italia*, Cannizzo was a Member of Parliament, his opponent, La Franca, was a mayor, Militello from Montemaggiore was *consigliere comunale* and Salemi Pace from the same township was *assessore municipale*.[43] Two historical situations in particular, after 1860 and after 1943, both marking a change in State government, resulted in the village strongmen receiving official recognition and honours from the new government simply because they too had been opponents of the old system. As a result, the position of many *mafiosi* was legalised for many years to come. (Reference should be made to the mayors appointed by the Allies on Vizzini's recommendation in 1943: Vizzini himself at Villalba, Malta at Vallelunga, Serafino Di Peri at Bolognetta, and others.)

(c) The functions discharged by the *mafioso* frequently enable him to present himself to the State organs as a collaborator in their tasks.

In 1886 a small polemical pamphlet was published at Petralia Sottana, entitled '*Mafiosi ! Protettori della mafia !*' This was the defence and counter-charge of Antonino Li Destri and Alessandro Milletari from Gangi, addressed to the hostile faction (the Mocciaro family) and to the *delegato di P. S.* Virgilio who had described the two authors as *mafiosi* and *protettori della mafia* and now had to accept the same labels. It contained the sentence:

> Those whom you call *mafiosi* and protectors of the *mafia*, you bastard Don Beppe Virgilio, are the men who liberated the mountains of at least 18 malefactors in less than two years. ...[44]

In 1881 a certain Damiano Mazzarese from Campofelice di Fitalia, an *uomo di rispetto* and landowner, had been placed under police surveillance by the Pretor of Mezzojuso. He submitted a number of appeals to the Prefect of Palermo for a withdrawal of the *ammonizione* and also turned for help to the Prince of Fitalia. In the Prince's letter to the Prefect (4 January 1882) we find the following passages:

> ... I take the liberty of drawing your attention to the services which Mazzarese has been performing for the police over a number of years since I have known him. ... After 1866, following the seven-day revolt

in September, Mazzarese co-operated with the Bersaglieri officials who had been dispatched to Campofelice di Fitalia from Palermo and whose names were Pistori and Silvio by handing over to them a number of fugitives who had been behind this bloody movement. The above-named officials can testify to Mazzarese's action.

About six years ago Mazzarese tipped off the *compagni d'armi* of Lercara Friddi that the brigand known as Tredici was hiding out at Campofelice di Fitalia. Acting on this the police secretly followed him and eventually arrested him at Mezzojuso, ... I would add that Mazzarese was the man who about two years ago informed the then warrant officer of the Royal Carabinieri named Scopeci of the whereabouts of the brigand La Bussa and then took part in tracking him down and killing him. ...

I do not wish to bore you any further with the details of all the small services which the said Mazzarese has performed for the local authorities at the risk of his life and property.[45]

Cannizzo at his trial also expressly boasted of his co-operation with the *carabinieri* which had led to the capture of two bandits. He had personally pursued a third one, Nobile, several times. Admittedly, it emerged in the course of the trial that all three belonged to the *cosca* of his adversary:

Presiding Judge: In pursuing this Nobile, did Signor Cannizzo show a personal interest or was he acting in the public interest?

Ambrasi: His efforts to seize Nobile were in his own personal interest and in that of his *partito*.

Presiding Judge: You speak of *partiti*, will you explain this to me?

Ambrasi: Cannizzo and the Cernigliaros were on the one side and the La Francas and the Scalias on the other.

Presiding Judge: In the sense that, if the first *partito* was interested in getting rid of Nobile, there was no such interest on the part of the other *partito*?

Ambrasi: They wanted to catch Nobile because he had made an attempt on the life of Cernigliaro.[46]

In a characteristic modification of *omertà* some *uomini di rispetto* collaborate with the State organs in order to manipulate them against their own enemies. At the same time this procedure had its functions in the process of legalisation.

(d) No *mafioso*, not even a novice, need apply actual physical violence all the time in order to assert his will. Mostly the realisation of this ultimate possibility is enough. But, of course, the novice has to resort to it far more

62

often than the established *mafioso*. The career of a *mafioso* might thus be described as leading from the position of executant to that of employer. Avoidance of personal application of force is a very essential part of legalisation. It is rendered possible by the formation of the *cosca* and the dependence of the 'picciotti', the novices, on a patron. The more established a man's reputation, the more readily this reputation will in itself be sufficient to achieve submission to his judgement, to a demand for payment, to the fixing of a price. His will, often merely hinted at as a wish or a possibility, commands obedience. The better, more extensive *partito* frequently ensures a bloodless decision in a potentially bloody dispute between *mafiosi*. The weaker man, who has fewer strings to pull, acknowledges the superiority of the other.

> He no longer has to open his mouth to shout because now he gives the orders, or he sends others. He no longer has to play his trump card in order to achieve what he wants.[47]

The effect of his reputation and the mobilisation of the two instruments of *cosca* and *partito* thus enable the *mafioso* to exercise his functions to a ripe old age. As for the end of a *mafioso*, since he is not defined by membership in an organisation but by a certain behaviour which enables him to discharge specific functions, such an end to his *mafioso* existence cannot take place through resignation but only by the abandonment of his behaviour pattern and the exercise of his functions. This can take place in three different ways—through peaceful natural death, through violent death, or through (voluntary or enforced) gradual withdrawal from the practice of his functions. A fourth possibility, which frequently represents only a temporary end, would be a prolonged term of imprisonment, but this solution is by no means typical and is worth mentioning only for the period after 1925 and after 1963.

The problem of succession to the position of largely monopolised power is likewise settled in an informal way and is closely linked with the nature of the former holder's end—sometimes by struggle against the former holder, sometimes by transfer, and sometimes by the clash of several candidates in the power vacuum which has arisen.

In the view held by the present author it is therefore a mistake to describe as a *mafioso* a man who has given up his *mafioso* behaviour, or perhaps the son or nephew of an *uomo di rispetto* who may well be a corrupt politician or a corrupt official but no longer operates with the threat of physical violence. Naturally, the boundaries cannot be clearly drawn, but it should always be remembered that *mafiosi* are not a special kind of human being, but men who act in a certain manner and are characterised solely by this manner of action. A man who does not act as a *mafioso* is no *mafioso*.

4 Legitimation and self-assessment

Legalisation has been discussed only as a structural characteristic, as a rapprochement of the *mafioso*'s position to the organs of State power in order to meet the dangers threatening from that quarter. Mention was made at the same time of the importance which this legalisation for the monopolisation of power *vis-à-vis* rising *mafiosi*. It must not therefore be confused with a legitimation of the *mafioso* position. True, it may contribute towards legitimation, but essentially legitimation stems from another source—from popular morality and from functional necessity. The structure of *mafioso* groupings as well as the functions of the *mafioso* will be discussed in separate chapters, where it will be possible to go into sufficient detail. Although legitimation is based chiefly on function, it will be discussed at this point because it establishes the status of a *mafioso* in society.

The words *mafia* and *mafioso* do not have a positive ring in Sicily.

> In fact, to say of a person in Sicily nowadays that he is a man, that has an honourable meaning, but to say that he is a *mafioso*, that has an entirely different meaning....[48]

This is what Mori writes. To an official the word *mafioso* is a bad word, denoting a criminal. But Mori here refers to the colouring which the word has among the people. And all indications are that he is right: no one likes to be called a *mafioso*, everyone tries to label his enemy so, hence for the Sicilian public 'mafioso' has the same meaning as 'criminal'. We may recall the polemical pamphlet published by Li Destri and Milletari at Petralia Sottana in 1886, in which the authors indignantly rejected the accusation of being *mafiosi* and *protettori della mafia*. Cannizzo said at his trial: 'I was alone and fought against the *mafia* both that in white gloves as well as that with a carbine....'[49] 'Mafiosi' are the other side; to characterise one's own personality the words favoured are more vague and less loaded: 'uomo d'onore, uomo di rispetto, uomo di panza, persona di petto'. Even the theoreticians of the secret society make allowance for this fact when they say that the organisation is not called 'mafia' by its members but 'onorata società'.

The term 'uomo di rispetto' in Sicily means precisely what we have described here as 'mafioso' and therefore reflects both the informal element and the normality of this type in Sicily in that it describes a man who, to a high degree, matches up to the universally valid personality ideal. This label in itself marks the beginning of legitimation.

Reference has already been made to the Sicilian ideal of human existence in both its nuances—the *gentiluomo* who has no need to perform manual work and the powerful *uomo di rispetto*. An essential characteristic of the

64

powerful man is not outward pomp but the mystery which surrounds him.

> The true man reveals himself above all by his silence, by the secret presence of a hidden power, by long and secret paths; he stands at the centre of other men who, like him, work in the shadows and he achieves recognition by the others as their centre.[50]

Someone possessing a secret or operating silently possesses a shadowy significance and importance; he can exploit hidden possibilities, he is respected, admired, envied and feared. The ability to settle problems by a glance, a word or a gesture lends a man prestige. He is not only feared but he is honoured; one acknowledges his superiority as justified. There are many terms for an honourable man, i.e. chiefly for a man who can keep a secret: 'picciottu d'onuri, picciottu onuratu, picciottu di sgarru, cristianeddu, cristianu di Diu, umiceddu di Diu'.[51]

The *uomo d'onore* must not bow to anyone: 'nun s'havi a scantari i nautru', he must not fear anyone else, 'nun si l'havi a ghiuttiri', he must on no account passively accept an affront. The mass of Sicilians who have to suffer humiliations day after day without a chance of revenge see a *mafioso* who has created for himself this chance of revenge or one whom no one even dares offend any longer, as the male ideal, the 'omu' par excellence. His reaction, however, his vengeance must on no account be direct or open; it must take place in that mysterious and opaque manner which magnifies the awe surrounding him; it must strike not blindly but deliberately. 'Si sarba la pezza pri quannu venu u purtusu', he waits until the moment of vengeance arrives.[52]

The bandit loves 'conspicuous consumption' of power (Veblen's expression does not only apply to the consumption of goods); he remains the peasant boy for whom power is not merely a matter-of-fact but he gets drunk with it and displays it again and again, he tries to impress others by the fascination of his outward appearance and his bravura. A report about the Rocca and Rinaldi gang states:

> They all dressed in blue cloth or in velvet and wore riding boots and most of them had red caps; nearly all of them had a silver winding watch and wore a ring with the initial R.[53]

Giuliano, too, wore a large conspicuous ring and invariably, even in the mountains, wore a white raincoat. At a time when he was fiercely pursued he would dine in Palermo restaurants and leave there notes bragging of his bravura. The bandit Leone, shot in 1877, also loved demonstrations of this kind:

Antonino Leone acted more recklessly than ever and let the rumour gain currency that he travelled from Termini to Palermo by rail at certain intervals and that he visited the performances of the Politeama whenever he pleased or felt like it.[54]

The *mafioso* is totally different. He likes to veil his power. One need only compare the pictures which exist of various bandits—the posture adopted by Giuliano, or Pietro Alvanese mounted on a horse, adorned and armed (facing p. 129 in Mori's book), with the photographs of, say, Vizzini or Russo—solid citizens in braces, their jackets informally over their arms. They control power and do not let power control them. Undoubtedly, 'fare figura' is important also to them; they enjoy the respect shown them, they enjoy power, but they do not wish to give rise to its discussion. They know very well that behind the veil of modesty power is felt to be all the more uncanny.

Montanelli describes an interview with Calogero Vizzini and quotes a few typical remarks by Don Calò:

> A photograph of me? Whatever for? I'm no one. I'm just some citizen. ... It is strange. ... People think that I don't talk much from modesty. No. I don't talk much because I don't know much. I live in a village, I only rarely go to Palermo, I know few people. ... And besides, I've grown old, over 70 years old.[55]

'Baciamo le mani, servo suo, sono il servitore di Voscenza'—this is how in Loschiavo's 'Piccola Pretura' the *mafiosi* salute the Pretor. And Turi Passalacqua, a character drawn from an *uomo di rispetto* known to Loschiavo, says at a meeting:

> I am the lowliest of the men here assembled, I am a poor countryman; but I believe I can speak for everybody.[56]

The simple man who nevertheless speaks for everybody—that is the typical *mafioso*: the man who, moreover, regards it as his duty to speak for others. An honest citizen whose behaviour is above reproach, a model for all to see. Mommo Grasso from Misilmeri acted the part of Jesus in the Good Friday play every year; and this is what the earlier quoted peasant from Mussomeli had to say of Russo:

> On the feast of the 8 September, the feast of the Madonna Maria Santissima dei Miracoli, he takes the alms bag and collects the money. He positions himself at a place near the church tower, and one man gives

him 500 lire, another 50, this one 1,000, that one 10, according to the person. He alone collects 150,000 lire and pays it to the feast commission, year after year.[57]

With surprise the *mafioso* rejects the accusation of being a criminal. Such accusations were used by journalists and *carabinieri* in order to ruin honourable family men. He himself regards his actions as in no way criminal but as a natural 'comportamento sociale', a behaviour which is simply indispensable to Sicilian society such as it is.[58]

At the cost of sacrifices and trouble, usually unselfishly, he will assume the duties of settler of disputes, protector, mediator and adviser, duties which have to be undertaken by someone if life is to continue—this is how the *mafioso* himself sees one of the most important facets of his function.

> I was born that way. I act without purpose. No matter who asks me a favour, I'll do him the favour because, I believe, that is what my nature prescribes to me. ... One man will come and say: 'I have a problem with Tizio, do see if you can settle the matter for me'. I summon the person concerned to me or else I go and visit him—according to what terms we are on—and I reconcile them. But I don't want you to think that I'm telling you this in order to brag. I certainly don't want to seem to be telling you this in order to brag. I am telling you this from politeness, because you have come all this way. I am neither vain nor ambitious. The people ask whom they should elect because they feel an obligation to get advice in order to show gratitude or recognition. They grope in the dark and they want to follow those who have been good to them. Tomorrow, for instance, I've got to leave my threshing flail, the animals, all my things, and drive to Agrigento to put in a good word for someone so they will let him pass some exams.[59]

This is how Genco Russo sees himself. Compare this with the following dialogue from Montanelli's interview with Don Calò:

> You know, I believe that if one holds a position like yours ...
> What position?
> I mean: in the opinion of the people.
> Oh! (Pause)
> The fact is, he replied after a while, that in any society there must be a category of persons who put things right again when they have become complicated.[60]

This self-assessment is a mixture of an honest conviction that one has a task, a duty, of a more or less subconscious rationalisation, and of deliberate embellishment; but the individual shades of this mixture cannot be clearly separated. Even if a neutral observer comes to the conclusion that the construction of a dam across the Jato river near Particino cuts across the objective economic interests of certain people, including certain *uomi di rispetto*, the sabotage action of the *mafiosi* may nevertheless appear to them as an action for the benefit of the community, for the preservation of tranquility and order:

> Naturally he had no intention of allowing anyone—even the big bosses at the head of the government—to turn the country topsy-turvy under the pretext of regulating a river course. He did not have to remind Mara that he was responsible to a great many leading figures for the state of affairs in the region under him.[61]

In his novel *The Day of the Owl* Leonardo Sciascia describes the extortion of a building contractor. When the contractor refuses to pay the protection money demanded he is shot in the piazza one morning. The *capitano dei carabinieri* interrogates the influential *mafioso* Pizzuco about the negotiations which he had conducted with the building contractor:

> Advice, *capitano*, advice. Disinterested advice, as a good friend. ...
> If you are in a situation to give advice this means that you are well informed. ...
> Well informed? ... Things which one hears here and there. I'm always travelling about because of my work. I hear one thing today and another tomorrow. ...
> And what did you hear that made you think it necessary to give advice to Colasberna?
> I heard that his affairs were in a bad way. And I advised him to seek protection and help. ...
> So you went to the trouble of giving advice to someone you scarcely knew?
> Well, that's the kind of man I am. When I see a man stumbling I am on the spot to give him a helping hand.[62]

If a man is too stubborn, if he absolutely insists on upsetting the normal order and the natural course of things, then quite simply he has to be coerced into a reasonable attitude and if, then, there is no other way he has to be altogether eliminated. Violence, therefore, is only the *ultima ratio* for the *mafioso*, a sacrifice which he makes for the benefit of the public weal. And what neutral observer could trust himself here to separate deliberate lie from rationalisation? The borderlines are fluid and the mixture of the shades differs

68

in each individual case. Besides, the observer must beware of falsifying the analysis of this structure of ideas by introducing his own values. Certainly for the persons on the fringe of a *partito* of a *mafioso* these rationalisations are an indispensable means for avoiding conflicts of norms.

Occasionally the *mafioso* is indeed a 'cavaliere a rispetto dei deboli';[63] as befits a real man he gives help to the poor, including economic help, and frequently such help is, or at least seems, totally unselfish.

> Any citizen, even a foreigner, needing a favour would only have to turn to one of the so-called *capi-mafia*. He can be sure that his request will be listened to with genuine sympathy. The *mafioso*, in fact, displays all possible anxiety to serve his new friend unselfishly, without demanding anything in return. He knows that his work is never unprofitable because it not only consolidates his reputation but also enlarges the number of persons devoted to him.[64]

In the above-mentioned biography of Antonio Li Destri the *delegato di P.S.* of Gangi writes:

> As he has the ambition to rule this community and therefore to win the next election, he now endeavours, together with his inseparable friend Milletari Alessandro, son of Michelangelo, a local lawyer, to get together a new agricultural co-operative which, it is generally said, numbers about 400 members to date. He does this in order to be appointed a municipal councillor and then to become mayor, and he opposes the ruling Mocciaro party.[65]
>
> It is not the urge to improve the condition of the lower classes of society which motivates the named gentlemen. ... They merely want to be cheered as the protectors of the poor and at the same time hope to overrun their administrative and personal opponents and to improve their own financial position.[66]

Calogero Vizzini bought three estates in the Villalba region after the first World War; he divided them up and handed them over—allegedly without making a penny—to a co-operative founded by him.[67] He could easily have had himself elected a Parliamentary Deputy at this stage but he preferred to keep in the background and instead advise both voters and elected officials. Surely it was no more than just and fair that one was devoted to such a benefactor, that one should strengthen his clientage, that one should increase his prestige, and that one should ask his advice before an election and follow it. Surely one had to be glad of the opportunity of repaying a man for his help?

Candida describes a scene in the Palermo fishmarket: A young man, to whom everyone shows great respect, appears at a fish stall and with his hands indicates the size of fish he wants. The stall keeper understands at once, wraps up a good fish in paper and hands it across the stall. Without payment and indeed without a word of thanks the man walks away.[68] Is one to assume that the young man sees this whole incident as simple extortion? It would probably be more correct to interpret his own attitude in a somewhat modified way: the fish is his due as a small collateral for protection provided. But it is not only in their self-assessment that the *mafiosi* are an élite and that their action appears legitimate. Their approximation to the personality ideal raises them above the mass, and many in the mass regard this exalted position as justified: 'People admire a man who is stronger, who is well-known —that's logical.'[69] And just as the *mafioso* himself, so the others similarly justify his actions by functional necessity and consider them legitimate.

> Once you get involved with the law—do you know what you stand to lose? If you have no money you can't do anything against the charge, the investigation or the lawyers. But if you settle the matter with the help of a mediator everybody saves money. One has a great deal of confidence in him because he possesses the ability to put things in order.[70]

And the *mafioso* legitimately expects some collateral action for the discharge of such a function:

> They are under an obligation. If someone acts as a mediator and reconciles the parties, then they have an obligation towards the man who reconciles them. ... The public thinks: I'll give him my vote because he deserves it, because he has been good to us. He advises us, he can see more clearly how he can give support to the people in order to do good. He is a man who does something for the people, who gives his help to the public. He will advise those people who are groping in the dark, who know nothing about life and the parties: look out, don't let so-and-so's party get on.[71]

One cannot therefore be surprised at the text which was fixed above the church door of Villalba on the day of the memorial service for Calogero Vizzini, the son of poor peasants, illiterate, nephew and brother of priests, a petty bandit at the beginning of his career, a wealthy *Cavaliere* at the end, a *gabellotto*, repeatedly charged with murder, the planning of murder, extortion and fraud, but almost invariably acquitted:

CALOGERO VIZZINI
With the ability of a genius
He raised the fortunes of the noble family
Clear-eyed dynamic, untiring

He gave farm labourers and sulphur workers prosperity
Constantly worked for the good
And made his name highly respected
In Italy and beyond
Great in his enterprises
Much greater still in misfortune
He always kept smiling
And today in the peace of Christ
Reunited with Death's majesty
He receives from all his friends and even from his enemies
The finest testimonial:
He was a *galantuomo*.[72]

Notes

[1] Cutrera 1900, p. 96

[2] Hobsbawm 1959, p. 37

[3] Quoted in Dolci 1960, p. 57

[4] Lewis 1964, p. 176

[5] ASP 1885, busta 83, cat. 20, fasc. 1

[6] Tomasi di Lampedusa 1959, p. 140

[7] Loschiavo 1956, p. 542

[8] Cutrera 1900, p. 95

[9] Filippo Cilluffo, quoted from Novacco 1963, p. 25

[10] The sayings in the Sicilian dialect are quoted from Vaccaro 1899, p. 689

[11] ASP 1880, busta 56, cat. 20, fasc. 28

[12] Significantly enough he was pardoned shortly after the sentence, cf. ibid.

[13] ASP 1885, busta 84, cat. 20, fasc. 55

[14] Letter of the Sotto-Prefetto of Corleone to the Prefect of Palermo of 19 December 1875, in ASP busta 85, cat. 20, fasc. 133

[15] Ibid., cf. also Ajello 1868, pp. 14, 16 and 17 on 'imputato No. 34, Valenza, Giuseppe fu Giorgio di anni 27, da Prizzi, possidente'

[16] Letter of the *delegato di P.S.* of Prizzi to the Sotto-Prefetto of Corleone (19. 12. 1875) in ASP, busta 85, cat. 20, fasc. 133

[17] Testimony of a Castellammare peasant, quoted in Dolci 1966, p. 308. Note how clearly *mafia* is interpretated here as *mafioso* behaviour, far removed from any idea of a secret society

[18] Letter of the Sotto-Prefetto of Corleone to the Prefect (19 December 1875) in ASP 1885, busta 85, cat. 20, fasc. 133

[19] Ibid.

[20] Ibid.

[21] Ibid.

[21a] The reader will notice that my observations on this point—as indeed on the *mafioso*'s career generally—may be seen as supporting the correctness of the labelling approach. When I wrote this book I did not yet know the labelling theory, but naturally the facts described here lend themselves perfectly to subsumption under the categories of this theory. After all, the labelling theory not only explains the attribution of negative stigmata but also a person's growing into coveted positions.

[22] Dr Salvatore Costanza, Trapani, in a conversation with the author

[23] Ibid.

[24] A peasant from Mussomeli in Dolci 1960, p. 57

[25] A peasant from Castellammare in Dolci 1966, p. 310

[26] A peasant from Castellammare ibid., p. 325

[27] The Prefect of Girgenti to the Minister of Interior on 30 June 1874, quoted in Russo (Ed.) 1964, p. 22

[28] Mühlmann 1962, p. 47

[29] Alongi 1887, p. 72

[30] Vaccaro 1899, p. 688

[31] Letter to the Sotto-Prefetto of Corleone of 17 October 1883, in ASP 1885, busta 85, cat. 20, fasc. 133

[32] In Dolci 1960, p. 69

[33] Denti di Pirajno 1965, pp. 44–5

[34] In Dolci 1960, p. 61

[35] ASP, Processo Cannizzo

[36] Processo Amoroso 1883

[37] ASP 1885, busta 85, cat. 20, fasc. 133

[38] Mori 1932, p. 41

[39] Greatly abridged from two letters of the *delegatio di P.S.* of Prizzi to the Sotto-Prefetto of Corleone (17. 10. 1883 and 6. 11. 1883) in ASP 1885, busta 85, cat. 20, fasc. 133

[40] Ibid., abridged

[41] Cf. Poma and Perrone 1964, pp. 16–164, Chilanti and Farinella 1964, pp. 42–55, as well as Pantaleone 1962, p. 148

[42] A peasant's testimony concerning Genco Russo in Dolci 1960, p. 60

[43] Cf. ASP 1880, busta 56, cat. 20, fasc. 28

[44] *Mafiosi ! Protettori della mafia!* Petralia Sottana, Tip. delle Nebrodi 1886, in ASP 1887, busta 100, cat. 20, fasc. 25

[45] ASP 1882, busta 69, cat. 20, fasc. 20

[46] ASP, Processo Cannizzo

[47] In Dolci 1960, p. 59

[48] Mori 1932, p. 78

[49] ASP, Processo Cannizzo

[50] Titone 1964, p. 256

[51] Pitré 1889, pp. 1–7

[52] Dialect quotations from Avellone and Morasca 1911, pp. 53 and 55

[53] D'Alessandro 1959, p. 97

[54] *Giornale di Sicilia*, 10 September 1878

[55] Montanelli 1958, pp. 280 and 282

[56] Loschiavo 1962, p. 285

[57] In Dolci 1960, p. 60

[58] Remark by the *mafioso* Zizzo from Salemi in an interview with Dr Costanza, Trapani. Passed on by him to the author

[59] Genco Russo to Danilo Dolci in Dolci 1960, pp. 68–9

[60] Montanelli 1958, p. 282

[61] Denti di Pirajno 1965, p. 279

[62] Sciascia 1964, pp. 108–9

[63] One of the features of the 'vero uomo' as given to Dolci by his interlocutors in the Spine Sante district of Partinico; cf. Dolci 1962, p. 337

[64] Cutrera 1900, p. 51

[65] ASP 1885, busta 84, cat. 20, fasc. 55

[66] ASP 1885, busta 85, cat. 20, fasc. 91

[67] Cf. Guarino 1955, p. 74

[68] Cf. Candida 1960, pp. 191–2

[69] Statement by a peasant in Dolci 1960, p. 65

[70] Ibid., pp. 63–4

[71] Ibid., pp. 63–4

[72] Gaja 1962, photograph facing p. 17

5 The Structure of Mafioso Groupings

The literature contains very little precise information on the relationship of one *mafioso* to another or to persons grouped around him who cannot properly be described as *mafiosi*. True, some authors make very definite statements: for them 'the *mafia*' is a tidily structured organisation, a secret society with initiation rites, a 'pontefice massimo' (Candida), a 'General Council' (Lewis), sub-leaders in charge of groups of ten, recognition passwords, etc. But after all that has been said so far about the peculiarities of Sicily's social structure and about the individual *mafiosi* it appears fairly certain that these theories make very little allowance for reality. They simply apply alien structure patterns to *mafioso* groupings.

Other authors reject the theory of a centralised organisation (cf. Chapter 2): '*La mafia non è precisa società segreta...*' (Bonfadini); '*Dallo spirito di mafia prendevano vita non un'associazione, che non è mai esistita...*' (Ciasca); '*Colla stessa parola (mafia) vien indicato in Sicilia non uno speciale sodalizio...*' (Mosca). Yet the positive statements of these authors on the structure of the groupings is also a great deal less definite: '*piccoli gruppi, più o meno organizzati, di malfattori, obbedienti a capi locali...*' (Ciasca); '*il complesso di tante piccole associazioni che si propongono scopi vari...*' (Mosca). There is agreement on a few points: Instead of a uniform organisation the existence has to be assumed of a great number of separate *associazioni* or *cosche,* each with a *capo* of its own. Relations between *cosche* are not uniform or regulated; there may be hostility or refusal to accept their existence, or co-operation. A customary distinction is that of *alta* and *bassa mafia.* Included in the *alta mafia,* in addition to the *capo,* are usually a number of persons who co-operate with the *cosca* without themselves displaying any *mafioso* attitudes—i.e. the protectors. The *bassa mafia* consists of the executors, the 'sicari' who often do not even know the meaning and purpose of an action committed by them at the behest of another person. The extant records rarely contain any details, seeing that they were written not by sociologists but by historians, jurists or journalists.

1 Cosca

Each group of *mafiosi* is allegorically represented by an artichoke whose trunk represents the leader and its leaves his followers. In fact, it is quite common in Sicily to describe a man regarded as a valuable person as 'lu trunzu ri l'omini' (the trunk of the man).[1]

The name *cosca* likens the *mafioso* to the trunk and the men grouped around him to the leaves of an artichoke. In addition to this term there are a number of others, such as *sodalizio, fratellanza, famiglia, compagnia, associazione, aggregato, cerchio, paracu* ('si sta bene sotto u paracu')[2], but none of these is as good a visual simile of the true relationships.

These, in so far as reliable conclusions can be drawn from the sources examined, are as follows. The *cosca* is not a group; interaction and an awareness of 'we', a consciousness of an objective to be jointly striven for, are absent or slight. Essentially it is a multitude of dyadic relationships maintained by the *mafioso* (m) with persons independent of each other ($X \ldots X_n$):

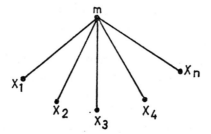

Instead of being a single person, X can also represent a small group, usually a family; in other words, via X, m reaches one or more further persons along a chain of dyadic relationships:

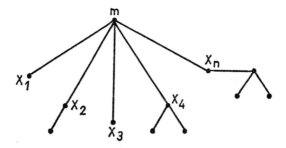

Within an X-branch there is frequently interaction, e.g. between the clients of a *mafioso* and his two sons, but the whole structure has no other cohesion than each person's link with m. None of the X persons regards himself as a member of an organisation, in a way that a bandit or a partisan regards himself as belonging to a gang or to a resistance group, i.e. to groups which can survive even after the elimination of the leader. Here the end of m at the same time means the collapse of the grouping.

76

In many localities there are associations or brotherhoods... without political line or political objective, without meetings, without any other link than dependence on one leader...[3]

...They frequently fall apart when key figures are arrested.[4]

This does not of course mean that X_1 to X_n do not know one another. On the contrary, they usually know very well who the other person is and in what relationship he stands to m but it is only the *mafioso* who mobilises them for joint action. The situation differs from one case to another: there are *cosche* which are quasi-groups in the meaning of Adrian C. Mayer,[5] i.e. a network of relationship chains which converge in the Ego and possess no lateral links, and there are other *cosche* whose nucleus is a group with strong interaction, constituted by kinship or friendship or both. However, the *cosca* is invariably more than just such a nucleus.

As a rule we find that the persons grouped around the *mafioso* do not represent a group but—chiefly in their opposition to another similar formation —feel a certain sense of belonging together, even if only in their shared dependence on one *capo*, and therefore are not a pure quasi-group either. These nuances should not be lost sight of whenever reference is made to a *cosca*.

As for the relations which bind a person X to the *mafioso* m, these may vary considerably in character; the range extends from a businesslike exchange relationship to kinship.

A purely businesslike relationship is represented, for instance, by the purchase of a service: m exchanges a certain sum of money for a service rendered by X. It may be that a *mafioso* hires a *sicario,* an assassin, and pays him for his deed. We find such an instance in the material about Valenza:

All three acted on instructions from Giuseppe Valenza who had paid each of them a sum of 200 lire in advance, with the proviso that he would pay a higher reward once the crime was accomplished according to plan.

As Sparacio had only been wounded Valenza did not want to give the executors the promised higher reward.[6]

In the Cannizzo trial a similar constellation is encountered: Giuseppe Reginella, a share cropper of the Cernigliaro brothers, hires three men in Monreale who were paid 100 lire by Cannizzo and 200 lire by Cernigliaro at Partinico before the murder demanded of them.

The exchange of *favori,* strictly speaking, is also a businesslike relationship. Let us assume that a small stock-raiser owns twenty sheep. To transport the small quantity of wool produced by them to Palermo would hardly be a paying proposition for him. To sell it locally in the village would yield too little. He therefore requests a much richer man, who is taking the wool of his 1,000 animals to the market, to take his wool along too. At some future date the man who has just been of assistance to him may ask him to cut down his neighbour's vines.

There are four factors which make such a business relationship invariably tend to transform itself into a clientage relationship—the asymmetrical nature of the relationship, its duration, its illegality and the manner in which the business was concluded. X is almost invariably the weaker partner, he is not only economically and socially on a lower level but also in the power hierarchy. He therefore tends to regard m as his patron; similarly it is natural for m to treat X not as a partner but as a man dependent on him. This asymmetry becomes the more marked the longer a relationship lasts, e.g. if the mentioned help with the wool transport is repeated year after year. The illegality of an action triggered off through this relationship in turn strengthens the position of the weaker partner. X is in a position to threaten m, the employer must not drop his executor after the deed but is obliged to perform his promised services and, moreover, will see the advantage of binding X to himself so he cannot become a danger to him in the future. This is why the executors invariably act in twos or threes, in order to be able to support one another *vis-à-vis* their employer. Finally, the business between m and X is not concluded in businesslike unambiguous formulations. As a rule the instruction is not spelt out explicitly but couched in hints—moreover, and this is very important, in the form of m asking X a favour:

> ... We were told that we were being asked a favour: there were enemies who had to die.[7]

This is what one of the men hired in Monreale stated at the Cannizzo trial. The services exchanged are given the character of favours by the mere fact that there may be a long time span between service and reward. Thus the economic support given by a rich man to a poor man at first appears as unselfish help:

> If, for instance, a shepherd has 30 or 40 sheep and stands with them on the road and cannot support them, then he will say to him: I don't know where to graze my animals. And the other will say: Take all your sheep to my pasture. And he will stay there for a month, or two months, and when he wants to leave he will let him go, even if the animals have fed on his grazing land. Half-wits, vagabonds, they all feed with him.[8]

Naturally Genco Russo, to whom the above passage refers, expects the shepherd or vagabond to feel beholden to him and to be anxious to prove his gratitude when the opportunity arises.

M may also protect X from the reach of the law, in which case he also speculates on making X 'his man'. Thus Franchetti writes:

> The more dangerous and notorious a malefactor, the greater is his risk of being arrested and sentenced, and the greater also is the master's endeavour to consolidate his power by protecting and saving the criminal, even if he has no material interest in doing so. Naturally the malefactor thus saved becomes his protector's man in the feudal meaning of the word: in a sense he has received from him his life as a fief and is now at his disposal to render him services.[9]

This is a very widespread method of building up a body of dependent persons. The Sotto-Prefetto of Cefalù has this to say about Li Destri and Milletari in a 'relazione sulle condizioni amministrative e politiche di Gangi':

> Whenever the police makes a discovery and strikes, the *alta mafia* hastens to take on the defence, to provide alibis and witnesses' depositions, to falsify public opinion in the piazza, to intrigue in prisons and offices, and to protest against the public power and officialdom. Even though it may not always achieve its objective of gaining impunity for those trapped, it invariably earns itself a higher respect in the village because of the protection it offers, because of the firmness of its principles, the power of its means, its tendency to practise retribution. It does exactly the same even with the bloody crimes committed by the gang of the *partito,* no matter whether these are robbery with violence or theft, or premeditated acts of vengeance against spies or the impulsive consequence of unsuccessful extortion.[10]

The starting point for the relationship may be a service performed by X or protection provided by m—invariably the one will bring about the other. And things very rarely stop at a single exchange; instead, an oscillating reciprocal relationship develops until, gradually, this has grown into a firm patron-client relationship.

Very often there is also an employment relationship between the successful *mafioso* and the men he attracts for his purposes, so that the former becomes the latter's patron in a double sense. The *cosca* of a *mafioso* thus almost invariably consists to a large part of his *garzoni, campieri* and *pastori.* And of course of his bodyguards *(guarda spalle).*[11] These are nearly always on a lower social level, *bassi mafiosi,* so that the clientage relationship represents the principal binding force in the *cosca.* One could almost define the *cosca* as that part of a *mafioso*'s clientage which has functions assigned to it for the discharge of *mafioso* tasks.

It may be that the relationship is described as 'amicizia', as friendship, or that the bond is strengthened by a ritual kinship. The 'comparatico', the godfathership, establishes—not only between godfather and godchild but, above all, between the godfather and the father of the godchild—in an artificial manner the relationship which in Sicily is the closest possible—kinship. And not only between equals but also between social unequals; indeed it is mostly the client who requests his patron to be godfather to his child. The *comparatico* thus is of instrumental importance.[12]

As a rule, however, the nucleus of the *cosca* consists of a few social equals, bound together by natural kinship or friendship, emotional or instrumental, i.e. of the family of the *mafioso* or of two or three friends.[13]

The sociogram of a *cosca* abstracted from a specific case, therefore looks something like this (V=kinship relations, F=friendship relations, P/KL= clientage relations):

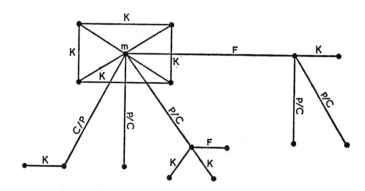

One becomes a member in the manner described gradually, and not through any kind of formal initiation. After all, the *cosca* is not a group to which initiation would be possible. It is formed instead by an indefinite number of very small informal groups which cohere by virtue of a central figure participating in each of them. The smaller the number of these individual groups, the more the whole develops the features of a group.

A word may be said here about the *mafioso*'s relations with the bandit. Although the bandit does not belong to the *cosca* he nevertheless frequently discharges executive tasks at the behest of an *uomo di rispetto*. Inasmuch as he does so he may be included among the *bassi mafiosi*. Nearly every bandit has one or more receivers, *manutengoli,* who are mostly *mafiosi*. Valenza was named as the *manutengolo* of the bandits Capraro and Di Pasquale; the Scalia and La Franca brothers, Cannizzo's opponents, used the bandit Nobile, and Li Destri was an 'antico manutengolo di briganti, e specialmente della banda dei fratelli Gulino'.[14] The Cavaliere Gaetano Salemi Pace, one of the two *capi-mafia* of Montemaggiore, likewise maintained good relations with bandits:

An old friend of the well-known brigand Valvo. ... How is it possible that nowadays no family ventures out into the country to picnic whereas he very often goes out with all his family without any fear?[15]

Nevertheless the relationship of the *mafioso* with the bandit always remains equivocal. On the one hand he acts as his receiver and as mediator between robber and robbed, or the family of an abducted person, and can therefore expect collateral services from the bandit. On the other hand, many typically *mafioso* functions are directed precisely against the bandits, such as the function of protection. Time and again bandits were fought by their *manutengoli* or even handed over to the police. Don Peppino il Lobardo, for instance, suffered this fate. After the Second World War many brigands who had executed instructions from *uomini di rispetto* lost their lives in mysterious ways. Some of them had previously got into open conflict with their former employers. Thus, in 1948, Giuliano shot the *mafioso* Santo Flores from Partinico.

Brief mention should also be made of a phenomenon which has not so far been touched upon—the fictitious *bassa mafia*.

The Marchese Pietro Mancuso, Conte di Geraci, owned an estate at Polizzi Generosa which he had put in the charge of the *soprastante* Vincenzo Mitra. On 24 August 1881 the *campiere* Gaspare Tripoli appeared at his house in Palermo and handed him a letter. This letter, a threatening letter demanding 6,000 lire from Mancuso, had allegedly been handed to the *soprastante* Mitra, for conveyance to the Count, by four persons armed with double-barrelled guns, wearing dark suits, with berets on their heads, and not speaking the dialect of the region—all of medium height and appearing to be about 30 years old. (A general and hence totally useless description.)

Mancuso refused to pay up and handed the matter over to the police.

This is what the *delegato di P.S.* of Polizzi Generosa gave as his opinion: '...I would observe that it is not improbable that this is a piece of play-acting by which the persons employed on the ex-feudal estate of San Giorgio are pursuing insidious objectives'.

The opinion of the *Comandante delle guardie a cavallo* was this: 'I must disclose to you that I believe little or nothing of the appearance of the four armed men and that indeed I very much suspect that behind this may be persons employed by Signor Mancuso on the ex-feudal estate of Tiborio and who are believed to be responsible for the burning down of a shed on that *ex-feudo*. Because they are now afraid and have been threatened by the Count that he would sue them and that, at the least, they might be deported to a prescribed place of residence, I assume that these persons wrote the letter word for word in order to dodge the charge of arson and perhaps also from other evil intent or from vengeance against the Signor Count Mancuso, and that—in collusion with Mitra—they made those four individuals appear who in fact do not exist for me.'[16]

In all probability, therefore, the bandits were fictitious—fictitious *bassi-mafiosi* who nevertheless lent as much weight to the threat as if they had been real. It is not clear from the material what objectives the *soprastante* was pursuing. One is tempted to see it as a ploy to force the landowner to sell his land.

In the famous case of the monks of Mazzarino a fictitious gang of bandits very probably played a similar rôle to the four armed men mentioned above. The situation here was as follows: Four monks from the local monastery and the monastery gardener Lo Bartolo pretended to be acting as mediators between the blackmailed pharmacist Colajanni and an alleged blackmailing gang from Barrafranca. The existence of this gang was never proved and it may be assumed to have been invented by Lo Bartolo, possibly in conjunction with the monks, so that the four pretended mediators must be seen as the true extortioners.[17]

2 Partito

One of the criteria which distinguishes the *mafioso* from other types, such as the bandit, is his relations with the exponents of formal rule. The sum total of these relations of a *mafioso* will now be called his *partito*. The *partito* has even less of a group character than the *cosca*; it consists of a surrounding circle of dyadic relationships, each formed by m and a partner p, whereby as a rule most of the p have no relations between each other. Frequently a *mafioso* is in a position to reach even more important persons by way of p.

A decisive factor in the central position of the *mafioso* in the *cosca* is the fact that there are no direct relationships between the persons of the *partito* and the *mafioso*'s clients, between p and X. Thus m derives his power within the *cosca* (and over a wider radius) from his connections with p and in turn establishes and maintains his position *vis-à-vis* p by the number of *bassi-mafiosi* X at his disposal.

In theory the formal governmental machine, the State, with its claim to the monopoly of legitimate physical coercion, is opposed and hostile to the private exercise of power by the *mafiosi,* who do not recognise this monopoly.

In practice, the *partito* relationships of the *mafioso* represent an arrangement between the opponents. By establishing links with certain officials the *mafioso* makes himself immune against the measures of the machine. In the final analysis the functioning of a State administration and of State justice depends on the actions of the men who hold these offices. If these bureaucrats are insufficiently socially minded, from the point of view of the bureaucracy, i.e. if they largely lack that specific public servant ethic (as we have found they do in Sicily), then the bureaucracy cannot function in an ideal manner.

Conversely, the weaker the bureaucracy, the looser the grip of the State governmental machine on the citizens, the more will an official find himself dependent on the support of informal holders of power for the smooth discharge of his business (maintenance of order, protection of property, elections). The businesslike exchange relationship which thus exists between partners, the performance and return of *favori,* becomes overlaid by an awareness of personal ties, by a sense of loyalty and friendship.

Even before 1812 the feudal baron would protect the *bravi,* and the landowner later would protect the *campieri* and *guardiani* employed by him and, if necessary, shield them from the reach of the State's judiciary. In these instances we are still dealing with a clear clientage relationship: the *bravo,* the *campiere* is the dependent weaker partner. Gradually, however, the balance changed: the new stratum of *gabellotti,* of small landowners and of middle class *mafiosi* possessed means of applying pressure on the landowner living in the city and the absentee aristocrat; added to the feudal obligation of granting protection there was now also fear. Or, in the case of the politician dependent on the votes of the electors, sober self-interest. It was largely these elections which gradually reduced the asymmetry of the arch of relationships between m and p. Indeed, the *mafioso* who controlled the votes in a constituency not infrequently succeeded in making the politician dependent on him. And through the politician he then influenced those parts of the State machine which might become a danger to him.

A rising young man anxious to make a career in the municipal administration or in national politics would be only too pleased to accept the offered support of an *uomo di rispetto* of whose great influence on the electorate he knew. His new electoral helper might have committed a murder, but the marked sub-cultural morality held also by the young politician would take no offence. Besides, his rival would use the same kind of people and if one rejected such means one would be certain to be defeated. The *mafioso,* whose services frequently do not have to be sought but who will offer them of his own accord, subsequently benefits from the influence which the Deputy has on the officials of the State, either directly or via a Minister. Sometimes the services of a *mafioso* may go beyond electoral help. An illustration is the case of the Deputy Raffaele Palizzolo who, as Director of the Bank of Sicily, in

1893 feared an investigation into his business management and (very probably) had Emmanuele Notarbartolo, who had collected evidence against him, assassinated.[18] Most interesting among the records of the subsequent trial are the services which the Deputy exchanged with certain *mafiosi*. He maintained relations with persons with previous convictions in Palermo, Caccamo, Villabate Alterallo, Resuttana and Ventimiglia Sicula, and some of these were employed as *curatoli* on his estate. Marchesano, plaintiff in a civil case brought by the Notarbartolo family, saw their importance to Palizzolo as follows: 'It was indeed Palizzolo who organised detachments of crooks to help him in the election'.[19] A *cosca* at Villabate is bluntly called by a witness an 'associazione elettorale'[20]. In a statement about Matteo Filipello, a former receiver of the bandit Leone, twice charged with robbery and abduction and twice acquitted 'per insufficienza d'indizii', under police surveillance since 1879 and Palizzolo's *curatolo* at Villabate, we read: 'He busied himself for his master, he was much concerned with the elections'.[21] More important, however, are the functions which the Deputy has as *partito* of a *mafioso*. A certain Salvatore Pesco from Caccamo, for example, repeatedly charged between 1869 and 1892 but always acquitted for lack of evidence, was placed under police surveillance in 1878 'as a *mafioso,* suspected of murder, abduction, robbery with violence and being a receiver for the most notorious bandits. ...'.[22] Palizzolo, in whose services Pesco was, intervened for him. In an attempt to have rescinded the restrictions of movement imposed on him he wrote to the Questor of Palermo on 24 December, 1878:

Dear Signor Questore,
    I have bought an estate situated two kilometres from Monreale and San Martino at the foot of the Castellaccio and called Trifirò. As I have to have a trusted person there I have chosen Salvatore Pesco, one of the two men from Caccamo who are at present on my other estate of Bellolampo, in the S. Croce area. Would Your Excellency permit me to make this change? In the hope that you will meet my request I thank you sincerely.

                                             Your most humble
                                             R. Palizzolo[23]

At Trifirò, however, Pesco was soon arrested again for implication in a money robbery. Palizzolo again intervened on his behalf and achieved his release. A letter which he subsequently sent to the Questor on 12 March 1879 is extant:

Dear Signor Questore,
    My bailiff has been set free and I hasten to express to you my sincere

84

thanks for the courteous efforts which you were good enough to make following my complaint.

Meanwhile my above-mentioned man informs me that the Questura now opposes his return to S. Croce, where I have need of his services. If, as always, you want to do me a favour you would have to sweep away this difficulty which I do not regard as excessively just.

Consider me your most respectful and devoted

R. Palizzolo[24]

A further letter by Palizzolo concerns Pietro Rini, who had been placed under police surveillance as a receiver for the bandit Leone. Of particular interest are the private remarks at the conclusion of the letter, emphasising that the addressee is here being approached not in his rôle as an official, but as a friend:

A certain Rini, who has been under police surveillance for years though I don't know why—resident in Caccamo according to the laws in force, was ordered to return to his birthplace. Since I considered this to be a directive from higher quarters, which you yourself merely implemented, I addressed myself to the Sub-Prefect with the request that he should rescind and revoke an order which indirectly causes difficulties also for me. I have handed over to Rini quite a bit of my land, as a tenant and share-cropper, and I don't know to whom I should entrust it if he has to leave; the more so as I have been summoned to Palermo by the Prefect in order to participate there in the work of the Provincial Parliament of which I am a Deputy.

An obliging letter from the Sub-Prefect, which has just reached me, informs me that my request has been granted—when that honourable representative of the Government had been examining the files concerning Rini it was realised that it was excessively harsh to bring the father of a large family to the verge of despair, especially as he has not even committed the worst offences in the world, as I am in a position to prove to you in a thousand different ways.

I trust therefore that you will not insist on those directives which were imposed on Rini and I thank you for this from the bottom of my heart since I too, as I have mentioned, derive a not inconsiderable advantage therefrom.

I am returning to you the novel of Ponson du Terrail which I have read. Without any satisfaction I confess that I found occurring in it all those improbable episodes with which the French school adorns itself. When I come to Palermo I shall send you a copy of one of my works in this genre and hope that you will write me your impressions when the opportunity offers.

And now let me squeeze your hand and consider me entirely yours

R. Palizzolo[25]

9 February 1876

Mention has been made in this book of the *mafioso* Damiano Mazzarese from Campofelice di Fitalia. The files concerning him, in the Archivio di Stato in Palermo, provide a good picture of a *partito* in action. In 1881 Mazzarese (together with his son-in-law Giuseppe Cirrincione) was placed under police surveillance. However, he was by no means prepared to accept the *ammonizione*. As an *uomo di rispetto* and a wealthy landowner he had influence and connections which he now mobilised. Enclosed with his own letter of protest to the Prefect was a resolution of the citizenry with sixty-two signatures

> As citizens of Mezzojuso as well as of the Ward of Fitalia we, the undersigned, confirm and declare that Signor Damiano Mazzarese, son of Vincenzo, resident and listed at Campofelice di Fitalia (Mezzojuso), has led a praiseworthy and immaculate life.[26]

Also enclosed with the letter was a certificate of good conduct issued by the Eletto Delegato who represented the Mayor of Mezzojuso in the Borgata of Fitalia. While the sixty-two signatures exerted only a diffuse pressure, this document represented the view of an official, i.e. the *partito* proper. Most probably the relationship between m and p was kinship—both Mazzarese's son-in-law and the Eletto Delegato were called Cirrincione—but the exact degree of kinship does not emerge from the material.

> I, the undersigned Eletto Delegato of Fitalia (Ward of Mezzojuso) confirm that Mazzarese Damiano, son of Vincenzo, proprietor, resident and listed in the above-named Ward, has displayed an entirely proper conduct, both politically and morally, and has never disturbed the public order.
>
> In confirmation whereof I issue the present document signed by me and sealed. Given at Fitalia this twenty-third day of November 1881
>
> The Eletto Delegato
> Domenico Cirrincione [27]

Having received these protests the Prefect demanded from the official of the Pubblica Sicurezza of Mezzojuso a report on the man on whom the *ammonizione* had been imposed. His opinion, expressed in a letter of 28 December, differed very considerably from that of the Eletto Delegato:

> ... Both Mazzarese and Cirrincione have had relations with brigands as receivers and extortioners; because of their *mafia* they impose their will on all citizens, and I have been assured that morally or actually they have participated in all crimes which have occurred in the area of Campofelice and the surrounding communes. It is incredible the number of crimes they are accused of, but from fear for their lives no one is prepared to state this formally. They have known how to pose as helpers of the police whereas in reality they were the traitors...
>
> Their prosperity comes from crime and not from sweat or hard work...[28]

Although this letter was confidential *(lettera confidenziale)* the Prefect passed it on to the Prince of Fitalia whom Mazzarese had already persuaded to take an interest in his affairs. One would probably not go wrong in assuming that Mazzarese's relations with the Prince of Fitalia were analogous to those between Calogero Sedara and the Prince of Salina in Tomasi's *Leopard*. Mazzarese was the upstart into whose possession considerable portions of the princely estates were gradually passing and who himself was not only a landowner but also the Prince's tenant. Mazzarese himself writes:

> I have a modest property—partly free, partly taxed—in the territory of Campofelice, a good part of which was bought from the Prince of Fitalia...[29]

The aristocrat had to reckon with the powerful upstart: he would rather have him as a friend than as an enemy and therefore intervened on his behalf with the Prefect:

> Administration of the estates
> of the Prince of Fitalia
>
> Palermo, 4 January 1882
>
> Most Excellent Signor Prefetto,
> I am returning to you the confidential letter of the police official of Mezzojuso and thank you for your courtesy in letting me see it ... I can assure you that I have known Mazzarese for a number of years and that he has always seemed to me an honest family man, totally devoted to agricultural pursuits so as to improve his family's position, and that until now he has been regarded by the authorities as an honest man. He has always been issued a gun licence ...

In conclusion I ask you to excuse me for writing such a long and boring letter, but I considered it my duty to unfold to you all that I know about the Mazzarese case in the sure knowledge that Your Excellency in his wisdom will attach due importance to the above-listed facts.

Please accept my ever highest esteem and my highest respect

Your most devoted
Prince of Fitalia[30]

These were two examples of *partito* relationships which we were able to attest in detail. Similar relationships may be assumed for any *mafioso*. They are used not only to ensure immunity from the judicial machinery but also for obtaining a gun licence, blocking official measures (like the construction of a dam), etc.

3   Faction

Grimaudo: Voi mentite; siete dipendente di Cannizzo.
Delisi: Mentite voi invece che dipendete dagli Scalia, coi quali avete comunanza di interessi.

(Processo Cannizzo)

Cosca and *partito* are groupings which can rarely be clearly delineated, either from one another or from the wider sphere of influence of a *mafioso* which also includes a halo of more passive followers and dependants. *Cosca, partito* and this more extensive circle together shall now be described as 'faction'. All three concepts serve the purpose of introducing a little more clarity into the description, but they are probably rarely used by those concerned. Just as 'uomo di rispetto, uomo d'onore' are used rather than 'mafioso', so the persons surrounding a *mafioso* are described as 'amici degli amici' and one of them as 'amico degli amici'. There is no rigid organisation, no group, let alone a 'società'—'friends of friends', that is an exact description of the fluctuating, oscillating bonds along the relationship lines described. If there is a certain feeling of belonging together among the followers of a faction, then this is related not so much to a common leader as to a clearly identifiable common adversary.

The root cause of enmity between *mafiosi* is the shortage of positions of power, while its immediate cause is frequently a private affair of honour, a quarrel over a woman, the refusal of a marriage proposal, disputes which grow into vendettas and bloody political clashes.

Your Excellency is not unaware that a long time ago (1848) Antonio

Rappa, motivated by amorous rivalry and favoured by the opportunity of the period and his position, killed Costa Erasmo and that the response to this murder was that of Salvatore Rappa. This led to hatred, hostility and acts of vengeance between the two families and these have ever since devastated this village. During the night of 11 November 1878 Francesco Di Marco (brother-in-law of Costa) was given a warning by shots from a firearm and presently those guilty were identified as Rappa Antonio (instigator) and La Bue Nicolo (instigated) and the cause of the crime was the campaign for the local elections ...[31]

On 15 April 1883 an attempt was made at Bagheria on the life of the mayor, Antonio Scordato. A certain Pietro Greco was accused as one of the instigators. On 12 July 1883 the Questor wrote to the Prefect:

> The hostility which has existed for a long time between Signor Greco Pietro and the mayor Cavaliere Scordato is due not only to the fact that in the local struggle for power they belong to opposing parties and their partisans now rally around them, but also to the fact that when a few years ago Greco asked for the hand of Scordato's daughter the Cavaliere refused it to him.[32]

The formation of factions may also be due to the rupture of a friendship. Thus Cannizzo and Scalia had originally been friends, just as Valenza and D'Angelo:

> When Giuseppe Valenza together with Pugliese's gang took part in the Alessi theft at Cammarata, his loyal friend and companion was the equally rich proprietor D'Angelo Luciano, son of Pietro, who, after the deed had been done, took a good part of the booty with him, without the knowledge of most of the gang, but he assured Valenza that he would share it with him, with Filippo Greco and another loyal comrade. But this did not come about because D'Angelo, after having withdrawn to the Malfarina region, refused the planned share-out. This gave rise to irreconcilable hatred between Valenza and D'Angelo, a hatred that was to have deplorable consequences.[33]

Around the two antagonistic *mafiosi* as nuclei the two hostile factions then take shape. Many people who belong neither to the *cosca* nor to the *partito* may be drawn into this polarisation—e.g. the doctors whose loyalty and discretion could become vitally important in the treatment of any wounded and the issuing of death certificates,[34] the village authorities, the lawyers, the bandits and above all the small criminals who are still at the beginning of their careers and seek protection from a *padrone*.

The switching of persons from the sphere of one *mafioso* into that of another also occurs. Frequently the spheres of influence overlap so that the loyalty of those affected fluctuates:

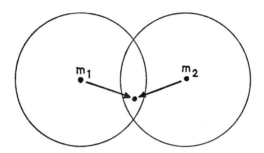

'The lawyer Alongi was said to be an intimate friend of the D'Angelo brothers, and particularly of Luciano, who had done him the favour of giving him the money for the purchase of a large vineyard.'

By the way he acted in public Alongi left no doubt about the fact that he belonged to the faction of the D'Angelo brothers. One day he was even warned that a rumour was current in Prizzi which might be very dangerous for him: this rumour stated that he had received instructions from Luciano D'Angelo to kill Valenza. Alongi was assured that Valenza himself would certainly have heard the rumour and would be taking appropriate measures.

The importance of verbal communication in the face-to-face group of the Sicilian village has been mentioned before; here we have an example of how decisively a 'voce' may determine the action of two men. On 17 December 1881, at six o'clock in the evening, shots were fired in the Corso del popolo at a group which included Alongi. Subsequent 'confidenze' confirmed the surmise that this had been an attempt on Alongi's life. However, no one had been wounded and it might therefore easily have been just a signal in the menacing language of the *mafiosi*—something to be discussed later.

'Following this attempt there were quarrels between Alongi and D'Angelo due to conflicts of interest, and these quarrels eventually culminated in open clash so that at present there is a civil action pending between them.' Valenza, who kept an eye on these developments, now tried to draw Alongi onto his side. He offered him a loan of 5,000 lire which would enable Alongi to break off altogether his relations with D'Angelo.

'But as the disputes between D'Angelo and Alongi turned to open struggle, Valenza reduced his generous offer and finally went so far as to say that all he was now prepared to do was to put in a word that might serve Alongi as a guarantee in case he had to borrow a sum of money to settle his dispute with D'Angelo.'[35]

Two further examples will be given below when Cannizzo's *cosca* is described.

Alongside bitter rivalry and feuds it may also happen that several *mafiosi* or *cosche* co-operate. Such co-operation, however, always has an ad hoc character; joint actions presuppose a common objective, agreements limited to a definite action. There is no long-term organisational link-up. Certain branches of the economy, about the monopolisation of which there may be very sharp clashes within a narrow geographical area, make co-operation across greater distances necessary with men employed in the same line of business. A case in point is the supply of vegetables: producer, middleman and retailer may be totally different persons. Another example is the cattle trade; the great importance of cattle markets for contacts between *mafiosi* from different regions has been described by Alongi. In fact he describes the 'fiere' as 'veri congressi interprovinciali della mafia, specialmente agricola'[36]. Similarly, cattle thefts, transport and realisation of stolen cattle or horses are not conceivable without integrated and concerted action by executors and *manutengoli* from different localities or even provinces. Such co-operation across three localities is described in a deposition made to the *delegato di P. S.* of Termini Bagno:

Sir: I am in the hands of the judiciary and have therefore decided to talk, since it is only from you that I may receive some mitigation.

A clique of criminals exists here in Termini. Its objective is the theft of cattle. Its leader in Termini is Leonardo Di Nuovo, son of Cosimo, field guard on the Torrazza estate. Relations are maintained with similar cliques in Mezzojuso and Corleone, in the first case with Como Salvatore, son of Antonio, in the second with Luca Patti, son of Giuseppe, field guard on the *ex-feudo* Pirrello (Corleone). The proceeds from the sale of the animals is shared out by our leader, i.e. he himself and those who committed the theft receive a double share, the others a single. The animals stolen in our territory and nearby are first driven to Mezzojuso to Como's place who issues instructions about where they are to be taken then, but as a rule they are taken to the *feudo* Pirrello, to Luca Patti. We receive no money at this handing over, but other animals which we drive to Termini and there hide in the houses of those less suspected by the police, while waiting for the certificates which Como, who has connections in many localities, gets for us.[37]

The participants, however, remain totally independent of each other, even though the relationship is maintained for a certain length of time, as for instance in the case quoted. Apart from arrangements within the framework of a definite action each separate *cosca* enjoys complete freedom of movement. True, some *mafiosi,* if they have an extensive *partito,* enjoy authority beyond their direct sphere of power. They may be asked by other *cosche* to arbitrate in disputes, or a candidate recommended by them may be supported by other *cosche* and he may then himself become a mediator between that *cosca* and a politician. But this influence invariably is confined to authority, i.e. it is based on the judgement of those acting upon their recommendation; it is not a case of command and obedience. The events following the Second World War more than ever before conjured up the image of a united 'Mafia'. The support given to separatism, and to the Christian Democratic Party by all *mafiosi,* the violent and brutal reaction of *mafiosi* everywhere to the peasant unrests, the series of murders of trade union officials—all these could be readily explained as the planned actions of a closed organisation. However, one will be nearer the truth if one assumes these actions to have been motivated by nothing more than a common interest in a specific historical situation: nearly all *mafiosi* had been made *gabellotti* by the threatened landowners, each one therefore, independently of all others, was responsible for protecting the land against the peasants. All of them had suffered under the Fascist dictatorship and welcomed the restoration of the democratic system which returned to them the instrument of power of communal and parliamentary elections and hence the *partito.* Because of their economic position they were opponents of the left-wing parties and logically supported the conservative Christian Democrats. Also, of course, because this party had the best chances of winning anyway—a *partito* without influence on the State machine is useless.

4.   Some false conclusions

Time and again one comes up against authors who suspect, or indeed claim to know for certain, that there is more behind the 'mafia' than meets the eye. The post-war situation, just touched upon, gave rise to a crop of books by authors on the Left, inspired by the hardships of the peasants and written as indictments. Naturally there was a temptation to present the conservative forces as a bloodthirsty Moloch. 'The mafia' was more easily comprehended and more easily attacked as a counter-type. Yet it seems that most of these authors—Sicilians—realised that this was just a polemical device: their information on the structure of 'the mafia' is vague and no concrete analysis is offered. They know what reality looks like, but the social and political clash calls for slogans. And these then acquire their own historical legitimacy.

However, there are other theories which cannot be explained quite so easily from the historical situation. Thus Ed Reid writes:

> Early in Sicilian history, when it was necessary to maintain extreme secrecy, the *Mafiosi* were divided into groups of ten with a group leader or *capo di diecina* (Chief of Ten) at the head of each. This kept members from knowing too much about the association. The group leaders were known only to each other. They reported to provincial chiefs and the chiefs to a supreme chief who resided—and still does—in Palermo...[38]

In America, too, he speaks of 'members of the mafia, whose allegiance is pledged only to the supergovernment of crime which has its capital in Sicily'[39]. This organisation, in his view, was founded on 30 March 1282, during the Sicilian Vespers, and its name developed from the battle cry: 'Morte alla Francia, Italia anela!'

Norman Lewis similarly always operates with the idea of a centralised secret society directed by a 'General Council'.[40] And Renato Candida speaks of the 'onorata società',[41] its 'pontefice massimo',[42] and its 'sotto-capi'.[43] The complicated process of rise and recognition is briefly simplified into an application for formal admission to the society, with a waiting period, trial performances, etc.[44] In addition the book contains some quite astonishing remarks about the *mafioso*:

> He has a way of seeing, thinking and living which is the exact opposite of how the honest citizen sees, thinks and lives... His eye never holds a gleam of goodness.[45]

Giuseppe Longo comments on this as follows:

> Thus the problem is simple once the machine has been identified: one high priest, four provincial leaders, since there are four *mafioso* provinces, about 150 local leaders. One knows who they are: let us arrest them, let us try them, let us send them to prison, and everything is solved. Why has this not been done? Or if it has been done why has it produced no results? Because evidently matters are not like that.[46]

Cutrera was the first to call the idea of the *mafia* being a closed organisation a 'gravissimo errore'.[47] The views quoted above are extremes, but certain wrong judgements are very widespread (Cutrera contributes his share). In discussing the structure of *mafioso* groupings an attempt should at least be made to explain the origin of these misjudgements.

It was pointed out at the beginning of this book that the word *mafia* in itself can be misleading. It came into use after 1860 when Italians were unable to interpret many phenomena other than in terms of the work of a secret society. The word gradually came to mean not a characteristic or an attitude but an organisation. And since nothing was known about this organisation extra-Sicilian models were transferred to Sicily.

The one to offer itself first was the Neapolitan Camorra. In official documents of the past century the terms *mafiosi* and *camorristi* are still used indiscriminately. It is thought that the *camorra* originated in the fourteenth century—'compagnia quae fuit in Kallari dicta de Gamurra'; the name has been derived from the Arabic 'Kumar', the game of dice forbidden by the Koran, or from the Arabic 'gamara', the place where such gaming takes place.[48] Over the course of time the society is said to have grown in number and, 'following the natural process of differentiation and division of labour', split into sub-groups or 'paranze'. Early authors still refer to a 'capo dei capi, un pseudo gran maestro o pontefice massimo', who, together with the *capi* of the sections, formed the 'Gran Consiglio'.[49] Here then we have both Candida's 'pontefice massimo' and Lewis's 'General Council'. But a writer as early as Alongi had this to say:

> The cliques in the city and in the prisons were independent of each other, each disposed independently over its revenue, laid down discipline and practised jurisdiction over its members.[50]

These statements about the Camorra, without any doubt, are largely speculation.[51] Their true nucleus probably is a phenomenon of big-city delinquency, separate gangs concerned with gambling and extortion, above all the typical protection racket. The centre of these activities was in jail. It is quite possible that fraternisation took place there, that novices were admitted to secret groups and that, in this connection, those famous initiation rites were practised which continue to be mentioned in the literature. The novice pricks his finger and lets his blood drip on a sacred picture which is then burned. Just as the picture cannot be restored, so the bonds among the sworn brothers can never be severed. This is followed by the kiss of brotherhood and the address *fratello* or *compare*. Now and again there is also mention of a shot fired at a crucifix.[52]

Many authors report the existence of various 'associazioni a delinquere' for the decade from 1870 to 1880. Some of these are claimed to have been known by name—the Fratuzzi of Bagheria, the Stoppaglieri of Monreale, the Oblonica of Girgenti, the Scattialora of Sciacca, the Scaglione of Castrogiovanni (Enna), the Fontana nuova of Misilmeri, the Fratellanza of Favara, and others. For all of these the same initiation rites are reported as for the

Camorra.[53] In addition there is frequent mention of recognition passwords in the form of a special dialogue, as for instance for the Fratellanza of Favara:

Question: Who is your God?
Answer: Aremi.[54]
Question: What is your aim?
Answer: The universal republic.
Question: Who was present when you were admitted?
Answer: Nice people.
Question: Who were they?
Answer: 1, 2 and 3 (the names of the brothers present at the ceremony are given).[55]

Or for the Stoppaglieri of Monreale:
'Does the dog's tooth hurt much?'
'Since the Feast of the Virgin.'
'Who was present?'
'Nice people.'
'What people?'
'Giuseppe Valentini, Francesco Polito and Pietro Puleo who admitted me as a brother.'[56]

The account of these initiation rites and passwords can be traced until they are encountered as characteristics of the secret society of the *mafia*. In following up the sources, however, one would have to go back not only to the Camorra but also to the masonic secret societies of the Kingdom of Naples (or rather to the rumours current about these). Thus the following ceremonial dialogue is reported from the 'setta dei fratelli Pugnalatori':

'The head.'
'Of the tyrant.'
'What do you hold higher?'
'Equality, fraternity, patriotism.'
'What do you hold more sacred?'
'Liberty or death.'
'What is your law?'
'God's ten commandments.'
'Quote them to me.'
'Death to all tyrants, their followers and henchmen, etc.'[57]

These patterns have become associated with the public idea of the structure of *mafioso* groupings in four different ways:

(1)   Through the writings of educated jurists—needless to say, non-Sicilians —who believed that they could recognise a familiar phenomenon in the scant information about the *cosca* and who interpreted and enlarged that scant information. One of these was Lestingi; Cutrera and subsequent writers took over Lestingi's information word for word.

(2)   Through individual witnesses giving evidence in trials of *mafiosi*. It is entirely possible that there were conspiratorial groups in the prisons and that these practised rites which resembled those in Naples or which were corruptions of the political-revolutionary character of the masonic rites. The only witness to describe the Stoppaglieri as a 'setta' and to pretend to know its ceremonies, was Salvatore D'Amico, who had spent many years in jail. None of the many other defendants seemed to know anything about them. Similar information about the Stoppaglieri in the writings of Alongi, Cutrera and all later authors are based on the evidence of this one man.

(3)   Through the terminology of the police and the law courts. The word *cosca* did not exist in official language and there was no other which would adequately describe the real state of affairs. Thus, in order to describe the *mafioso* groupings, the term 'associazione di malfattori' had to be employed, with all the implications of a firm group suggested by 'associazione'. As this terminology was known to those writing denunciations, and as they knew what would appeal to the police, these formulations are then time and again found in anonymous letters: 'una associazione segreta... il Presidente della detta società... in Altavilla esiste una setta di malfattori cosi detta società dei Fratuzzi'.[58] The prosecutor in the Amoroso trial refers to Salvatore Di Paolo as the 'segretario generale della Associazione'.[59]

(4)   Through newspaper reports or the novelettish treatment of trials. During the second half of the last century—and indeed even during the Fascist era— *Giornale di Sicilia* regularly devoted part of its pages to law court reporting. Trials which had caused a particular stir were freely reported, the action being condensed and simplified, rather in the manner of serialised novels. (In addition this paper also published the official trial reports as special issues, as for instance the Amoroso trial. These, needless to say, were different in character.) Readers' requirements were similarly satisfied by the *Le cronache delle Assise di Palermo,* published by Giuseppe Di Menza. Sometimes the material was turned straight into adventure stories. Thus the events disclosed in the Amoroso trial were issued as a thrilling and sentimental cautionary tale, written in the present tense, in Scalici's book *Cavalleria di Porta Montalto o La Mafia siciliana* (Naples 1885). The Amoroso and Mendola brothers

here call themselves *fratuzzi,* which is explained in a footnote as follows: 'Nota associazione di malfattori intesa Fratuzzi, vezzegiativo di fratelli, come fratellucci'[59a] (a well-known association of malefactors, known as *fratuzzi,* which is a pet name for brothers, something like little brothers). 'Cavalleria di Porta Montalto' is printed in the book in heavy type and understood as a proper name (the Amoroso brothers lived near the Porta Montalto in Palermo) and Salvatore Amoroso is described as the 'capo squadrone'.

Time and again we find statements from one of these sources being included uncritically in an otherwise carefully compiled book. Both Alongi and Cutrera are guilty of this mistake.[60] Thus Cutrera writes about the so-called *Fratuzzi* of Bagheria:

> The *Fratuzzi* were subdivided into detachments with each detachment consisting of ten men and its leader known as *decimoprimo.*[61]

If one reads the records about the incidents at Bagheria[62] one asks oneself with amazement where Cutrera could have obtained his information. All that emerges from them is the existence of two factions of the usual kind, grouped respectively around the mayor Scordato and around Pietro Greco, and the fact that in their quarrels they resorted, among other things, to murder. But in the very next line Cutrera quotes Lestingi's statements about the *fratellanza* of Favara, and here, all of a sudden, we find the same subdivision into columns of ten. Ed Reid's information undoubtedly also comes from this source (or from Cutrera). The non-Italian authors in turn accepted the information of Sicilian standard works without critical examination.[63]

Just as the charges of Left-wing authors or the blood-and-thunder stories about the *mafia* by romantic authors, the books of American writers on 'the mafia' spring from a definite readers' need. Thus the idea of a 'supergovernment of crime which has its capital in Sicily' (Reid) offers satisfactory explanations for the many disturbing events taking place in the United States. Gangsterism, mysterious murders, the astonishing power of the 'Mano Nera' or 'Cosa Nostra', the strange inability of the police and the judiciary—all these become understandable if one knows that the nerve centre of this underworld lies far away on the other side of the ocean, outside one's own sphere of power, and that the short, dark southerners with their unfair methods are controlled from some distant centre (as with the Jesuits at one time) and that it is all the fault of the Italians whose duty it would be to cut off the dragon's head.[64]

5. The system of norms

Any discussion of the relationship of *mafioso* persons must include the norms which govern these relationships.

Those who assume the existence of a well-organised secret society will be tempted to look for codified rules applying to its members. Such rules have in fact sometimes been 'discovered'. Montalbano lists the following:

(a)   The duty of those associated to help one another to revenge in blood any affront suffered.

(b)   The duty to try to achieve the defence and freedom of any member who has fallen into the clutches of the judiciary.

(c)   The right of members to a share, in accordance with the wise judgement of the leader, in the proceeds of extortion, robbery expeditions, thefts and other crimes jointly committed.

(d)   The duty to keep a secret; the punishment for those violating it is death by decision of the competent adjudicating organ of the *mafia*.[65]

―――   True, most of the authors state that such 'Statuti scritti', as Montalbano quite seriously calls them, have never existed. If one bears in mind the structure of *mafioso* groupings it will seem pointless to look for a codified law governing *mafioso* attitudes. Just as there are no initiation rites, since there is no such thing as a formal organisation, just as passwords are not necessary when the collaborating *mafiosi* know each other personally, so the attitudes of *mafiosi* and of others to them are governed solely by the sub-cultural norms valid anyway. Franchetti is the first to point out:

> ... As for the guarantees which one would have to look for in other countries whenever like-minded people associate and precisely lay down their mutual duties and rights—these he (the *mafioso*) finds in the customs of the population.[66]

These sub-cultural norms are not a law (in the meaning of Weber), i.e. they are not enforced by a specially available staff of people using physical or psychological coercion, but they are conventions. They are guaranteed 'through the likelihood, in the event of deviation within a definite circle of persons, of encountering a (relatively) universal and in practice appreciable disapproval'.[67]/ All specifically sub-cultural attitudes, not only *mafioso* ones, are conventionally guaranteed in this manner. The internal order of the family, for instance—fidelity of wives, virginity of daughters, support of relations by emigrants—is sanctioned by withdrawal of good will, by ridicule and disgrace, by expulsion from the family, or even, ultimately, by killing at the hand of a husband, brother or father; but these cannot be seen as a staff of persons specially held available for these actions. These sanctions are applied by individuals and even then quite irregularly. It is an interesting point that the application of these sanctions is in itself conventionally guaranteed: the man who does not punish his unfaithful wife becomes the butt of ridicule; the man who does not fulfil his obligation of blood vengeance becomes an object of contempt.

Montalbano's 'laws' (b) and (c) are contained in the general expectations which a friend has of a friend, a ritual kinsman of his *compare,* and a client of his patron and vice versa. Whenever *mafiosi* stand in this kind of relationship to one another it is a matter of course that they will help each other in trouble (especially against the State organs) and that economic arrangements between them are conducted with mutual trust. A *compare* simply does not cheat a *compare*—after all, the whole purpose of this ritual kinship is the extension of a relationship of absolute trust—and in any event a patron would naturally protect his client. (When D'Angelo failed to share out his booty he was violating not the laws of an institution and therefore becoming liable to its punishment, but he was breaking a relationship of friendship and therefore made himself liable to vengeance by the affected Valenza party.)

The 'laws' (a) and (d) are contained within a conventional system of norms valid for, and felt to be binding within, the entire sub-culture—the system known as 'omertà'. The word *omertà* comes from the Sicilian *omu,* meaning man. Its main connotation is the idea of a true man: in the Sicilian view a real man knows how to make himself respected through his own efforts, defend his property through his own efforts, if necessary restore his honour and that of his family through his own efforts, and solve problems and controversies through his own efforts without having to seek the help of others or have recourse to any kind of State organ.[68] The encouragement of a private use of violence—Montalbano's item (a)—is clearly implied. It is also reflected in local sayings, altogether, proverbs frequently offer the best definitions of sub-cultural norms. 'A cu ti leva lu pani levacci la vita', if a man takes away your livelihood you take his life; or 'Si moru mi drivocu, si campu t'allampu', if I die I'll be buried, if I live I'll kill you.[69] It follows for an *uomo d'onore* that he absolutely refuses any kind of co-operation with the judicial organs of the State—not only if he is directly concerned in a case but also if he is only indirectly concerned. It is not therefore just a fear of terrorisation which keeps silent the witnesses of a deed punishable under State law, but also a conviction that it is the business of the victim, or his relations, to take the matter into their own hands. If the State organs were to be effectively involved, the person concerned would in a sense be robbed of the chance of proving himself an *uomo di sostanza*.

The first aspect of *omertà*, the encouragement of the use of violence, is crucial for the legitimation of *mafioso* behaviour; the second—Montalbano's item (d)—makes such attitudes possible by screening off all uninvited intervention. The rule of silence, which is universally valid for all Sicilians, is particularly strong among the accomplices of a deed without, however, requiring any special codification. Time and again one encounters the praises of silence and contempt for garrulity:

> The following fable is familiar to all Sicilians. Once upon a time Speaking and Eating asked King Solomon which of them should dominate man's mouth, and Solomon decided that Eating should dominate man's mouth and not Speaking, for fear that Speaking might become man's downfall. Ever since, a man has been the more successful the less he speaks.[70]

> L'omu chi parra assai nun dici nienti,
> l'omu chi parra picca è sapienti.[71]
> (The man who speaks much says nothing;
> the man who speaks little is wise.)

> Bell'arti parrari picca.[72]
> (To speak little is a beautiful art.)

> Cu è surdu, orbu e taci,
> campa cent'anni 'mpaci.[73]
> (He who is deaf, blind and dumb
> lives a hundred years in peace.)

Sometimes a proverb emphasises the protection which one is affording others by keeping silent:

> Lu parrinu cummogghia lu calici,
> e nui ci avemu a cummigghiari l'unu cu l'autru.[74]
> (The priest covers the chalice
> and we must cover one another.)

> La tistimunianza è bona sinu a quannu nun fa mali a lu prossimu.[75]
> (Testimony is good so long as it does not damage your neighbour.)

Quannu cc'è lu mortu
bisogna pinsari a lu vivu.[76]
(When there is a dead man
one must think of the live one.)

Sometimes the witness is merely asked to keep silently out of an affair that is none of his business:

Zoccu nun ti apparteni né mali né beni.[77]
(If something does not concern you, say neither good nor bad about it.)

Chiddu è lu bonu chi vidi e taci.[78]
(A good man is he who sees and keeps silent.)

Time and again one reads of instances when people have acted in accordance with these commandments. One such example is an attempted murder in Caccamo one December afternoon in 1882:

Pugliese, attacked at closest quarters, received the first shot, fell to the ground and called for help—but the assassins closed in on him, fired again and then turned to flight. When he saw that no-one had come to his aid—the street was deserted—he succeeded with an effort in dragging himself to the nearby house of a certain Tranfo, where the local police eventually found him gravely wounded.[79]

Dolci's informant in Mussomeli mentions a man called 'Tanuzzu u mutu' because throughout five years in prison he had pretended to be mute to avoid giving evidence.[80]

A popular song says:

E lu iurici mi chiama a lu spurtellu:
– rimmi la virità ca ti nni mannu –.
– E-gghè la virità la rissi o cunfussuri,
e-nnò a-ttia, sbirru e nfanuni –.[81]

(And the judge called me to the counter:
Tell me the truth and I'll let you go.
I tell the truth to my confessor
but not to you, *sbirro* and traitor.)

There is a proverb which runs:

L'omu ch'è omu nun rrivela
mai mancu se avi corpa di cortella.[82]
(The man who really is a man never reveals anything,
not even under dagger blows.)

Cutrera (quoting Pitré) recounts a legend from Cefalù: a young man is charged with murder. Accompanied by a priest his mother goes to the grave of the murdered man and the priest commands the dead man to confess the name of the culprit. And although the accused man is in fact guilty, and the dead man knows it, the dead man replies:

Lu mortu: Patri, no cci arrispuniu;
Stu giuvini è 'nfamatu attortamenti;
Cu fu chi m'ammazzau, lu sapi Diu;
Nun mi spiati, cà nun sacciu nenti.[83]

(The dead man: No, Father, he replied to him;
That young man is being slandered.
God knows who it was murdered me;
Do not ask me—I know nothing.)

In the legend *omertà* extends even beyond death. And indeed contempt for the informer, the 'nfami', the 'spia', is so deeply rooted in real life that in any collaboration with the State organs, i.e. in actions conforming with the norm system of the superimposed culture, this system of relations deserves particular emphasis. Thus we find the following significant sentence at the beginning of an anonymous letter:

As a citizen and not as a spy I feel an urge to enlighten the judiciary.[84]

Alongside the positive sanctions, i.e. the respect enjoyed by the *omu dipanza,* the silent man, we find also negative sanctions. Very massive threats against those infringing the norms are encountered in popular sayings:

Chi mangia zucca muore appiccato.[85]
(He who spies (eats marrow) dies strung up.)

Zucca, zucca – chi parla va sotto.[86]
(Marrow, marrow – he who talks is buried.)

Una parola male detta,
ne viene una vendetta.[87]

(One wrong word
entails vengeance.)

Chi non si fa l'affari suoi,
con la lanterna va cercando guai.[88]
(He who does not mind his own business
looks for trouble with a lamp.)

In their practical sanctions the *mafiosi* have developed a rich scale of a menacing language which employs both verbal and symbolical signals. If a landowner does not want to employ a certain *campiere,* if a market gardener refuses to pay a certain sum of protection money, if someone offers money for a piece of land whose price the *mafioso* wishes to keep low, if someone is reluctant to sell, if a witness threatens to give evidence—in all such cases those concerned are first given some good advice, the well-meaning advice of friends. If they disregard these 'consigli' more or less explicit verbal threats may follow. If, for instance, a peasant refuses to sell out, the *mafioso* may say to him: 'I understand, *massaro,* I understand. You were born here and—you want to die here.'[89] Such threats may also be uttered in anonymous letters.

Next come the first 'avvertimenti', symbolical warnings: a cross made of pebbles, laid out on the field of the threatened person, or a rectangle representing a bier. A bullet, a clove of garlic or a small heap of salt are other hints of impending dangers.[90]

The next stage is actions resulting in considerable material damage—the famous 'taglio d'alberi' or 'taglio di viti', the cutting down of olive trees or vines. In those regions where these are not cultivated the *taglio* is replaced by fire-raising, destroying barns and sometimes the entire grain harvest.

If a man still refuses to yield he may find a donkey or a mule with broken legs on his land, or a beheaded dog or a sheep with its throat cut outside his door.[91] All these are threats usually practised by the *mafiosi* against others. In disputes amongst themselves the methods frequently harden far more quickly. If any sanctions are used other than killing, they are immediately directed against the person himself. A few deliberately missed shots can be an *avvertimento.* A traitor receives a cut across the face, known as the 'sfregio'. These *sfregi* are so typically *mafioso* that an *amico degli amici* is described in the Sicilian language of gestures by a thumb quickly drawn across the cheek, like a knife. Yet even so these are not password signals of a secret society. This form of punishment is a phenomenon widespread throughout the south of Italy:

The customary threat among southerners is in fact: 'I'll carve your face up, I'll mess your face up'; ... the *sfregio* is also used against unfaithful wives or even wives suspected of infidelity.[92]

Other forms of mutilation also occur—for instance the cutting off of a hand:

> ... The case of Caravotta whose hand was cut off in revenge and who has remained silent to this day.[93]

A man using this kind of threat will not shrink from applying the ultimate sanction: 'Cu t'amminazu, t'ammazza'[94]—he who threatens you will also kill you. Killing, sometimes combined with mutilation, for instance the cutting out of the tongue of a traitor, is the customary informal enforcement. The dangers threatening *mafioso* actions both from the State and from other *mafiosi* render quick, resolute and vigorous action necessary in disputes within a *cosca* or between two *cosche*. Killing has therefore often been compared to the execution of a death sentence without previous appeal. But this surprising act of ultimate brutal violence is needed to lend validity to the norms whose observance is not supervised by an enforcement staff. The objectively slight forces of sanction behind *omertà* are multiplied by the technique of terror, by the spreading of an atmosphere of fear which paralyses any attempt at non-conformist action. An important aspect of this technique is the public character of the acts of terror: unless they were known in circles beyond those directly affected they would represent an ineffective weapon. It is not as an individual punishment or as an act of revenge but as a symbolical demonstration of what might happen that the terror act acquires its importance.

6. Some structure patterns

In conclusion a few sociograms are added below, to stand as examples of what has been said above. Those participating in a definite action are surrounded by circles. The date of the action is given. Explanations of each sociogram are appended in its accompanying commentary.

K = kinship
RK = ritual kinship
F = friendship
IF = instrumental friendship
P/C = clientage relationship (P = patron, C = client)

(i) *Salemi Pace*

Source: ASP, 1880, busta 56, cat. 20, fasc. 28. Report of the *delegato di P. S.* of Montemaggiore entitled: 'Capi mafia di Montemaggiore con ramificazioni

104

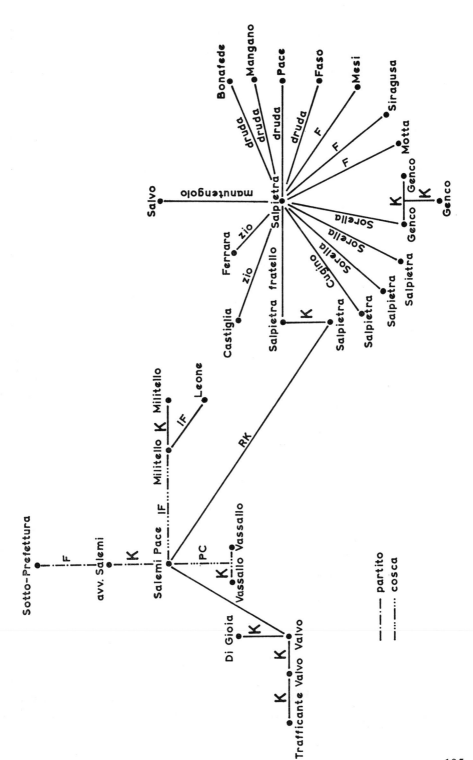

partito
cosca

105

in altri comune persino con impiegati addetti alla Sotto-Prefettura di Termini Imerese. Salemi Pace Cav. Gaetano, Militello G. Domenico di Vincenzo.'

Cosca: Gaetano Salemi Pace, *Cavaliere, farmacista, assessore municipale.* Among his employees are the twin brothers Gaetano and Francesco Vassallo, 24, who are named also as *manutengoli* in the list of suspects. A friend of his is Domenico Militello, 41, *possidente, Consigliere Comunale, ammonito, camorrista, mafioso, manutengolo dei briganti.* His brother Federico has no occupation and is 'sospetto in genere'.

Militello on one occasion mediated between Salemi and the bandit Valvo: 'Salemi is an old friend of the notorious brigand Valvo with whom he once had a quarrel. Thereupon Militello Domenico by means of a banquet restored peace.'

Bandits: The Salemi Pace case was chosen in order to illustrate the links with bandits. Yet in spite of its title the report is concerned less with *mafiosi* than with all persons suspected of collaboration with the bandit Salvatore Salpietra. The sociogram therefore shows, above all, the network of relationships maintained by a bandit in his native village. Salpietra was taken as the Ego and his relations with the persons set out in a circle around him, bottom right, are seen from his point of view. *Druda* means mistress, *sorella* sister, *cugino* cousin, *fratello* brother and *zio* uncle. Salemi Pace was the godfather of Salpietra's nephew, the son of Salpietra's brother, and in this manner he consolidated the relationships which he maintained with the whole circle. He had once had a clash with the *delegato di P. S.* 'because the latter had not issued a gun licence to certain former receivers, *mafioso* crooks, whom he had recommended ...'

Partito: The *delegato* Mattiolo had thereupon been transferred. 'Mattiolo's transfer was a disgrace to the village and to the Government; he had deeply penetrated into the web of the locally invariably strong *mafia*.'

Militello had once brought the wounded horse of a bandit down from the mountains in order to cure it. Because of his connections with the bandits the police arrested him. 'But he pulled all strings for his rehabilitation and also used the lawyer Salemi Pace Giuseppe, Gaetano's brother, who lives in Termini and has good relations with the sub-Prefecture.'

(ii) *Giuseppe Valenza*

Source: ASP, 1885, busta 85, cat. 20, fasc. 133 and Ajello 1868, pp. 14, 16 and 17.

Cosca: The nature of the relationships in Valenza's *cosca* are hardly ever indicated. An attempt has therefore been made to explore the *cosca* by way of the recorded joint actions:

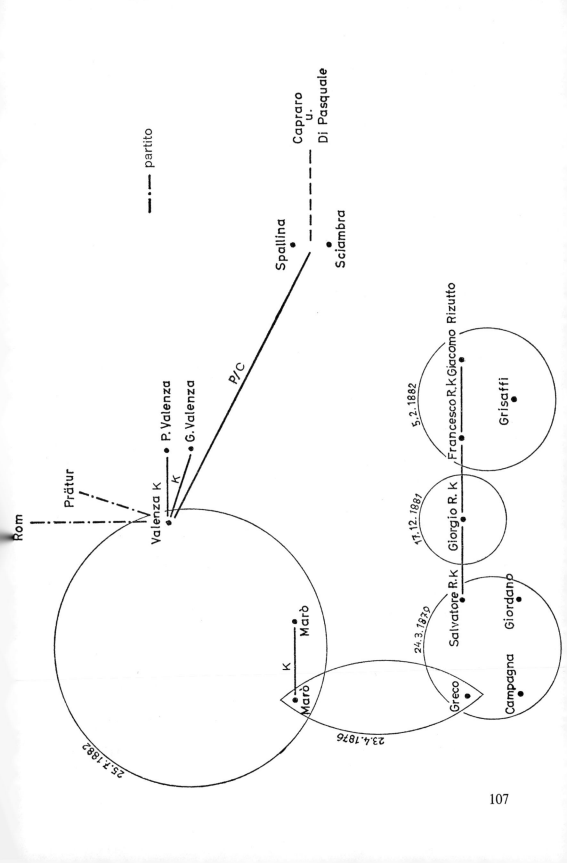

107

23.4.1876: Assassination of Castrenze D'Angelo; participants Francesco Marò, 34, and Filippo Greco, 48.

4.3.1879: Assassination of Antonino Comparetto; participants Filippo Greco, Salvatore Rizzutto, 24, Salvatore Giordano; accessory Giuseppe Campagna.

17.12.1881: Attempt on the life of the lawyer Alongi; participant Giorgio Rizzutto, 19.

5.2.1882: Attempt on the life of Paolo Sparacio; participants Francesco and Giacomo Rizzutto and Francesco Grisaffi, 24.

25.7.1882: Attempt on the life of Vincenzo Macaluso and Sebastiana Fucarino; participants Giuseppe Valenza, Francesco Marò and Salvatore Marò, 26.

Filippo Greco had previously participated with Valenza in the activities of Don Peppino's gang.

The brothers Rizzutto are described as 'fidi satellitti', on another occasion 'fidi sicari'. Most probably there was a clientage relationship with Greco, the Rizzutto family and the Marò brothers. There certainly was one with Michele Spallina and Giuseppe Sciambra. In the 'Copia dei cenni biografici' we read: '1874: He took a certain Spallina Michele and a certain Sciambra Giuseppe from Palazzo Adriano into his services and with their help supported the notorious bandits Capraro and Di Pasquale'.

As for the relationship with Sciambra we read in Ajello 1868, p. 16: '... Sciambra da Palazza Adriano amico di Valenza e da costui condotto'. As with Greco, Valenza was connected with Sciambra by ancient bonds dating back to the days of Don Peppino il Lombardo. Elsewhere Spallina and Sciambra are named as *campieri* of Valenza.

Pietro is Valenza's brother and Giorgio is Valenza's son. On 16 March 1884 the *sotto-prefetto* of Corleone wrote to the Prefect:

Only today this official has passed on to the Royal Prosecutor a statement by a witness dealing with the pressures and the threats emanating from Pietro and Giorgio, the brother and the son of the detained Giuseppe Valenza from Prizzi and directed against the State's witnesses involved in the various cases now pending against the last-named.

Bandits: Relations with Don Peppino il Lombardo and the bandits Capraro and Di Pasquale have already been mentioned.

Valenza, a wealthy property owner from Prizzi, is considered a very dangerous subject ... He is forever travelling about his extensive property, mostly at night and invariably unarmed as he has nothing to fear from malefactors and brigands whose friend and protector he is.

Partito:

... In my opinion that man ought to be placed under police surveillance. However, at present, it would be no easy matter to achieve this objective because a change would first be necessary in the personnel of the Prizzi Pretura. I have already notified the Centrale Ufficio of the need for measures against the court clerk Vizzimisi and even more against the court bailiff Vajana who is described as a bad lot. It must also be pointed out that the Pretor, Signor Accarelli, though a proper and honest person, was of weak character and incapable of energetic action ...

Valenza therefore had a great deal of influence on the officials of the judicial machinery. His relations with Rome and his acquittals 'per intrighi' have been mentioned in the text.

(iii) *Cannizzo–Cernigliaro–Scalia*

Source: ASP, Tribunale Civile e Penale, Palermo, Fascicoli dei Procedimenti di Corte di Assise, Anno 1877, No. 47: processo Cannizzo. Also two letters lying loose in: ASP, 1885, busta 85, cat. 20, without fascicolo: *delegato di P. S.* of Partinico to the Questor of Palermo (30 May 1885) and Giuseppe Reginella to the Questor (19 May 1885).

Cosca: The material contains information on the structure of two *cosche* confronting one another. Their nuclei are, on the one hand, the brothers Antonino and Gioacchino Cernigliaro and, on the other, the brothers Benedetto and Francesco Scalia, both parties wealthy landowners and proprietors of mills.

Cannizzo works closely with the Cernigliaro brothers, he is their friend, and as he himself participates in some of their actions may be considered as belonging to the *cosca*. At the same time, being a Deputy, he represents the *partito*. Directly dependent on him are his employees Scuma and Uberto.

Giuseppe Reginella, 53, and his son Francesco, 37, are tenants of the Cernigliaro brothers. Angelo Geloso is a brother-in-law of the Cernigliaros and at the same time stands in a client–patron relationship to them as he is employed on one of their estates at Monreale. Di Paola is a cooper (bottaio) from Partinico and lives in Palermo. Di Paola and Geloso are friends; Curcio and Mandala are drawn into the services of the Cernigliaros through Geloso.

110

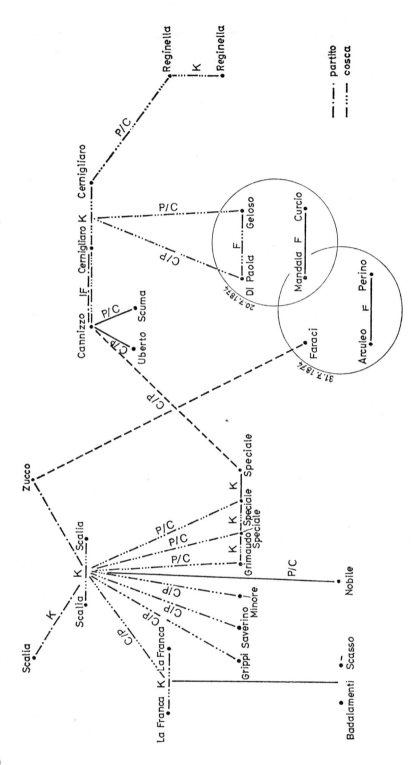

partito

cosca

Perino, Arculeo and Faraci are enlisted both via Mandala and via Di Paola; Curcio, 41, is a shoemaker from Monreale; Mandala, 32, a baker, and Faraci, 31, a gardener, are likewise from Monreale. Perino, 23, a citrus fruit merchant, comes from Villafranca, and Arculeo, 30, likewise a citrus fruit merchant, from Palermo. The last two appear to be working for the Cernigliaros only occasionally: they represent the *bassi-mafiosi*, the hired tools.

Faraci stands in an incipient clientage relationship to the lawyer Zucco; he had once been defended by him and now feels beholden to him.

In the Scalia *cosca* there are two small sub-groups formed by bonds of kinship: the La France brothers, one of whom is the mayor, and the three Speciale brothers. Ignazio Speciale holds Scalia land in *gabella*; Vito Speciale is a bodyguard of the Scalias. In the attempt on their lives on 31 July 1874 he, together with Grippi and Saverino, accompanied and defended the Scalia brothers and the lawyer Zucco. Grimaudo, a cousin of the Speciale brothers, was collector of the *dazio di consumo*, the consumer goods tax collected at the entrance to every locality; the Scalia brothers had leased this tax for Partinico.

A *pecoraio*, who is specially mentioned, and the brigand Nobile, who frequently stays at the Scalia's house, occasionally serve as *bassi-mafiosi* without belonging to the inner *cosca*. Acting on a tip-off from Cannizzo the *carabinieri* caught the bandits Scasso and Badalamenti who thereupon instantly demanded to see the mayor La Franca.

Incidentally, Benedetto Scalia was sentenced to *ammonizione* on 14 May 1877 (i.e. three years after the events described in the trial) 'come persona sospetta per mafia ed altro'.[95]

Alfonso Scalia is a cousin of the Scalia brothers, 'uomo onesto' as Cannizzo states, 'ma faceva parte della famiglia'. He is a candidate in the elections to the Chamber of Deputies and, if elected, would constitute a powerful *partito* relationship for the Scalia brothers.

Gioacchino Speciale has relations with both *cosche*. On the one hand, his brothers are in the service of the Scalias, and he himself seems to work for them. On the other hand, Cannizzo emphasised the friendship (probably a clientage relationship) which had linked him with the father of the Speciale brothers. Speciale testifies:

> After his son's death the notary Cannizzo summoned me in the evening. I visited him at the bank the following morning and we sat in his room. He began by speaking of the old friendship between him and my father which, he said, he wanted to continue with me. The talk was about his son's assassination, and he said, boasting of his effective connections, that he must avenge his blood. Nothing else was talked about, and this conversation went on for hours.

Emergence of Factions and Disputes: To emphasise the strength of the feeling of belonging to a faction we refer to the dialogue quoted as a motto on p. 88.

The enmity between the Scalias and the Cernigliaros had three causes:

(1) Slights and jealousy; Francesco Scalia himself said about the 'antichi livori':

> The hatred began with an event a good many years back. A brother-in-law of mine, who is now dead, Russo, offended the Cernigliaro family; we all disapproved of this action, including myself, as it simultaneously affected my sister, Russo's wife. From revenge Cernigliaro pinned on my brother the instigation of the murder of a certain Vutano. My brother-in-law was innocent. I yielded to my sister's entreaties and looked after the defence of my brother-in-law who was released. From then on Cernigliaro was my enemy.
> *Presiding Judge:* And Cannizzo?
> *Scalia:* At first Cannizzo was my friend, but he then got the idea that I might have been the author of a *taglio d'alberi* on his estate and he laid an action against me. But even before that he had been drifting away from me. He had been getting closer to the Cernigliaros. Thus began the disturbances which became extremely violent in view of the electoral struggle for the seat in the town hall.

Cannizzo had this to say about an attempt on the life of Gioacchino Cernigliaro: 'That attempt was attributed to La Franca because he had been after a woman whom Cernigliaro later married'.

(2) Economic conflicts seem to be the more deep-seated causes: the two wealthy families were quarrelling about pieces of land and were rivals in the milling business.

> Francesco Scalia: Later there was the quarrel with my brother Benedetto about the land by the Cambuca and the attempted murder of my brother when Cernigliaro fired a rifle at him.
> The witness Ignazio Provenzale: In Partinico there was a milling company; later the Cernigliaros built additional mills which brought benefits to the town but not to the company. The benefits for the town came from the competition which the Cernigliaros constituted for the old mill-owners, the Scalias.

(3) Political clashes: Cannizzo and La Franca were opponents in the com-

munal elections, and Cannizzo and Alfonso Scalia subsequently in the Parliamentary election. Scalia has this to say on the subject: 'The enmities became even more "cordial" because of the election of Deputies.' But the true 'cordiality' of the atmosphere only emerges from Cannizzo's words:

> Among the other candidates I saw Gen. Alfonso Scalia, the cousin of these Signori Scalia, an honourable man but nevertheless a member of the family whose target I was. I locked myself in my house so as not to be murdered.

In addition to the attempt on Benedetto Scalia and Gioacchino Cernigliaro, mentioned above, a whole series of clashes are described in the trial records:

1865: Cannizzo suffered a *taglio di agrumi*.

3.10.1873: Cannizzo's son was shot dead in Partinico. Cannizzo suspects the La Franca brothers of having given the orders and the bandit Nobile of having been the executor; he now personally starts to pursue him.

1874: Shortly after the start of the electoral campaign a warrant was issued for Cannizzo's arrest—as Cannizzo himself puts it, 'per una vile calumnia'. A former employee of the communal administration, whom Cannizzo had once dismissed in his capacity of *assessore communale* and who had thereupon entered the services of the Scalia brothers, had invented a 'storiella'. 'They needed in addition a man of authority who would co-operate with them to my detriment, and they found him in the person of the Pretor of Partinico who hurried to issue a warrant of arrest.'

The following testimony of a witness, which in spite of its businesslike conclusion reads like the commentary of some brilliant humourist, might stand as a motto over the discussion of the role of politics in *mafioso* behaviour:

> As for the notary Cannizzo, a warrant was issued for his arrest. He escaped. Later this warrant, issued by the official Pretor, was countermanded by the Examining Magistrate because Cannizzo had been elected a Member of Parliament for the Partinico constituency.

20.7.1874: Angelo Geloso invited Curcio and Mandala from Monreale to Partinico *(propose una gita di piacera in Partinico)*. They were joined by Michele Di Paola. They were treated as guests at Giuseppe Reginella's house and kept hidden for a few days. They were then taken to a barn of the Cernigliaros and from there the Scalia brothers were pointed out to them: 'It was explained to us that a favour was expected of us since one had enemies who had to die'. They received 100 lire from Cannizzo and another 200 from Cernigliaro. However, the planned attempt was prematurely discovered by the opposing party.

> Grimaudo: In the month of July, on the 20th or 21st, I was passing the forge of the locksmith Cammarata and there saw two individuals, and subsequently yet another stranger, sitting in the company of Giuseppe Reginella. As he is a kinsman of the Cernigliaros I smelt some plot against the Scalias. So I went to see them, to warn them.
> Presiding Judge: In short, there is no one in Partinico who is not hatching some plot either against the Cernigliaros or against the Scalias.
> Grimaudo: It was generally said that the Scalias were in danger.
> Scalia: With grave suspicion I went along with Benedetto Scalia to that place, and saw the four men walk away.

At Reginella's house the assassins were subjected to serious reproaches (rimproveri e minacce) for having lacked the courage to commit the crime.

31.7.1874: Michele Di Paola states in evidence that on 30 July he had met Curcio, Mandala and Geloso at Curcio's house: 'At that meeting it was proposed to kill the brothers and a generous reward was offered.'

The Scalias, who had been staying in Palermo for a number of days, noticed on the 29th and 30th that they were being watched by Arculeo.

On the 31st the attempt of the 20th was repeated. As the Scalia brothers, accompanied by the lawyer Zucco, were stepping out of his house they were fired on. The Scalias' bodyguards, Vito Speciale, Grippi and Saverino, returned the fire and the assassins took to their heels. The court established that the executors were Mandala, Perino, Arculeo and Faraci. Faraci, however, had not fired because he had recognised Zucco as his former defending counsel.

Defamation also plays a part in the disputes. Cannizzo was called 'Barabba' in Partinico. 'Cannizzo protests and states that in his community he is addressed by his proper name and Christian name, and that the addition of Barabbas is an invention or rather a slander thought up by his enemies.'

Mention was made above of the case of the lawyer Alongi who switched from D'Angelo's sphere of influence to that of Valenza.

Two more such cases of switch-over are attested from Partinico. They confirm that there is no such thing as a group with enrolled members but that the relationships within the cosca network are in a continuous state of flux, of moving together and moving apart.

Seven years after the Cannizzo trial, eleven years after the events revealed

114

in its course (from which the position of the *cosche* in the sociogram was reconstructed), Giovanni La Franca was facing a court in Palermo, charged with the attempted murder of Giuseppe Reginella. The two were still enemies but they had exchanged their positions: Reginella had fallen out with the Cernigliaro brothers, who now supported La Franca in the trial.

The *delegato di P. S.* of Partinico writes:

> Reginella Giuseppe was one of those who participated wholeheartedly in the bitter struggle between the well-known families of Scalia and Cernigliaro. At first he belonged to this latter's *partito* but subsequently dissociated himself from him, and later became a declared enemy of the Cernigliaros because they remained firmly convinced that Luigi Cernigliaro had been arrested through a denunciation by this very Reginella.

On the other hand, Cernigliaro seemed to be the one who was trying to draw La Franca into his sphere of influence. The reason—as Reginella stated in his letter to the Questor—was as follows:

> Signor Cernigliaro's activity is due to a different reason: his son Giuseppe wants to marry the daughter of Signor Vincenzo Rosso but he opposes this. Since the mother of the accused is a kinswoman of the young lady, Cernigliaro uses the mother of the defendant in order to obtain information and so to facilitate the desired marriage. That is why Cernigliaro is now looking for a lawyer for him in Palermo ... and why he is busying himself in all directions and in every other possible way which Your Excellency is sure to understand. The accused would not have the money for two lawyers and all the rest: it is Cernigliaro who looks after everything...

The two power centres thus continue to exist and remain rivals. But for the elements within their spheres of influence, i.e. in their *cosca* or faction, fluctuation is entirely possible:

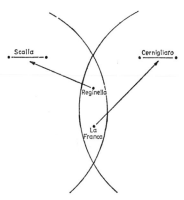

(iv) *Amoroso*

Source: Processo dei fratelli Amoroso e compagni. Resoconto del Giornale di Sicilia. Palermo 1883 (protocol of the trial).

Cosca: The nucleus is formed by family relationships. It consists of the five Amoroso brothers: Michele (44, *possidente, industrioso, sensale*), Emanuele (40, *possidente, trafficante*), Salvatore (34, *giardiniere*), Gaetano (29, *industrioso*) and Leonardo (26, *industrioso*). It is interesting that not the eldest brother but Salvatore is universally described as the *capo,* as the most violent and the one with the best relations. They all live in Palermo, near the Porta Montalbo, but they follow their occupations in the market garden zone of the Conca d'Oro. Salvatore, Gaetano and Leonardo are charged with murder.

Emanuele's wife Rosa is the sister of the Mendola brothers: Antonino (30, *giardiniere,* with a criminal record of five years' imprisonment for a murder 'per onore della famiglia') and Carmelo (25, *giardiniere*). They are, therefore, related to the Amoroso brothers but also show them great respect and followed their instructions '*per una certa temenza che gli Amoroso loro ispiravano*'. The Mendolas are enemies of another of Amoroso's accomplices who, like them, has participated in many of the actions—Girolamo Caratello, 34, employed by Amoroso as a *garzone.* Just because the men who can be counted as belonging to a *cosca* know one another this does not necessarily mean that they are friends.

A friend of Caratello's is Giuseppe Lopez (40, *guardiano d'acqua*). His participation in Amoroso's actions appears to have been only occasional.

Not so in the case of Lo Verde, 27, who is both a friend of Caratello's and related to the Amorosos by ritual kinship: 'Erano amici; anzi Salvatore Amoroso doveva cresimare il Lo Verde'. Salvatore Amoroso, therefore, was his godfather.

Through Lo Verde the Amoroso brothers have relations with Bonafede (Lo Verde and Bonafede had been charged in connection with the kidnapping and the murder of the wealthy landowner Catalfamo from Termini Imerese) and with Giacomo Lauriano (40, *fontaniere*), who himself is an influential *uomo di rispetto* with an extensive *partito.* Lo Verde is likewise on friendly terms with Vincenzo Mini (67, *guardiano*) and his two sons Giacomo and Antonino, 37 and 24, both *giardinieri.* The Mini family also stands in a close clientage relationship with the Amorosos: they are employed on a property owned by Michele.

Salvatore Di Paola (40, *fattore*=bailiff) is a friend of the Amoroso family.

Salvatore Gambino, 36, was temporarily employed by the Amorosos and participated in many of their actions. Through him the Amoroso brothers have relations with Angelo D'Alba, 24, his brother-in-law, an assassin who hired himself out to a variety of employers—including a certain Cataldo and

116

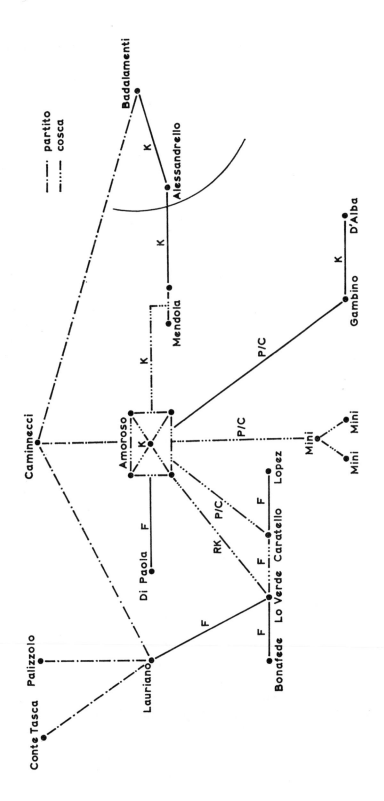

partito

cosca

117

a certain Spatola, both of whom had acts of personal vendetta performed for them by D'Alba.

The Amoroso brothers are on hostile terms with the Badalamenti family who represent the opposing *cosca*; however, there is not enough information available to reconstruct a sociogram. Antonino Amoroso, a sixth brother, had been killed by Gaetano Badalamenti; Antonino Badalamenti had been killed by Salvatore Amoroso and Francesco Bonafede.

The Amoroso and Badalamenti families had originally been on friendly terms and had both worked for the Deputy Caminnecci; later, however, they had fallen out, allegedly over the extortion of a priest practised by the Amorosos and obstructed by the Badalamentis.

The case of Gregorio Turetta, one of the guards employed by Badalamenti and murdered by the two Mendolas, provides an example of fluctuating allegiance:

> At one time Gregorio Turetta, a courageous man and capable of any bold deed, was an intimate friend of Salvatore Amoroso; but later a deep quarrel developed between them and Turetta joined the opposing party.

Ignazio Allessandrello, brother -in-law of the Badalamentis and their employee, was gravely wounded during the assassination of Antonio Badalamenti (who, incidentally, had just been discharged from prison after having served a sentence for participation in the abduction of a certain Parisi). He is at the same time Mendola's brother-in-law and thus has relations with both groupings.

Partito: The Amoroso trial also provides some interesting *partito* examples. Among others, two Deputies gave evidence for the accused.

The Honourable Valentino Caminnecci (37, *proprietario, Deputato al Parlamento*) had relations with Lauriano, Di Paola, with Leonardo and Gaetano Amoroso and with Antonino Badalamenti. On this point a passage from his interrogation is significant:

> Presiding Judge: On what occasion did you make Lauriano's acquaintance?
> Witness: On the occasion of the elections.
> Presiding Judge: And what do you know about his attitude?
> Witness: I have no new observation to make on this now.
> Presiding Judge: When?
> Witness: 1879. He worked in my house at Salaparuta. Then I remember that he was in prison because of some trial which has slipped my mind.

Presiding Judge: What picture had you of him throughout the period he was close to you?

Witness: He was a person on whose morality it never seemed to me proper to pass any observation.

Avv. Figlia: I would like to hear your present opinion of Lauriano.

Witness: I cannot at present answer with a clear conscience. In view of this trial it seems to me that I cannot form an opinion of Lauriano until after sentence has been passed by the jurors.

Presiding Judge: Are you acquainted with Di Paola?

Witness: I believe I made his acquaintance when I made Lauriano's acquaintance, and I regarded him as a good boy. So much so that I got him a job with the firm of Parisi.

Gaetano Amoroso: Would you please ask the witness if he knows me and if he once put in a word for me to save me being put under police surveillance?

Witness: I do know him and I remember the incident—I intervened on his behalf and on that of a number of others who were all on a long list of people to be placed under police surveillance. This happened quite shortly after the assassination of one of the Amoroso brothers. I got the authorities to quash the proceedings which did not seem to me appropriate.

Gaetano Amoroso: Do you remember that you once applied for a gun licence for my brother Leonardo?

Witness: I do remember. But I don't know whether the Questor actually granted him one.

The witness Curion, a police inspector, made a statement about Caminnecci's relations with Antonino Badalamenti. He had gone to the hospital in order to interrogate the mortally wounded Badalamenti.

I approached Badalamenti and when I had nearly reached the bed the director of the hospital told me that no one could speak to the injured man until he had been examined by the doctors. I saw a gentleman in riding boots and with a riding crop in his hand talking to the injured man and found this astonishing. I therefore said to the director: 'If I, who am a police inspector, am not allowed near the wounded man, will you remove that gentleman also. And I asked who he was. I was told: Valentino Caminnecci, the Member of Parliament.'

Conte Tasca, a wealthy landowner, submitted a written affidavit in favour of Lauriano: 'Count Tasca says that he knows Lauriano as an honest man who lives by his work.'

119

And finally, also as a witness to exonerate Lauriano, there appeared none other than Raffaele Cavaliere Palizzolo, the Member of Parliament repeatedly mentioned in this book earlier:

Witness: I have known Lauriano for years.
Presiding Judge: In what connection?
Witness: Lauriano is a well-builder. I have frequently had to employ him for the water in my villa at Malaspina. In contrast to the usual behaviour of our well-builders he has always shown himself a good and honest man. I was subsequently told that he had been arrested several times and stood trial. But as I saw that the court each time suspended proceedings and discharged him, and as I saw that he always had official authority to carry arms, I thought that he was nothing but the victim of some persecution and had been picked on unjustly.

Notes

[1] Cutrera 1900, p. 63

[2] Boissevain 1964

[3] Pietro C. Ulloa, *Procuratore Generale del Re* in Trapani, on 3 August 1838, to the Minister of Interior in Naples, quoted in Pontieri 1945, p. 192

[4] Boissevain 1964, p. 48

[5] Cf. Mayer 1966, pp. 115–16

[6] Letter of the *delegato di P.S.* of Prizzi to the Sotto-Prefetto of Corleone (6 November 1883) in ASP 1885, busta 85, cat. 20, fasc. 133

[7] Carlo Curcio in ASP, Processo Cannizzo

[8] Statement of a Mussomeli peasant about Genco Russo in Dolic 1960, p.64

[9] Franchetti 1925, p.138

[10] Letter to the Prefect of Palermo (18 July 1885) in ASP 1885, busta 85, cat. 20, fasc. 91

[11] 'Vincenzo Lauria's right hand was a failure in his job; he spent all his time with the *mafioso*.' This bodyguard was moreover said to have once committed a murder. After his master's death he had to work on the land. (According to an informant from Alcamo.) Montanelli has this to say about Don Calò's bodyguard: 'He appeared to be alone. But in fact he was followed at a distance of a few paces by two young men in velvet jackets and with coppolas on their heads, who never left him out of their sight and who never exchanged a single word either with each other or with anyone else.' (Montanelli 1958, p. 280)

[12] Cutrera 1900, pp. 58–9

[13] Examples are the five Amoroso brothers, the Scalia brothers, the La Franca brothers, Cannizzo and his friends, the Cernigliaro brothers, the friends Salemi Pace and Militello in Montemaggiore, Li Destri and Milletari in Gangi (an instrumental friendship through common enmity towards the Mocciaro family), Giuseppe Valenza, his brother Pietro and his son Giorgio in Prizzi, the four Mannino brothers from Monreale, *gabellotti* accused of 'intimidazione' and 'atti di maffia' (cf. ASP 1887, busta 100, cat. 20, fasc. 109) and many others

[14] *Delegato di P.S.* of Gangi to the Prefect (19 July 1885) in ASP 1885 (busta 85, cat. 20, fasc. 91)

[15] 'Capi mafia di Montemaggiore con ramificazioni in altri comune persino con impiegati addetti alla Sotto-Prefettura di Termini Imerese', a compilation by the *delegato di P.S.* of Montemaggiore in ASP 1880, busta 56, cat. 20, fasc. 28

[16] ASP 1881, busta 64, cat. 20, fasc. 62

[17] Cf. *L'Ora* of 13, 14, 16, 17 and 20 July 1962, as well as Alessi *et al.* 1965 *passim*

[18] Cf. Romano 1966, pp. 200–5, and Novacco 1963, pp. 231–47

[19] Marchesano 1902, p. 364

[20] Ibid., p. 339

[21] Ibid., p. 526

[22] Ibid., p. 325

[23] Ibid., pp. 323–4

[24] Ibid., p.324

[25] Ibid., pp.328–9

[26] ASP 1882, busta 69, cat. 20, fasc. 20

[27] Ibid.

[28] Ibid.

[29] Ibid.

[30] Ibid.

[31] Letter of the *delegato* of Borgetto to the Prefect (20 April 1881) in ASP 1881, busta 63, cat. 20, fasc. 7

[32] ASP 1887, busta 100, cat. 20, fasc. 116

[33] Letter of the *delegato* of Prizzi to the Sotto-Prefetto of Corleone (6.11. 1883) in ASP 1885, busta 85, cat. 20, fasc. 133

[34] Cf. the part played by the doctor in Loschiavo's novel *Condotta di paese*, Loschiavo 1956, especially pp. 250–2, 320, 335 and 337

[35] Cf. the letter of the *delegato* of Prizzi to the Sotto-Prefetto of Corleone (6 November 1883) in ASP 1885, busta 85, cat. 20, fasc. 133

[36] Alongi 1887, p. 71

[37] Letter to the Sotto-Prefetto of Termini (26 May 1884) in ASP 1885, busta 85, cat. 20, fasc. 107.

A note on the terminology: 'associazione di malfattori', as the interrogated here calls the group of cattle thieves, is of course the official term used by the police; certainly those concerned would not see themselves in this light. The uncritical acceptance of such official formulas often results in misunderstandings concerning the true structural character of *mafioso* groupings; cf. also §4,. It is interesting that the *associazione* included a family called Teresi with five and a family called Calderone with six participants; hence the *cosca* engaged in *mafioso* activity consists of a number of groups constituated by bonds of a different kind.

[38] Reid 1964, p.34
[39] Ibid., p.29
[40] Lewis 1963, p.233
[41] Candida 1960, p.110
[42] Ibid., p.11
[43] Ibid., p.12
[44] Ibid., pp.102 ss.
[45] Ibid., p.24
[46] Longo 1957, p.51
[47] Cutrera 1900, p.127
[48] Cf. Alongi 1890, pp.22–7
[49] Alongi here quotes Monnier and Forni, cf. Alongi 1890, p.42
[50] Ibid., p.43
[51] I should like to give one example of how such erroneous judgements may come about. In a footnote on p.33 Alongi says:

> In January 1888 Professor F. S. wrote to me: I firmly believe that the *camorra* should be studied not only among the delinquents but also among those who escape the sanctions of the penal code—e.g. among local administrations, among journalists and above all in the school system. Thus a regular *camorra* has been organised here in the higher schools, of a kind unknown in other towns. The State and municipal schools are insufficient for the acceptance of all pupils; a large part of them is therefore compelled to attend private institutions. The Minister demands that the local administration should open new schools—but the heads of the private schools are so powerful that they can force the mayor's office to turn a daef ear.... L.C. in fact assures me that there is another kind of *camorra* which concerns itself with textbooks.

An outraged schoolmaster who describes an act of corruption by a term otherwise reserved for violent crime. A factual author who briefly records the fact. A third author, reading Alongi only cursorily, may then present the matter as follows: The *camorra* takes over the schools and textbook production. Just as it has been said: The *Mafia* takes over the flower markets.

[52] Ibid., p.41

[53] Cf. Lestingi 1884, pp.454–5, Cutrera 1900, pp.119–20, Alongi 1887, pp. 140–1, *et al.*

[54] The name of a playing card

[55] Lestingi 1884, p.456

[56] Di Menza 1878, p.239

[57] Caso 1908, pp. 9–10

[58] From anonymous letters in ASP 1881, busta 64, cat. 20, fasc. 146, and ASP 1882, busta 69, cat. 20, facs. 191

[59] Processo Amoroso 1883

[59a] Scalici 1885, p.35

[60] Cf. Alongi 1887, pp. 140–2 (Recognition passwords), Cutrera 1900, pp. 116–64 (Misunderstandings concerning the structural character of *mafioso* groupings, recognition passwords, etc.)

[61] Cutrera 1900, p.122

[62] ASP 1887, busta 100, cat. 20, fasc. 116

[63] In the treatment of so difficult a problem as *mafioso* behaviour it is quite usual for one author to copy another. I should like to quote but one example here because it is important also for another reason.

The judgement of *mafioso* behaviour by the Fascists and Mori's measures are always sharply criticised by the Communists. However, the consistent struggle against *mafioso* behaviour stems for both of them from a strong emphasis on State power. Liberals and Conservatives, by way of contrast, have always found some form of arrangement with the *uomini di rispetto*. Thus the example demonstrates not merely the manner in which one author takes over the ideas of another (in the present instance almost verbatim plagiarism).

Mori wrote in 1932:

> A special characteristic (of the *mafia*)—and of particular interest to us— is the fact that in the relations between criminals and population it ranges itself alongside the State power. The result is that, where three concepts exist elsewhere in the field of *difesa sociale* against criminal activity, there are four in Sicily—State, population, *mafia,* criminals.

(Mori 1932, p.76.)

Giuseppe Montalbano wrote in 1953:

> A further characteristic aim (of the *mafia*) is that in relations between ordinary criminals and the population it ranges itself alongside the State power. In consequence, whereas in countries without a *mafia* there are three concepts in the field of *difesa sociale* against criminal activity

and its suppression—State, population, delinquents—there are four such concepts wherever a respectable society flourishes—State, *mafia, population*, delinquents.

(Montalbano 1953, p.540.)

Montalbano in this paragraph does not quote Mori, whom otherwise he execrates. Among other things he accuses him of confusing *mafia* and *banditismo*. And since Montalbano in turn is one of Hobsbawm's principal informants the same opinion is encountered also with the English sociologist: 'One of the commonest misconceptions about Mafia—perpetuated in such works as the ineffable Prefect Mori's Last Battle of the Mafia...— is the confusion between it and banditry.' (Hobsbawm 1959, p.40.) This is simply a false statement. Mori explicitly differentiates between the two phenomena ('Dal canto mio, ritengo che la mafia sia cosa distinta e separata dalla malvivenza...' (p.78) and implicitly throughout his book.

⁶⁴ Cf. Barzini 1965, p.282

⁶⁵ Montalbano: *La mafia siciliana* in Tocco 1959, pp.86–102, quotation on p.90. The following passage further clarifies Montalbano's view:

The four points listed were specifically laid down in the statutes of the various (old and new) associations of the *mafia*. Gradually, however, as actions began to be (however hesitantly) laid against the criminal organisations, the *mafia* had to forgo written statutes so as not to furnish documentary proof of the criminal association. Together with the written statutes, the formalities accompanying entry into the *mafia* associations also gradually disappeared; the norms became traditional in the sense that they were kept up and handed on by tradition.

Thus a proto-*mafia* is assumed here to have existed at some point in the past, with formalised intitiation rites and firm written rules, and the complex reality is seen as a watered down version of a much simpler original state of affairs.

Statuti scritti seem a curious assumption for the Sicilian countryside if only for the reason that illiteracy must surely be assumed to have been even more widespread the further back one goes into the past.

⁶⁶ Franchetti 1925, p.116

⁶⁷ Weber 1964, p.24

⁶⁸ Cf. Ciasca in *Enciclopedia Italiana* vol. xxv, p.345

⁶⁹ Quoted in Alongi 1887, p.76, and again in Boissevain 1964, pp.44 as still in current use

⁷⁰ Anonymous: *La Mafia,* manuscript in the *Biblioteca della Società Siciliana per la Storia Patria* in Palermo, n.d.

71 Ibid.

72 Ibid., cf. also Duyzings 1964, p.35, who quotes the saying from a village tavern in Villalba

73 Pantaleone 1962, p. 193

74 Cutrera 1900, p.29

75 Alongi 1887, p.76

76 Ibid.

77 Ibid., cf. also Boissevain 1964, p.45, and Uccello 1965, p.24

78 Boissevain 1964, p.45

79 Letter of the Prefect of Palermo to the Ministry of Interior (18 December 1882) in ASP 1882, busta 72, cat. 20, fasc. 12

80 Cf. Dolci 1960, p.58

81 Uccello 1965, p.89

82 Uccello 1965, p.23

83 Cutrera 1900, p.34

84 ASP 1885, busta 85, cat. 20, fasc. 127

85 Pitré 1889, p.2

86 Ibid.

87 Dolci 1966, p.87

88 Ibid.

89 Loschiavo 1965, p.306

90 Alongi 1887, p.145

91 Cf. Lewis 1965, p.27. No further attested instances of these types have been found. They are not as frequent as, for instance, the *taglio,* which is continually mentioned in the files.

92 Alongi 1890, p.46

93 Alessi *et al.* 1965, p.10

94 Boissevain 1964, p.44

95 Cf. *Giornale di Sicilia* of 21 October 1877

6 The Functions of Mafioso Behaviour

Mafia is neither an organisation nor a secret society, but a method. In his social relations the *mafioso* has recourse to physical violence or threatens such recourse. By means of this private application or threat of violence, declared illegal by the State, the *mafioso* not only achieves a personal material or prestige gain but also discharges certain functions within the sub-cultural system by entering the service of others. Although the two aspects—personal advantage and function within the system—are nearly always intertwined in concrete instances, in the sense that, for instance, the *mafioso* when performing a system-preserving action (protection of an estate against the peasants) is thinking chiefly of his own profit (as a *gabellotto* his enrichment through high share-cropping dues, and consolidation of his position *vis-à-vis* the landowner), we shall nevertheless treat these aspects separately for the purpose of systematic examination.

1. Functions for the individual mafioso

1.1. *Social rise*

> Presidente: Vi chiamavano Jacuzzo?
> Lauriano: Chi Jacuzzo! ... Giacomo, Don Giacomo.
> (Processo Amoroso)

As has been pointed out, the *mafioso* reflects the personality ideal of the Sicilian by being powerful, by commanding respect, and by being able to lead the life of a gentleman unhampered by manual work. In his lifetime his actions have earned him an enormous increase in prestige and a steep rise up the social ladder. A small peasant or cowherd has become a *galantuomo*, Jacuzzo has become Don Giacomo. And he has achieved all this not only through improving his material conditions but largely also because from the outset he has tried to match up to the attitudes expected of an *uomo d'onore*. This includes, above, all, total and absolute observance of the norms of *omertà*. Any matters of honour, any slights, refusals or business disputes are settled by him without recourse to the State organs. He does not flinch from the obligations of blood vengeance and punishes those who have offended or robbed him.

Above all, his position and his power enable the *mafioso* to act the part of patron, of protector, of the noble chivalrous cavalier who unselfishly helps the weak. Cutrera writes that any citizen can turn to the *mafioso* with a request for help:

> He is certain of having his request listened to with genuine sympathy. Indeed the *mafioso* mobilises all his efforts to be of service to his new friend—unselfishly and without claiming any service in return.[1]

However, Cutrera adds, the *mafioso* is not quite as disinterested as he pretends to be; he knows that any help he offers enlarges his clientage. Nevertheless, his action is valuable in itself in that it provides the *mafioso* with considerable psychological satisfaction. Cutrera describes the regular audiences given by *mafiosi* at their homes.[2]

Barzini, who was himself well acquainted with Calogero Vizzini, provides an excellent account of the morning conferences given by Don Calò at Villalba:

> Punctually every morning Don Calò came out of the little door on to the square and walked peacefully up and down, his hands behind him, talking to his brother, the Monsignore.
>
> From the shadows of the walls and out of small side streets now emerged the people who had arrived earlier, some of them from a long way off, and who had waited in order to speak to him. They were peasants, old women with black shawls on their heads, young *mafiosi*, men of the middle class. Each one walked a short distance with him, when his turn came, and explained his problems to him. He would listen, then call one of his followers, give a few instructions, and summon the next supplicant. Many kissed his hand in gratitude as they left him.
>
> Later he would sit at his table in the café on the piazza and continue with the day's business while sipping an espresso: a middle-aged peasant or cattle dealer like many others. ... His magnanimous and protective manner, the respectful salutations of the passers-by, the entourage around him, the humility of the people who approached him, the grateful smiles on their faces when he spoke to them—all these suggested a scene from the ancient past, a prince holding court and dispensing justice in the open.[3]

All the peolpe who approach him in this way seek his help as a mediator in their affairs; the *mafioso* discharges important functions for the others. But in the whole style in which this is done he becomes 'the prince holding court'; the scene becomes not just a demonstration but simultaneously an enjoyment of prestige and respect. 'Era una personalita aristocratica, era un signore, stava sempre al bar parlando colla gente', an informant from Alcamo told the present author about Vincenzo Lauria.

More important and fundamental to his social rise, needless to say, is material enrichment. In a variety of ways the *mafioso* succeeds in assuring himself of an income or in greatly enlarging his income by the application of threats of violence or by the exploitation of violence in the service of others. The multiplicity of a *mafioso's* sources of income may be divided into two basic types: on the one hand direct robbery, theft or extortion, and on the other the improvement or monopolisation of earning opportunities in a regular occupation.

(a) While engaging in activities of the first type the *mafioso* differs only slightly or not at all from the bandit. Cattle theft, abduction, smuggling, robbery with violence[4] and threatening blackmail letters[5] are in fact modes of activity more typical of the bandit. However, they are recorded time and again in connection with men who, by all other criteria, must be labelled *mafiosi*. Usually *mafiosi* appear in an executant rôle in such actions only at the beginning of their career; later they are far more often marginal figures, employers or, above all, receivers, capable through their connections of obtaining new papers for stolen animals or controlling the slaughterhouses where the carcases are processed. In certain historical situations individual *mafiosi* can enrich themselves especially rapidly by large-scale thefts, illegal trading and other activities: between 1915 and 1918 during the First World War, the army's demand for horses offered many opportunities; after 1943 it was principally the black market; in both wars money was made by helping illegal emigrants. The mere usurpation, the open taking possession of rights or objects—the victims being too frightened to object—can similarly often yield considerable profit. This procedure is typical of *mafiosi*. A case reported from Castellammare in 1849 may serve as an example: a *mafioso* family appropriated the water intended for the municipality.

> Ten thousand inhabitants were engaged in a noisy demonstration in front of the town hall. I was deafened by the public uproar, they were all shouting: Water. Ten thousand inhabitants who had to slake their thirst, cook their meals and wash in five *penne* of water. The cause of the curses, quarrels and family brawls was a dirty spring at which I was obliged to post a sentry because every single litre of water was a problem ... There was water. The municipality had spent 9,000 ducats to bring it into the town, but a robber's greedy hand and the lethargy of the administration had resulted in an exceptionally disgraceful malversation to the detriment of the population, of public order, of justice and of the dignity of

the Government and of its representative. About two miles from a locality called Pozzillo a canal had been under construction since 1790, which united several springs and from which about 30 *penne* of drinking water flowed to Castellammare by various ducts; and in order to achieve this the municipality had spent 9,000 ducats. The canal runs past the property of the Marcantonio family, and with unparalleled insolence they had blocked the canal on the far side of the country house, tapped it in its upper part and used the water for irrigating their gardens. In one of the clearings they built a well from which they sold the water at one *grano* or something like it per quarter; and they made an additional profit from the fact that, apart from the water, the inhabitants also had to pay for a beast of burden unless they wished to perish.[6]

Damiano Mazzarese from Campofelice, who has been mentioned before and who was put under *ammonizione* in 1881, writes in his letter to the Prefect:

> These very people describe him as arrogant because—resorting to his rights and to the practice of the *piatti dominicali* (domanial contracts)— he claims the land owned by others; a right granted to him by his titles and the valid law.[7]

From this letter and from one of the *delegato di P.S.* of Mezzojuso the following state of affairs may be deduced: Mazzarese lends money. If a debtor cannot repay his debt he takes possession of his land. The barons had done the same in the past but they had simultaneously been creditors and the enforcing authority of the formal law. Mazzarese, however, appropriates the *diritti dominicale* (domanial rights) to his debtor's land without having been assigned this right by the formal organs of the law.

The typical *mafioso* form of making money, of course, is the exacting of tribute for protection allegedly offered, i.e. for refraining from causing damage. This has been characterised by Max Weber as an impermanent revenue based on extorted services[8]. Fundamentally this form does not differ from ordinary blackmail by means of the *lettera di scrocco*; only its peculiar euphemistic cover, the endeavour to keep on a friendly footing with the extorted person and to appear in the rôle of a man of honour or indeed a helper —all this is typical of the *mafioso*.

> Let us assume A has bought a vineyard. On his first visit to the country to inspect his new property he is greeted very courteously by two or three men passing by. The following day the oldest of the three pays a respectful call on him. He congratulates A on acquiring such a fine property and wishes him luck for the future. He also praises the nearby village.

True, there was much talk of thieves but those were calumnies. What few criminals there were could very easily be kept in check by a man of respect. In any event he wished to offer A his services whenever he should find himself in any difficulty. Provided he did not disregard the advice of honourable men his property, his family and himself would be as safe, by day or night, as in the bosom of Abraham.

By talking politely and courteously about ways and means of avoiding dangers he lets the new arrival understand that such dangers exist. If the proprietor returns the courtesies of the *mafioso* he will ask him to recommend his vineyard to the protection of his friends, and, just to show how obliged he feels for the advice and help, will arrange for some money to reach him. In this case he will continue to be greeted respectfully in the village and will be able to live in peace.

In the opposite case, if A pretends not to understand, the *mafioso* will resort to the numerous possibilities of the language of threats mentioned above, culminating, in the extreme case, in the abduction of a child or a murder.

But these extreme measures are very rare. Once the dignified characters who at first had saluted him so cordially had shown themselves distinctly cold and once the first irregularities have been reported from his vineyard, A will almost invariably invite the *mafioso* and ask him why he visited him so rarely seeing that he would like to welcome him to his house as a friend much more frequently. Eventually he will ask him to do him a favour and look into those events in the vineyard. The *mafioso,* who naturally pretends not to know anything about it, will declare himself delighted to perform such a selfless service for his friend.

(b) Alongside these cases, where direct profit is obtained through violence or threats, there are others where a man's income derives from a regular occupation but where his earning possibilities within that occupation are substantially improved or downright monopolised through violence or threats. This is possible in virtually any occupation but it is entirely typical of *campieri, guardiani* and *fontanieri*. We may illustrate this with our earlier fictitious example. In this case now the *mafioso* would advise A to appoint him or one of his protégés as *guardiano* for the vineyard. In other words, A could not freely choose his employee from among a number of applicants but on the other hand would have the assurance that the mere respected name of his *mafioso* vineyard guard would protect him against greater damage. Nor could he dismiss his *mafioso* guard whenever he pleased without finding himself the object of warnings in the language of threats. In this manner the *mafiosi* limit the free flow of business in the labour market and ensure for themselves a certain measure of social security.

In the Amoroso trial the witness Pietro Gaudino testified as follows:

In 1881 I was a policeman, and one day Di Chiara told me he owned an orchard of 15 *tumuli* and was looking for a policeman who had hung up his uniform because he wanted to appoint him as a guard on his property. I offered my services. He told me that Salvatore and Emanuele Amoroso had stolen more than 10,000 lemons from him. The next morning Salvatore, who had been the guard before me, came and said to me: 'What are you doing here?' 'I'm guarding the property', I replied. He pushed off, muttering, and came back the following day. One night I heard a shot. In the morning a gentleman called on my wife and told her to leave the village unless she wanted to lose her life. One day Salvatore came and had a talk with Di Chiara; afterwards he dismissed me on some excuse or other.[9]

And the proprietor of the orchard added the following evidence:

Presiding Judge: But when the Amorosos were guards of the orchard things disappeared?
Witness: Yes, but those were people from outside.
Presiding Judge: And why did you take a former policeman as guard?
Witness: No one else would come. For hoeing, yes—but I couldn't find anyone for a guard.[10]

By pressure on his rival, and also by pressure on the landowner, Salvatore Amoroso thus maintained his position. Two other cases were revealed in the course of the trial—one of murder and one of attempted murder, the victims in both cases being rival *guardiani*.

Monopolisation proceeds by the same pattern in all other occupations. Alongi quotes the example of a dealer who called on a landowner at harvest time and informed him that he wanted to buy his crop. He already had customers, friends, all lined up, who could sell it further, and he had already arranged a fixed price in order to speed up the whole business. The alarmed owner inquired the price. In reply to his protestations that he could get far more for his crop in the market the *mafioso* merely observed that it was also possible that it was stolen en route to the market, or that some criminal might set fire to his barn, etc., and that it was surely far more advantageous for him, the owner, if he, the *mafioso,* took all further risks upon himself.

Moreover, surely the owner would not wish him, the *sensale,* to go back on his word to his buyers. The owner eventually had to agree and his losses represented the profit of the *mafioso*.[11]

Usury with money and water,[12] overcharging for all kinds of merchandise handled by *mafiosi*, monopolisation of the vegetable trade and the consequential obstruction of the building of dams, the unlawful occupation of the most favourable spot in the market, monopolisation of orders for a building firm or of licences for the retail of motor fuel—all these are ways and means by which the *mafioso* can improve his economic position. His sources of income are practically as numerous as the economic activities of the Sicilians; only the most important ones can be listed here.

In terms of social history the most important application of *mafioso* power is found in the field of fixed-rent tenancies and land transactions. Here it has been the principal factor in the rise of a new though small middle stratum. In Chapter 3 it was explained how the stratum of *gabellotti* had turned its actual position of power to economic advantage. Owing to the weakness of the State the landowner had behind him no coercive force either during the conclusion of tenancy agreements or as a guarantee of contracts concluded. The *mafioso* large-scale tenant, though economically the weaker partner, almost invariably was in a position of the stronger partner in terms of power politics. This power-political strength which, initially without economic foundation, was based solely on the physical violence at the disposal of the *mafioso*, became a decisive regulating factor in economic relations: the tenancy sum fixed by the *gabellotto* in his own favour, mostly well below the true market value, and the long term of tenancy enforced by him, usually well beyond the customary four or five years, gradually, in the course of time, led to the transfer of a substantial part of the economic wealth in the countryside into the hands of a small bourgeois middle stratum. (We need only recall the quoted passages from Mori, dating from 1932, to the effect that in the Province of Palermo alone 28,000 ha. of land had yielded an additional 18 million lire in tenancy dues once the power of the *mafiosi* had been broken.) The unscrupulous exploitation of sub-tenants, of course, was another factor in this, and here too the major part was played by real *mafioso* power rather than by economically-based power.

The *mafioso* enjoyed great advantages not only as a tenant but also as a buyer. By the application of *mafioso* means, he succeeded in intimidating possible competitors at auction sales and then fixing the price as the only buyer.

In this way *mafioso* behaviour became a method of social advancement, of rapid social rise within one generation. It must always be remembered that most *mafiosi* had not been born into a well-to-do middle class but had acquired wealth only in the course of their own careers.

Vincenzo Catanzaro was very poor to begin with, and on the run. Nowadays he owns land, a large herd of cattle and sheep, and a new house where he meets sinister figures who come from all points of the compass.[13]

The estate left by Nino Cottone of Villabate, a former butcher's assistant, was estimated at about 2,000 million.[14]

The children of the *mafiosi* begin life as middle class; frequently their father can give them a good education and often he endeavours to keep them out of *mafioso* life and ensure for them a peaceful bourgeois existence. Vincenzo Laurea's son is a lawyer, his nephew became a doctor. Genco Russo's sons both studied law. Vanni Sacco's sons obtained official positions in public institutions. Battaglia had begun as a pottery worker but his son studied in Naples. These are but a few examples of the general trend.

In Sciascia's novel *The Day of the Owl* the captain of *carabinieri* says to his *mafioso* opponent Don Mariano Arena:

And you have made sure that your daughter has a future surrounded by wealth ... I know that she is at present at a finishing school in Lausanne, a very expensive, very famous one ... I suspect you will find her greatly changed. More refined, full of sympathy for everything that you despise. Full of consideration for everything that you show no consideration for ... Besides, you are doing all you can to make sure your daughter does not become like yourself, that she will be different ... And if one day you don't recognise your daughter then, in a sense, you will have paid for the riches which you have acquired by violence and fraud.[15]

This is strongly reminiscent of Calogero Sedara in Tomasi's *The Leopard,* who had sent his daughter to a finishing school in Florence and later married her to a prince, the girl who was the granddaughter of Peppe 'Mmerda, a miserable share-cropper adequately described by his nickname.

A Sicilian proverb shows that the people know how such wealth is acquired: 'Lu riccu havi lu patri a lu 'nfernu chi prea pri iddu'.[16] The rich man has his father in hell where he prays for him—i.e. he would never have acquired his wealth unless his father had made it from crime and if he had not himself enjoyed the protection of hell.

1.2. *Protection against State organs*

La Mantia Rosario, assente, non fu citato perchè ignoto il suo domicilio e perchè trovasi, dalle informazioni avute, al Giappone o alla Cina.

(Processo Amoroso)

All the activities leading to the described results for the *mafioso*, i.e., reduced to a formula: the use and threat of physical violence, are declared illegal by the formally valid law. It is in the nature of the State to claim for itself the monopoly of legitimate physical violence; the consequence is the persecution of all private application of violence. It is necessary, therefore, for the *mafioso* to escape this pursuit, to make himself immune to the intervention of the staff of persons enforcing the State's claim, i.e. the police and judiciary. To a large extent this task is performed by the *partito* relationships of the *mafioso*; this has been discussed before. On the other hand it is the activity of the *mafioso* himself which results in the State organs being paralysed in their function. Intimidation and if necessary liquidation of witnesses are an important component of *mafioso* behaviour. This intimidation, together with the sub-cultural normative system of *omertà*, results in a situation when many a victim of robbery or extortion, and more particularly the witnesses of such actions, desist altogether from reporting it. In his report on Li Destri and Milletari the *delegato di P.S.* of Gangi writes:

> Because of their boldness and ruthlessness these malefactors have created such fear in the minds of the owners that the most serious crimes committed to the detriment of the latter are hushed up. Thus I have been told in confidence that a large number of threatening letters have been sent to various gentlemen here—but no one wanted to report this crime.[17]

It is not always possible to keep all incidents from the police quite so effectively. Murders, in particular, cannot easily be passed over in silence; the police discover suspects, the courts start an investigation against them. The typical end of any trial of a *mafioso*, acquittal for lack of evidence, is due to the fact that the various witnesses heard in court are witnesses for the defence. Admittedly, incriminating testimony is sometimes given in the preliminary investigation, but this as a rule is later retracted. To understand this phenomenon one must realise the situation of a witness and the double threat under which he is. Suddenly he is arrested as a suspect, as an accomplice or as a person who had knowledge of a crime; suddenly he finds himself helpless in the hands of the hated police. The great psychological and physical pressure applied to him through the brutality of the first interrogations[18] makes him temporarily lose his orientation by his familiar norms of behaviour. But once he has got over his first shock he sees the much more massive danger threatening him from the *mafioso* or from the *cosca* of the accused. The powers of his familiar environment once more determine his course of action.

Only to-day this official has sent to the Royal Prosecutor a testimony by a witness which deals with the pressure and the treats issuing from Pietro and Giorgio, the brother and the son of the detained Giuseppe Valenza from Prizzi, and directed against the State's witnesses involved in various proceedings now pending against the latter.[19]

In court the witness cannot remember anything:

Witness Cammarata: I don't remember.
Presiding Judge: You have the air of one who is not too anxious to speak the truth.[20]

2. Functions within the sub-cultural system

Mafioso behaviour may be viewed not only in terms of what it achieves for the individual *mafioso* but also with regard to the functions it serves within the entire sub-cultural system. To this end it is necessary to include in our examination also those other people for whom the actions of the *mafioso* are of importance.

The importance of informal relationship chains in Sicily has already been emphasised.[21] The Sicilian solves many of his problems through a series of inter-linked dyadic relations formed either by kinship, or freindship, or a patron–client relationship. Such chains exist in large numbers in a great variety of latent forms, any particular one being brought into play in response to a specific need. They derive their importance from the fact that the impersonal machinery of the bureaucracy is not competent for the solution of many problems, that because of its inability to act or the slowness of its measures or else the financial burden they represent for the supplicant they cannot be resorted to; alternatively the desired solutions may lie altogether outside the bounds of legality so that the formal machinery has to be avoided for that very reason. In a sub-culture in which the bureaucracy and the formal legal machinery serve the requirements of the superimposed culture a greater recourse to personal relationships is to be expected.

For the present analysis it is important to know how the *mafioso* is involved in such a chain. His intervention is sought in order to exert coercion in the direction of the desired solution. The *mafioso* does this by actualising his permanent power opportunity into a specific threat or violence situation. It is typical that A, whose direct connection to C has remained unsuccessful, now interposes the *mafioso* as a mediator m. He forces C into a behaviour agreeable to A. A might be a politician, for instance, and C ... n might be his electors:

The party A may own a spring and the party C may be planning the con-

136

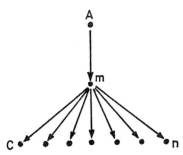

struction of a barrage. All attempts by A to influence C direct or by way of another chain, such as officials (x) who might sabotage the plan, have failed. A therefore turns to a *mafioso* who intimidates C by a murder or an act of arson and thus makes him desist from his plan:

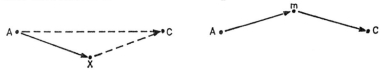

(The dotted lines represent the unsuccessful attempts and the continuous line successful influencing.)

It may also happen that two parties, unable to reach agreement on a certain question, both turn to the *mafioso* and request his mediation. In that case the sociogram would have the following shape:

The following case from Alcamo was reported to the author: A paid court to a girl B. Her father C did not approve and approached both A and his father D but without achieving any success with his intervention. He thereupon involved the *mafioso* Vincenzo Lauria ('una personalità aristocratica, un vero signore') who was then able to correct A's behaviour by direct contact and also via D:

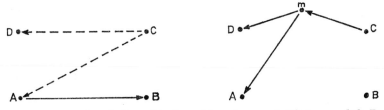

The reverse situation is found in Loschiavo's novel *Gli inesorabili*. Peppino Bellia (A) has seduced Rosina Dell'Aira (B) and refuses to marry the girl. Rosina, an orphan, asks help from a relation C who is a client of Don Salvatore Sparaino, the old *capo-mafia* of Gangi. The latter summons Peppino and his father Disma Bellia (D) to his house. Asked what a father should do if his daughter had been seduced with a subsequently broken promise of marriage, Disma Bellia, who believes one of his own daughters has been seduced, replies: *'Oh ! Santo di pantanone ! Gli sparerei in fronte se in quarantott'ore non riparasse !'* Sparaino thereupon discloses to him the true state of affairs and very discreetly implies a threat by arrogating to himself the rôle of father: 'Rosina è orfana ed io sono il padre di tutti'.[22]

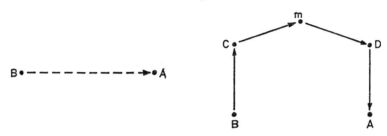

Salvatore Palazzolo quotes a case which shall be our last illustration because it represents a somewhat more complex and very interesting chain of relationships.[23] In 1913 a doctor A from Palermo settled in Caltanissetta and there set up a practice. However, several months passed without a single patient X calling on his services. He thereupon went to Palermo and asked a friend B, a senior civil servant, to help him. The civil servant listened to his story and then got on to a butcher C whom he knew. The *macellaio* wrote on a piece of paper: *Il dottor ... è amico mio,* signed the sentence and sent the doctor to another butcher D in Caltanissetta to hand over this message. This the doctor did and from that moment his difficulties were over.

No doubt another doctor E had monopolised the income opportunities in his area with the help of a *mafioso* (D or m), in the manner described also in Loschiavo's novel *Condotta di paese.*[24] The butchers frequently are themselves *mafiosi* or at least maintain good relations with *mafiosi* because of the important part they play as receivers of stolen livestock. Connections among them are frequently close.[25]

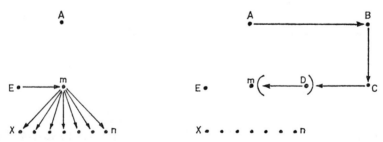

The principal motive of the *mafioso* in interposing himself in such a chain is material gain or increased prestige. At the same time he is very conscious of performing a task for the community as a whole, of contributing to the maintenance of order, i.e. to the preservation of the existing economic and moral system.

> We are not as you think, rebels, but genuine men of order.[26]

> When you are old, very old, and the *massaro* Turi, the *capo-mafia*, is no longer alive, you will perhaps judge this *massaro* more fairly and may think that his laws, which were not decreed by the State, were laws of nature and that he applied them with good will. ... Shake hands—I am a *galantuomo*.[27]

These sentences of Passalacqua from 'Piccola Pretura' are, as the author emphasises, an almost verbatim reproduction of a remark by the *mafioso* Bevilacqua to the young Pretor Loschiavo. We may also recall Russo's and Vizzini's assessment of themselves and, more particularly, Vizzini's words:

> The fact is that in any society there must be a category of persons who put things right again when they have become complicated.[28]

Having seen how a *mafioso* exercises his functions we shall now systematically set out these functions in the Sicilian sub-culture.

2.1. *Protective functions*

It was explained in Chapter 3 that the *bravi* of the barons by no means lost their *raison d'être* with the end of feudalism. The Bourbon State did not succeed, any more than did the Italian State later, in guaranteeing a truly effective protection of persons and property. This inability of the State's coercive power to discharge its order-maintaining function made private self-help an indispensable necessity for the property-owning classes. The *bravi* continued to exist as *campieri, guardiani* and bodygaurds. In periods of crisis the rebellious peasant *squadre* found themselves confronted by so-called *controsquadre* consisting of all kinds of elements, but organised mostly by *uomini di rispetto*. This was true in 1820, in 1848 and in 1866.[29] Although *mafiosi,* especially young *mafiosi,* also played a part in the peasant detachments, the typically *mafioso* attitude was primarily one of defending the existing state of affairs.

The owners of country estates and herds of cattle, of citrus fruit plantations and vineyards always found themselves compelled to employ men who were capable of deterring thieves and bandits either with a rod of iron or simply by the fear they instilled. The importance of this fact for the career of a *mafioso,* the rôle which the landowner plays for the *mafioso,* has been mentioned above; we must now emphasise the exceedingly important function which the *mafioso* discharges for the landowner. The protection which the *mafioso* provides for the property of his *padrone* is principally directed against *ladri* and *banditi,* i.e. against elements wishing, within the existing system, to improve their personal prospects. The punitive actions of *mafioso* protective power are terror actions and as such simultaneously have a deterrent effect. Time and again we read that most cattle or crop thefts are suffered by the smaller entrepreneurs who are not under the protection of well-known *uomini di rispetto.* The high murder statistics listed in Chapter 3 must not be seen simply as a high incidence of crime. Acts which enter the official statistics as criminal actions, measured by the criterion of the formal law, are better understood as sanctions of an informal legal system if one realises the general problem of sub-cultural peculiarities and the need for self-help within the sub-cultural social system. The divergent assessment of one and the same action, on the one hand as a crime and on the other as a judicial action, an assessment therefore which depends on the social system in which the action is viewed as embedded, is of course an abstract distinction. Reality time and again shows that *mafiosi* and State organs co-operate in fiighting banditry and that the *mafiosi* are accepted by some officials as order-maintaining factors.

In the examples quoted above (Chapter 4, §3.3) Li Destri, Mazzarese and Cannizzo expressly pointed to their merits in participating in judicial action. They are 'persone le quali resero senza ombra di interesse questo servizio alla giustizia'.[30] And there are quite a few officials who openly acknowledge such respected persons, who act 'without a shadow of personal interest', as extended arms of the State power:

> When the Questor of Caltanissetta received a number of peasants and the Deputies La Marca and Colajanni in June 1949, he was surprised to hear them protest against the acts of violence of the *mafiosi* in the region of the *ex-feudo* Pescazzo. He defended the *mafia* (which, in his opinion, had deserved well for public order and was a guardian of social peace) by exclaiming: The *mafiosi* are in every respect true men of the State.[31]

The best-known instance of a large-scale joint action against the bandits is the co-operation of Pubblica Sicurezza, *carabinieri* and *mafiosi* during the period after the Second World War .[32] On the other hand, compromises are frequently made between *mafiosi* and bandits. The bandits may be working for a *mafioso* as *bassa-mafia* and then be protected by him, or by other *mafiosi,* against the State. The receivers of the bandits are likewise mostly *mafiosi*. Finally, a *picciotto* who has participated in the activities of a bandit gang may be led by circumstances to embark on a *mafioso* career and become an *uomo di rispetto*.

Far more consistent and uncompromising has been the reaction of *mafiosi* to a different threat to the existing economic order—viz. the revolutionary aspirations of the peasants. Naturally, since these aim not merely at the improvement of the individual within the system but at a fundamental change of the entire system itself, they are far more dangerous to landowners and large tenants.[32a]

Thus the Fasci of 1892–4 among other things, aimed at a change in the tenancy pattern. By means of direct contracts between landowners and large tenants' co-operatives the large and intermediate tenants were to be eliminated. As the small peasants would then be able to negotiate with the landowners as a united body their dependence on the landoweners would have been greatly diminished.

The Fasci tried to support their demands by strikes and demonstrations which frequently—especially about the turn of the year 1893–4—resulted in bloody clashes and intervention by the State power. For certain localities it has been proved that the troubles had been provoked by *mafioso* elements and that the *campieri* had fired on the peasants even before the intervention of the *carabinieri*; this was the case in Giardinello (10 December 1893), Lercara (25 December 1893) and Gibellina (2 January 1894).[33]

After 1918 the same demand was revived with increased vigour. The Government, which in 1894 had been able to take tough measures, now had to show itself more conciliatory *vis-à-vis* the co-operatives made up of ex-servicemen. Landowners, *gabellotti* and *campieri* were now more than ever compelled to defend their privileges by their own efforts. In 1920 alone four trades union officials and organisers of co-operatives were murdered: Lorenzo Panepinto in S. Stefano Quisquina, Alongi in Prizzi, Salvatore Bonfiglo in Erice, and Mormino in Palermo.[34]

After 1943 the landless peasants demanded not only better tenancy conditions but also the share-out of the land, i.e. a fundamental change in ownership patterns. The land reform laws, introduced by the Fascist Government and renewed by the post-war Government, lent the movement considerable momentum. In many localities the peasants resorted to spontaneous seizure of fallow land and partitioned it symbolically among themselves. In their struggle against the organised peasants, the co-operatives, the trades unions and the left-wing parties, the conservatives had recourse to the customary means—terrorist murder and threats. Between 1945 and 1965 altogether 41 exponents of the peasant movement were murdered—30 of them during the crisis years of 1946 and 1947. The best-known incident, however, was the raid performed by the bandit Salvatore Giuliano, at the behest of others, on a May

141

Day demonstration of peasants from San Giuseppe Jato and Piana de Greci at Portella delle Ginestre on 1 May 1947, when 11 persons were killed and 56 wounded.[35]

A method far more frequently used than actual application of violence, of course, was the threat of violence. In March 1945 Giulia Florio D'Ontes, Princess of Trabia and Butera, appointed Calogero Vizzini bailiff of her estate Miccichè at Villalba. The 'Libertà' co-operative had demanded the sequestration of the estate. Her application was simply filed by the High Commissioner for Sicily with the note 'da archiviare' but the co-operative dissolved itself shortly afterwards when Don Calò had advised the peasants to do so. The Princess Lanza di Trabia made Genco Russo bailiff of her Polizello estate at Mussomeli.[36] It is worth quoting from a statement made by Pompeo Colajanni in the Regional Parliament in order to gain an idea of the universal scale of such protective measures:

Corleone:

Feudo Donna Beatrice, 32 *salme,* owned by the Palazzo brothers who had been abducted several times; *gabellotto* Lo Bue Carmelo, a well-known and dangerous *capo-mafia* from Corleone, previously arrested and deported.

Feudo S. Ippolito, 415 ha., owned by the Cavaliere Antonio Ferrara; chief supervisor (but perhaps rather more than a chief supervisor, allowing for the opacity of relationships and the resulting lack of precise information on the true nature of the agreement) Leggio Francesco, a well-known *mafioso,* at present deported.

Feudo Rao, 50 *salme,* owned by the widow Mangiameli, *gabellotto* Pennino Michele, whose father was shot dead in America in dramatic circumstances, himself a well-known *mafioso* repeatedly arrested and on the run for prolonged periods.

Feudo Chiatti, owned by Signor Provenzano; *gabellotto* Sabella Mariano, with previous convictions and deported.

Feudo Patria, about 180 *salme,* owned by the Duke Papè di Pratameno; *gabellotto* Leggio Biagio, a *mafioso* who had served five years of deportation, at present under arrest.

Feudo Strasatto, owned by Signor Pappalardo; *gabellotto* Liggio Luciano, a well-known *mafioso* on the run, against whom an order of arrest had been issued for numerous crimes.

Roccamena:

Feudo Caffarinni, 170 ha., owned by the Cavaliere Giambalvo; *gabellotti* Di Giovanni Chiccia, the brothers Raimondi, Cirrincione, well-known and dangerous *mafiosi.*

Feudo Gamberi, 159 ha., owned by Sparacio Mirto Serafini; *gabellotti* Giornado Leonardo and Casato Gioachino, at present deported.

Feudo Galardo, 300 ha., *gabellotto* Collura Vincenzo known as Criscione and his son, both *mafiosi*...[37]

2.2. *Mediatory functions*

One of the most important functions of the *mafioso* is that of mediator between *ladri* and *banditi* on the one hand and those threatened or harmed by them on the other. Pietro Ulloa wrote as long ago as 1838:

> As soon as thefts take place mediators appear on the scene and offer to arrange for the recovery of the stolen objects. The number of these arrangements is infinite.[38]

This mediatory rôle is particularly important in the numerous cases of cattle theft. The robbed person as a rule turns not only to the *delegato di Sicurezza,* but also to a man whom he knows to have connections in all circles of the population, and especially among the delinquents, and who is respected. The State rarely identifies the culprits. Even if it does it frequently cannot bring them to book because it is hamstrung by numerous legal restrictions *(in dubio pro reo)*. It can hardly ever replace the loss. The *mafioso,* on the other hand, often knows the thieves even before the theft is committed; in his subsequent steps he is not bound by any restrictions and an error of justice is no grave matter for him. Above all, he is concerned less with the culprits than with the stolen property and in most cases is able to restore it.

Mori estimates that in 75 per cent of all cases the State's agencies achieve absolutely nothing, that in a further 15 per cent they find the culprit but in only 10 per cent do they also discover their loot. Quite apart from these faint prospects of success, the robbed proprietor, if he resorts to the State organs, suffers a number of further disadvantages: it costs him time and money to make the journeys to identify his animals, to testify, to attend the trial, etc. Moreover he may have to face reprisals from the criminals. Mediation by the *mafioso,* on the other hand, according to Mori's data, remains unsuccessful in only five per cent of all cases. The owner loses only about a quarter or one third of the value of the stolen property, a sum which goes to the *mafioso* as a 'present' and part of which is passed on by him to the author of the robbery.

> ... Whereas the State power demands that the robbed person should talk (which is not always healthy for him) the *mafia* simply demands

143

that he should keep quiet (which undoubtedly is more comfortable and more useful).[39]

In the event of abduction, mediation by a *mafioso* can be a matter of life and death for the abducted person. If the police get on the track of the bandits they may be tempted to get rid of their dangerous witness.

Finally, intervention by a *mafioso* is sought also for negotiations on the sums demanded in threatening letters. Naturally such cases hardly ever become known but they may be assumed to be very frequent.

> In 1880 the Baron Antonio Callotti from Castelbuono received a threatening letter whose writer attempted to extort from him 8,000 lire. The *delegato di P.S.* of Castelbuono in his letter to the Prefect (4 July 1880) expressed his surprise at the baron's reaction. He no doubt suspected some mediation behind it:
> 'This regrettable blackmail at present appears a little odd and mysterious ... A demand is made for 8,000 lire but 370 lire are sent instead and whoever it is contents himself with this sum without further ado ... The day stipulated in the threatening letter is Thursday, 1 July, but the money is sent the following Friday, and the four who were supposed to have been at the appointed place on Thursday are still there the following Friday. ... In short, a concatenation of circumstances which makes the affair rather strange and mysterious.'[40]

The *mafioso* also discharges the functions of mediator in matters of civil law: he becomes a 'giudice di pace'. A creditor, for instance, may use the coercive power of the *mafioso* in order to get a debtor to pay up. A debtor, on the other hand, may request the *mafioso* to get his creditor to grant him a longer period of grace.

> One man will come and say: 'I have a problem with so and so, do see if you can settle the matter for me.' I summon the person concerned to me or else I go and visit him—according to what terms we are on—and I reconcile them.[41]

This is how Genco Russo sees the procedure. The parties thus avoid the expense and the time involved in a law suit. Besides, the *uomo di rispetto* can solve the matter much more quickly. And behind his arbitration there is always his effective power which neither party can escape.

Besides, a number of disputes cannot be brought before an official court anyway. These are the cases in which one party demands from another a course of action in line with their sub-cultural norms, a course of action not covered by formal laws. Unless one of the two parties resorts to direct self-

144

help the only arbitrator who also has the power of enforcement is the *mafioso*. One such example was quoted from Loschiavo's novel *Gli inesorabili*, where the *mafioso* forces a young man to marry the girl he has seduced.

A third type of mediatory function is that in which the *mafioso* appears as *intermediario* between influential persons or communal or State authorities on the one hand and those who have to approach such persons or authorities on the other. Broadly speaking the recommendations of the *mafioso* here correspond to the functions which a patron has to discharge *vis-à-vis* his clients. The extent to which the *mafioso* here adopts the position of a patron looking after his client emerged earlier from the account of the audiences given by him.

> If someone has to have a document issued to him, some paper, then he will almost invariably turn to him (Russo) rather than the municipality. He writes out a slip of paper and the mayor will instantly. ... To get some certificate or other a woman may have to wait six months, or the staff may be absent from this office or that, but he just goes there and they do everything at once.[42]

2.3. *Economy-regulating functions*

The major part of the actions of a *mafioso* also has an economy-regulating function. This need not be discussed in detail but the mere fact is worth emphasising once more.

The monopolisation of earning opportunities in an occupation, protection of ownership relations, influence on market conditions (the well-known institution of the 'piazza assicurata', the market stall protected by a *mafioso* in return for payment), disruption of the building of a barrage, i.e. guarantee of water and vegetable trade monopolies, the socially and historically significant intervention in land transactions and the individual cases of mediation in debtor–creditor relationships—all these features of *mafioso* action contribute to the regulation of economic relations in the Sicilian social system.

3. Mafioso behaviour and politics

Nearly all *mafioso* actions are instrumental for the securing of positions of power. Even the political institutions of the superimposed system of the Italian State can, in their specifically Sicilian modification, be converted into props of informal local power positions *(partito)*. On the other hand, the *mafioso* may often decisively strengthen the position of the holder of a formal position of power so that his actions must be seen also in their effect on the system as a whole. These preliminary observations are necessary if, in conclusion, we are to investigate those functions which the *mafiosi* may gain in the struggle for power over the institutionalised Government machinery.

It has been said before that the *mafiosi* build up their *partito* relationships by lending their support to candidates in communal and parliamentary elections. This support can assume three principal forms:

(1) votes can be won by force or by the threat of force;
(2) a candidate can be given money;
(3) individual voters controlling a great many votes among their clientage or kin and who will use these for a definite candidate can be granted certain *favori*.

It is above all the first method which is of particular importance for the behaviour of the 'classical' *mafiosi* of the late 19th and early 20th centuries. The second method is typical of the *nuovi mafiosi* and will be discussed in the following chapter. The third method is practised by the *mafiosi* not so much in their rôle as *mafiosi* (and, if so, through their *partito* relationships) as in their rôle as landowners or *gabellotti*. We shall here deal mainly with the first method and show its great variety of technique.

The most direct form of the use of violence in the electoral campaign is the physical threat directed at the opposing candidate:

> Among the other candidates I saw Gen. Alfonso Scalia ... a member of the family whose butt I was. I locked myself up in my house so as not to be murdered.[43]

> During the night of 11 November 1878 Francesco Di Marco was given a warning by shots from a firearm and the offenders were later identified as Ratta Antonio (instigator) and La Bue Nicolo (instigated), and the motive for the crime was the campaign for the local elections. ...[44]

Such violent measures against a political enemy may be applied in times of crisis even outside an electoral campaign. We need only recall the events of the period following the last war, the assassination of socialists, communists and trades union leaders, and the carnage of Portella delle Ginestre. However, such occurrences are the exception; the rule, as elsewhere, is intimidation by the threat of violence, and this is usually directed not against the candidates but against the voters.

The history of fraudulent manoeuvres which, ever since the plebiscite of 1860, have falsified the election results for Sicily reveal one general trend:

146

from a direct control of the electoral process, which had been entirely possible up to the Fascist era, the activity of the *mafiosi* increasingly turned towards indirect pressure on the electors, towards a specifically *mafioso* propagandist persuasion and intimidation.

(a)   The most primitve form of electoral fraud is the so-called 'pastetta' or 'coppino' (as the term is in the Province of Trapani): the number of votes is arbitrarily enlarged by the completion of voting papers for dead persons, the sick, emigrants, or illiterates (who did not possess the vote prior to 1913) until the desired result is achieved.[45] The technique of 'scheda girante',[46] on the other hand, requires collaboration between the chairman of the electoral commission and a 'grande elettore', a clientage patron, often a *mafioso*. (As a rule these two are on good terms since the chairman of the commission is appointed by the Prefect on the recommendation of the local administration.) This technique of the 'circulating voting paper' works like this: all papers have to be placed in an envelope before being dropped into the ballot box, and these envelopes have to be signed by the election official. The *uomo di rispetto* gets hold of such a signed envelope before the election; on election day he assembles all the voters dependent on him at his house, or in a *cortile*, a courtyard surrounded by several houses, where he treats them hospitably. He then motions the first one up to him and hands him the envelope which already contains a completed voting paper. The voter has to take this to the polling station where he is officially handed an envelope by the electoral official. He then secretly switches the two and drops the previously prepared one into the box. With the new envelope he returns to his patron's house, where the process is repeated. The voters thus manipulated dare not object; they are as a rule economically dependent on their employer and, even more, afraid of his field guards and herdsmen who might 'withdraw their protection' from their vineyards or livestock. Another form of electoral manipulation makes it possible to control whether the voters have in fact cast their votes in accordance with certain recommendations. To this end the voting paper, though marked for the same candidates, are variously completed:

> About 200 electoral papers are completed in divergent manner, with all kinds of titles and qualifications, combined in such a way that not two papers are exactly the same. Thus one may read: Saporito Ricca, Saporito Carini, Saporito Gagliano, Commendatore, Member of Parliament, former Provincial Councillor, baron, former Under-Secretary of State for Finance, etc. In this way a coach and horses were driven through the secret ballot.[47]

This is what Salvemini writes about the 1904 elections at Campobello di

147

Mazara. Whenever three votes can be cast, as was the case in later elections, and when the candidates are listed both by name and by numbers, an even greater variety of combinations is possible. The employer remembers the combination or special turn of phrase on the paper he has given to his share-cropper, supplicant or debtor and is thus able to check on every one of them.

As for the electors whose votes have not been made sure of beforehand, an attempt is made to influence them in the act of voting. And not only by offering them glasses of wine inside the polling station. Time and again we read that *uomini di rispetto* hang about the polling box, that some of them are even armed, that men known as violent criminals and employees of a *mafioso* form a so-called 'posto del bloco' outside the polling station or in front of the polling box itself, that they stop the voters, talk to them menacingly, sometimes beat them up and accompany them right into the booth. Salvemini refers to 'gente armata di bastone'[48] and Candida to 'tristi e malvagi figuri'.[49]

In a speech in Parliament on 23 November 1899 De Felice-Giuffrida accused the Government Party (Giolitti) of having discharged a number of criminals from detention just before the elections and of having permitted others to carry arms in order to promote, by their activities, the chances of the Government Party candidates.[50] But the Opposition Party employed the same techniques and therefore not infrequently clashed with the organs of the State. In his report 'Disordini avvenuti in Montemaggiore in occasione delle elezioni amministrative' the *delgato di P.S.* of Montemaggiore writes to the Prefect:

> On 19 August of this year, towards 12 noon, the constable-on-foot De Marchi Carlo, in charge of the post at Montemaggiore, was called by the office of Signor Legrenzi Giuseppe, chairman of the local electoral bureau, in order to intervene with two subordinates by force of arms in the hall where the municipal council was being elected. He was to maintain order which was being somewhat disturbed, by party quarrels, by the electors Salemi Cav. Gaetano ... pharmacist and Chianchiana Gaetano ... landowner, both of this locality.
>
> As soon as the above-named representatives of State power had entered the hall the chairman commanded them to remove the two above-named electors from the immediate neighbourhood of the ballot box. However, having been politely requested to obey, they refused and claimed that they were entitled to remain there. Meanwhile they got into dispute with the above-named chairman who ordered their arrest. ...[51]

Even quite recently some *mafiosi* have succeeded in having electors accompanied, under some pretext or other, all the way into the booth. Navarra in Corleone, for instance, issued certificates to hundreds of people to the effect that they were blind or short-sighted and therefore had to be assisted in the act of voting.[52]

(b) Such irregularities, however, have been progressively stopped. Pressure on the voters has become more diffuse. Attempts are made to create a general atmosphere of fear and then identifying a particular candidate with *mafioso* power, so that many people will not dare vote against him.

> On Saturday night, the eve of the elections, there was shooting outside the village, and my brother, who was curious and leaned out of the window, was grazed by a bullet. During the two weeks before the election many of us dare not sleep at home. The people are afraid. ...[53]

The people are afraid, they feel insecure, they still do not believe that elections are secret. True, since the Second World War the *mafiosi* have lost direct control over the ballot box, admittedly the secrecy of the vote is assured, but their conviction of the obscure power of the *mafioso* can nevertheless continue to govern the elector's course of action. So long as the voters believe that the elections are not secret then will they bow to the advice of the *uomo di rispetto* no matter whether their votes can in fact be checked up on or not. In Dolci's *Inchiesta a Palermo* we find significant answers to the question of whether voting was secret:

> Secret, yes. But you know who everyone votes for. ... The elections are secret but one knows all the same. ... Yes, they are secret but the secrecy of the vote is invariably violated by the *mafia* and their representatives. ... They say that they can always find out for sure. ...[54]

This kind of subjective view of the situation renders the voters susceptible to the 'advice' of persons of authority. Many call on the *mafioso* of their own accord in order to be advised and, in this manner, to perform an act of homage:

> The people ask whom they should vote for because they consider it their duty to be advised, to show their gratitude, their recognition: they feel unsure and want guidance from persons who have been good to them. ...[55]

This is stated by Genco Russo.
  Sometimes the mere demonstration of good relations between a candidate and the well-known *uomini di rispetto* is enough:

For the electoral campaign of 1946 [...] arrived at Salemi towards morning, with five or six car-loads of people most of whom were of *mafioso* appearance. He got out in the Piazza Libertà and immediately met a number of people who had been awaiting him. A group formed, including [...], Santo Robino, *capo-mafia* of Salemi; Ignazio Salvo, son of Alberto, a man with a well-known criminal record; Vincenzo Mangogna, a very dangerous and violent *mafioso,* sentenced for murder; Luigi Salvo, son of Alberto, back from America; Foreddu Robino, who was subsequently murdered in America and was involved in the drug trade; Alberto Agneci, a *mafioso,* subsequently put to death in America, fried, all because of drugs; Mariano Licari, a big *mafioso* from Marsala, now in prison for kidnapping. A short way off from [...] stood *mafiosi* of middling importance, curious spectators and campaign helpers.

After exchanging the warmest greetings [...] and the others remained there for a while and conversed before the eyes of the entire population and then made their way to Christian Democrat headquarters. ... After a while [...] stepped out on to Professor Favara's balcony to address the meeting. With him on the balcony were Ignazio Salvo, one or two other *mafiosi* and the then secretary of the Christian Democrat Party.[56]

Towards the end of May, during the election campaign, he (Genco Russo) had dined together with the Minister Zaccagnini and the Deputy Lanza and they had then walked out arm in arm.[57]

As a rule, however, they do not confine themselves to joint public appearances. Frequently the *mafiosi* appoint themselves election agents, go from door to door, distribute propaganda leaflets and hand out good advice ('Ti raccomando [...], che è cosa nostra'[58]), frequently very urgent advice, accompanied by threats. Not infrequently these threats are heightened by the *mafiosi* doing their propaganda work at night:

Mancino turns up during the day and he also turns up at night, when he does not want to be seen in some place or other; and, of course, if a man hears a knock at his door at night and then sees Mancino standing there ... who can tell what such people are after?[59]

Alia is a centre of the *mafia*. Here in Alia the votes for [...] went up, they almost exactly doubled, from 203 to 403, when Ditta Vincenzo, *capo-mafia* and a close friend of Genco Russo's and Matteo Vallone's, likewise an old *mafioso,* up to his neck in cattle thieving and on the *feudo,* with more than 15 years' imprisonment and deportations, became his election agent, i.e. shortly before the 1958 elections. Although these *ma-*

fiosi with their group had supported the Liberals and Monarchists in the post-war period, in 1958 they arranged for the distribution of, and themselves distributed from door to door, reproductions of ballot papers on which the number and name of […] were marked with a cross … and many people said Yes and many timid people eventually voted in the way they had been told to. They also visited the houses at night in order all the more to terrify people.[60]

Far less numerous are the cases of *mafiosi* themselves figuring as candidates of a political party, as for instance Genco Russo in the 1960 communal elections at Mussomeli for the Christian Democrats. They prefer to stay in the background and concentrate chiefly on developing good *partito* relationships.

Notes

[1] Cutrera 1900, p. 51

[2] Cf. ibid., p. 52

[3] Barzini 1965, pp. 279–80

[4] As already mentioned in connection with Valenza, Battaglia and Vizzini

[5] One example, at least, of a blackmailing letter should be quoted here; after all, these letters are typical of the bandits and of the youthful *mafiosi*. Even when the mediatory role of the *mafioso* is discussed presently, sight should never be lost of this kind of threat as the starting point of *mafioso* mediatory action. A copy, made by the police, of the *lettera di scrocco* received by the Baron Calogero Alongi of Petralia Soprana in 1883 is contained in ASP 1883, busta 72, cat. 20, fasc. 98. It runs as follows:

> Signor Don Calogero Alongi
> We come to ask you because we have need of a small sum of money if you comply with our request we shall content ourselves with what you send us if you do not close your heart to us, otherwise a curse will come upon you and the animals and the children.
> We know for certain that can spare a sum of not less than 400 ounces if it is good we shall content ourselves with this sum otherwise we shall think of something, the money must be silver or notes of two and five lire. Keep away from the judiciary, in two days you must send the money up to the *monte di Santuario* a person with a white handkerchief on his head must come up from the side and when he arrives he must stop by the tower.
> If you want to know who is asking you for this sum we are young people from Gangi and other colleagues.

That is enough *adio adio* and we ask you

always

[6] Letter of the Commandant of Gastellammare del Golfo to the Prince of Satriano (23 September 1849) in *Archivo di Stato di Trapani, Corrispondenza di Polizia* 1849, *Collocazione provisoria*

[7] ASP 1882, busta 69, cat. 20, fasc. 20

[8] Cf. Weber 1964, p. 147

[9] Processo Amoroso 1883

[10] Ibid.

[11] Cf. Alongi 1887, pp. 146–7

[12] For usury with water cf. in particular *Atti della Giunta per la Inchiesta Agraria e sulle condizioni della classe agraria (Inchiesta Damiani)*, vol. xiii, 1, 1884, pp. 412 ss.

[13] Statement by a peasant in Dolci 1966, p. 259

[14] Pantaleone 1962, p. 229

[15] Sciascia 1964, p. 139

[16] In Cammareri Scurti 1896

[17] Letter to the Prefect of 19 July 1885, in ASP 1885, busta 85, cat. 20, fasc. 91

[18] Cf. the description of such an interrogation in Loschiavo 1956, pp. 201–11

[19] Letter of the Sotto-Prefetto of Corleone to the Prefect (16 March 1884) in ASP 1885, busta 85, cat. 20, fasc. 133

[20] ASP, Processo Cannizzo

[21] Cf. Boissevain 1964 and 1966 *passim*

[22] Cf. Loschiavo 1956, pp. 494–6

[23] Cf. Palazzolo 1958, pp. 37–8

[24] Cf. Loschiavo 1956, pp. 197–416

[25] Cf. Alongi 1887, pp. 111–32

[26] Loschiavo 1962, p. 119

[27] Ibid., p. 162

[28] Montanelli 1958, p. 282

[29] Cf. Novacco 1963, pp. 113–14

[30] D'Alessandro 1959, p. 48. Naturally this customary euphemism begins to have an ironic ring with D'Alessandro

[31] Montalbano 1958

[32] Cf. chiefly Pantaleone 1962, pp. 151–3, and Montalbano 1953, pp. 541 ss. The best-known individual instance from the past century is undoubtedly that of the Questor of Palermo, Giuseppe Albanese, who jointly with the Prefect Medici conducted a campaign against banditry; in the course of it the bounds of legality were frequently transgressed.

Thus the bandit Termini was murdered in Monreale on Albanese's orders on 11 December 1869. The Prosecutor General Diego Taiani collected evidence on the case and in 1871 had the Questor arrested on charges of instigation to murder. Only the intervention of the Ministry of Justice prevented a trial. Taiani thereupon resigned and shortly afterwards was elected a Member of Parliament.

Cf. Montalbano 1953, p. 541, Novacco 1963, pp. 172–3, and—for the text of Taiani's speech in Parliament on 11 and 12 June 1875, when he reported on the case—Russo (ed.) 1964, pp. 135–77.

[32a] Cf. chiefly Blok 1969

[33] Cf. Romano 1959, pp. 450–8, and Romano 1966, pp. 216–19

[34] Cf. Novacco 1963, pp. 276–7, and Montalbano 1953, p. 540

[35] Cf. Dolci 1966, p. 306, Duyzings 1964, pp. 151–3. For the Salvatore Carnevale case cf. Ballola and Narzisi 1956, for Giuliano principally Maxwell 1963, also Pantaleone 1962, pp. 155–82, and Sansone-Ingrasci *passim*

[36] Cf. Pantaleone 1962, pp. 117–18

[37] The text of Colajanni's speech is in Tocco 1959, pp. 72–80, the quotation is on pp. 76–7. Colajanni supplies further information on San Giuseppe Jato, Marineo and Contessa Entellina

[38] Letter of 3 August 1838, in Pontieri 1945, p. 192

[39] Mori 1932, p. 98; cf. ibid., pp. 96–8. For the excellent description of the circumstances of such *mafioso* mediation and the total impotence of the State organs cf. Loschiavo 1962, pp. 9–14

[40] ASP 1880, busta 56, cat. 20, fasc. 15

[41] In Dolci 1960, p. 68

[42] Statement by a Mussomeli peasant in Dolci 1960, p. 65

[43] Statement by Cannizzo in ASP, Processo Cannizzo

[44] Letter of the *delegato di P.S.* of Borgetto to the Prefect in ASP 1881, busta 63, cat. 20, fasc. 7

[45] Cf. Vaina 1911, pp. 140 and 159, Salvemini 1962, pp. 123–4 and 126

[46] Cf. Salvemini 1962, p. 125

[47] Salvemini 1962, p. 128

[48] Salvemini 1962, p. 126

[49] Candida 1960, p. 89

[50] Cf. Russo (ed.) 1964, pp. 471–87

[51] ASP 1882, busta 69, cat. 20, fasc. 121. Incidentally, the Salemi mentioned here is the one discussed earlier on.

[52] In Corleone people talk to this day of the blind electors of Navarra: on election day hundreds [*sic*] of men and women were struck blind; they pretended to have lost their sight in order to enable Navarra's *mafiosi* to accompany them into the polling booth and check up on their ballot. Pantaleone 1962, p. 140

[53] Dolci 1961, p. 190

[54] Statements in Dolci 1961, pp. 255–6

[55] In Dolci 1960, p. 69

[56] Statement in Dolci 1966, p. 255. Unfortunately it is only possible to quote very short excerpts from the evidence conerning the relations of (…), the Christian Democrat Deputy from Castellammare, with various *mafiosi*. The entire dossier (loc. cit. pp. 241–74) is exceedingly revealing for the subject here under discussion. Time and again the same techniques are encountered: a joint appearance in the café, at a stroll in the piazza, or on the balcony, distribution of leaflets, the giving of advice, etc.

[57] Statement in Dolci 1960, p. 60

[58] Statement in Dolci 1966, p. 273

[59] Ibid., p. 256

[60] Ibid., p. 265

7 Mafiosi and gangsters

Many authors have tried to write the 'history of the mafia'. But once the term 'mafia' has been properly understood the problem of a history appears in a new light. Since there is no organisation, no secret society called *mafia,* one cannot write the history of such an institution. All that can be traced is the behaviour pattern of *mafiosi* in various historical situations, the rôle they played in the history of Sicily. Thus, the so-called 'histories of the mafia' are for the most part histories of Sicily, of the peasant movement, of the successes and failures of the various political parties, etc., combined with reports of a few sensational trials.

An examination of the rôle of the *mafioso* in Sicilian society from a historical point of view shows that four fairly well-defined periods can be distinguished.

First of all there is the period of the origin of the *mafioso* type, as dealt with in Chapter 3. From the unification of Italy roughly to the beginning of the Fascist era the position of the *mafioso* is an essential characteristic of Sicilian social structure and the functions performed by him are of unchanging importance for the sub-cultural system. Chapters 4, 5 and 6 systematically presented the phenomena of that period, the 'classical' period of the *mafiosi.* The suppression of *mafioso* activity during the Fascist regime is to be dealt with in the concluding chapter; the fact that the *mafiosi* were almost completely eliminated with the strengthening of the State power lends considerable support to the thesis that *mafioso* behaviour must be seen as a necessary from of self-help.

It is the purpose of the present chapter to outline briefly another phenomenon—that of the 'nouvi mafiosi', the 'giovane mafia', the 'mafia gangsteristica'.

In a sense this phenomenon has always existed. Even the 19th century authors speak of young *mafiosi* at the beginning of their careers being radical and frequently criminal by comparison with their elders who have 'arrived' and who have monopolised, legalised and legitimated their position. The concept of 'nuova mafia', however, has acquired another meaning and now describes the (real or reputed) organisations of Italo-American or Palermo gangsters who develop their illegal activity in the fields of bootlegging, gambling, prostitution, drug trafficking, the control of big markets, the building trade, etc. These are no longer young people who, at a later stage in their careers, will succeed to the positions of a Mazzarese or Vizzini, but something new and different in kind. This type of the new *mafioso* has emerged in connection with the emigration of millions of Southern Italians to the USA, the formation of a specific sub-culture within American society, assimilation to new social, economic and technological conditions, and finally re-emigration to Sicily—in short, a process of extensive cultural exchange. The Sicilian who emigrated to America at the turn of the century found himself in a country where the pioneering spirit, the myth of the robust self-made man, was still very much alive. He came to a world where it was up to the individual to seize his chance and make his fortune, even though by not altogether legal means, by bending the law or, if necessary, by using force. In his competition with the old-established and favoured immigrants (English, Scandinavian or Germans), the Southern Italian at first found himself in a very unfavourable situation: he came from an agrarian society, he did not understand the language of the country, and his social prestige as a Catholic and dark-haired southerner was exceedingly low.

Nevertheless, over the next few decades, the Italo-Americans succeeded in improving the status of their ethnic group. A not inconsiderable part in this rise of the whole group was played by two typical kinds of careers which led individual self-made men to wealth and political power—organised crime on an ethnic basis and a political career similarly rendered possible by support from the entire ethnic group. Both these methods had already been practised by the Irish and the Jews.

Unfortunately it is not possible here to deal in detail with Italian immigration to America. But a few important facts are worth pointing out: among the millions of immigrants there were many young *mafiosi, picciotti,* who had to flee from the reach of the State organs. Illegal immigration, however, did not mean the conclusion of their careers; on the contrary, in the United States they found conditions which greatly favoured *mafioso* activity. The national groups immigrating into America, and in particular the Italians, formed sub-cultures within the American society, and the exponents of these sub-cultures were very much aware of their cultural peculiarities. In addition to relations of kinship and friendship a further unifying force among the immigrants was this marked sense of ethnic community. The *compaesano* from the same place of origin, in whose vicinity one would frequently settle, became a *compare.* This circumstance on the one hand lent a new, ethnic cohesion to *mafioso* groupings and, on the other, created an atmosphere of *omertà* which favoured their activities, a sub-cultural *omertà vis-à-vis* the American State and its security organs.

Mafioso actions were first reported towards the end of the last century, but these were initially of importance only within the Italian population group: Italian merchants were made to pay protection money for fictitious protection, and there were fierce struggles for a monopoly in certain branches of business, such as the trade in Italian fruit, Italian cheese and Italian wine.

It was the clashes between the Matranga and Provenzano families for the control of the port of New Orleans, which also led to the death of a police lieutenant and to the lynching by the population of eleven Sicilians acquitted of this murder by the courts, which first focused the attention of the American public on these events.

The Italo-American gangster may be described as a *mafioso* because he shares certain characteristics with the *mafioso* of Sicily. At the same time the differences must not be overlooked; undoubtedly he owes his label not so much to the features he has in common with the *vecchio mafioso* as simply to his Sicilian origin.

Even more so than the Sicilian *mafioso* the Italo-American gangster comes from the lowest social stratum. His parents as a rule were peasants and, in the United States, worked mainly as unskilled labourers.

Sometimes a *nuovo mafioso* had started his career back in Sicily and emigrated as an adult, generally illegally. Thus Nicola Gentile, who later wrote his own biography, upon arrival in New York in 1903, already possessed good connections which made it possible for him soon to play a part in the lucrative textile trade.[1]

A case of the same type is mentioned in the documents about Valenza. A certain Gaspare Amato from Prizzi had been instructed by the D'Angelo brothers to murder Valenza. But he used the reward, paid to him in advance, for fleeing to America:

> He undertook the task but only on condition that the agreed sum of 300 ounces, that is 3,825 lire, was paid to him in advance. This was in fact done. But when the moment of action came he was so terrified of Valenza, this rich man who, by his *mafioso* relations, instilled a great deal of fear, that he added to the above sum a further 300 lire which he possessed and, instead of trying to kill Valenza, got himself a passport and fled to America.
>
> He returned to Italy with the intention of using what money he had left for dispatching a consignment of carob and vegetables to New York in order to start up an export business in this kind of merchandise to America where he planned to settle eventually...[2]

Here we see clearly the close links between his old and his new career.

Most of the later gangsters, however, came to the New World as children and started their criminal careers in the great cities of the USA. One of these was Salvatore Lucania, alias Lucky Luciano, who was born at Lercara Friddi but grew up in Brooklyn, New York, and started his career in a new field of activity—illegal horse betting and bootlegging.

The career followed the customary pattern. At the start stood an act of violence:

One day I was asked by Conti, whose guest I was, to remove a certain dangerous and unscrupulous man who had defiled himself with numerous and dangerous crimes.[3]

For a man who wishes to command respect from young criminals it is absolutely indispensable that he should not flinch from any act of violence:

All leaders are cruel. Unless you are cruel you don't become a leader.[4]

If the culprits are discovered at all they are frequently acquitted for lack of evidence. The successful ones soon manage to find admission to a *cosca*—now a gang—and to associate with other powerful gangsters with far-reaching connections. By eliminating all rivals for the leadership of the gang, by creating a devoted bodyguard of killers and by making *partito* connections the *nuovo mafioso* similarly endeavours to monopolise his position of power in a certain sphere of influence. A parallel process is that of monopolisation of profit chances within a certain economic sector.[4a]

The principal foundation of the power of the *nuovo mafioso* is the group of killers whom he has rallied around him and whom he is able to employ unconditionally. In an interview which Nick Gentile gave to the Palermo journalist Chilanti we read:

Gentile: Power was already in my hands.
Chilanti: What did your power consist of?
Gentile: I had organised a group of young people in order to protect the Sicilians. These young people were under my command.[5]

Just as the *bassi mafiosi* in a *cosca*, the killers are also held together chiefly by their common dependence on a *capo*.[6] Occasionally, however, an additional bond is their common origin: Gentile refers to the struggle between two gangs (Massaria and Maranzano in New York) as a struggle of 'sciaccatani' against 'castellammaresi'[7] and elsewhere he speaks of the 'predominio dei licatesi in Cleveland'.[8] Admittedly this factor would play a major part only in the first or at the most the second generation of immigrants.

The Italo-American gangster further consolidates his position by maintaining good relations with other *nuovi mafiosi*. Wherever possible he will look for bonds of kinship in order to reinforce business connections with more powerful ones.[9] The most important factor in this is the mutual trust which exists among kinsmen.

In some cases a gangster will pay tribute to others, a percentage share in a certain transcation, in return for if not support then at least neutrality with regard to the transaction in question. A certain La Gaipa had proposed to

Gentile that he would jointly with him organise the drug traffic from New York into Texas and Louisiana.

> I informed Vincenzo Mangano that I had an opportunity of a business connection with Charles La Gaipa who would put up the entire capital necessary for the purchase of the merchandise and give me 40 per cent of the profit. You decide, I said, how this is to be shared out between yourself, Joe Biondo, Anastasia and myself.[10]

These relations should be seen rather as arrangements between one big firm with a daughter company and other big firms without immediately speculating about the existence of some super-concern under central management. It is impossible within the framework of this short outline of the American scene to discuss all those theories which postulate such a central organisation[10a]. Probably the individual American *cosche* (families) are bigger and more widely remified than the old Sicilian ones and their range of activity is more extensive. Likewise, arrangements concerning a certain line of business seem to be better defined and more durable. But there is no doubt that the arguments put forward in favour of a central organisation are open to the same criticism in respect of their genesis and social function as those dealt with, concerning Sicilian conditions, in Chapter 5, paragraph four.[10a]

In order to explain the powerful position of the *nuovo mafioso* and above all his success in forging *partito* relationships it must be realised that he enjoys a high status within the Sicilian population group. The Sicilian immigrants see him as the poor boy from Castellammare or from the slums of Brooklyn who has made good, gained wealth and influence, and who in his person has fulfilled the wishful thinking of every individual. And although he ruthlessly exploits his fellow countrymen, he ultimately contributes to the rise of his whole ethnic group.

In Chicago Mike Merlo, a well-known gangster, was president of the 'Associazione fra i siciliani', a kind of leisure club whose members were thousands of workers, artisans and small traders.[11] In all large American cities the immigrants, feeling helpless and isolated in an alien world, sought psychological and material support in such clubs. And these clubs, as a rule, were totally dependent on certain successful fellow-countrymen, very frequently *mafiosi,* who in this way, among other things, controlled a large number of votes. These votes they then directed to be cast for Italian candidates or for candidates whose friendship they were anxious to gain. In this way the Italian section of the population, acting in concert—and often organised by *uomini di rispetto*—gained decisive influence on the municipal politics of many big cities (New York, Chicago, Kansas City, Los Angeles).

Added to this traditional form of relations between *mafiosi* and the holders of institutionalised power, a form already known from Sicily, now came a new one, typical of the *nuovo mafioso*—the enlistment of politicians, judges, and district attorneys by way of financial support for their election campaigns or even by straightforward bribery.[11a]

One instance among hundreds was the intimate relations between Frank Costello and certain New York politicians.[12] Costello (Francesco Castiglia) had originally become rich through bootlegging. In the 1930s Huey Long, the Governor of Louisiana, had asked him for financial support and in return licensed him to set up gambling machines in his State. In the 1940s he wielded a decisive influence on the Democratic Party of New York City (Tammany Hall).

> The most remarkable event—which was revealed by the bugging of Costello's telephone—was the 'thank you, Francesco' conversation conducted by Thomas Aurelio, who had just been appointed to the Supreme Court, in 1943. He ascribed his appointment exclusively to Costello.[13]

Instances of the same process, i.e. the purchase of *partito* relationships, though on a more modest scale, are found also in Gentile's autobiography:

> Faster than can be related and regardless of cost I penetrated every social set of Kansas City and earned the respect of the public and the friendship of the Mayor. Through his private secretary, a young, bright and active Jew, I made a business proposition to the Mayor in which he was to be my partner. Thus, under his protection, I operated securely.[14]

> The ill-famed quarter was continouusly watched by a strong police detachment. The policemen entered the bar, drank a whisky and received the *'mazzetta'*. It was exactly the same with those on night duty. In addition there was yet another group of policemen, fifteen officers of the homicide commission, who assured us of their protection. Their commander received 500 dollars a month.[15]

These direct contacts with the police, this multiplicity of straightforward bribery on the lowest level of *partito* relationships, seem to be far more typical of the USA than of Sicily.[15a]

A further important power factor which some *mafiosi* created for themselves was their influence on relations between employers and employees. First through their power over Italo-American workers and—more recently almost exclusively—through fraud and violence they succeeded in gaining control of many trades unions and, with their help, in exerting powerful pressure both on politicians and also on employers. To the politicans they would sell

160

the votes of the union members and to the employers the assurance that certain enterprises would be kept free from strikes.[16]

In the discussion of structural problems mention has been made of the functions which the activity of the *nuovo mafioso* may discharge by the interposition of himself as a mediator B in the relations between A and C. Again this mediatory rôle is that of a dealer trading in violence and placing it in the service of one party in order to exert a certain pressure on the other. This becomes particularly clear when the *mafioso* stands between employers and workers or between trades union officials and union members. Intimidation, beatings, bomb attacks and murders are by no means rare in these relationships. And it is significant that the *mafioso* is almost invariably in the service of the entrepreneur or the official, i.e. he again discharges a ruling function.[17]

With the modern gangster, however, the importance of this kind of function is almost entirely eclipsed. His activity is almost exclusively determined by the objective of personal enrichment and personal social rise. The occupations he chooses are characterised by the same basic features as those of the *vecchio mafioso*—they require no training, no formal education, no regular work; they are full of risks, invariably connected with speculation, and stand on the borderline between legal and illegal activity. But it is only the character of these occupations which is the same; their sphere, needless to say, is a totally different one in a modern industrialised and consumer society. Thus the Italo-American gangsters are found above all in the transport business, in the fruit and vegetable trade, as importers of olive oil and cheese, in the building trade and in real estate. Their vast profits, however, come from dealings in certain drugs and intoxicants and from the entertainment industry—from the production, smuggling and sale of alcohol during Prohibition, later from dealings in drugs, from gambling machines, horse betting and pimping. Alongside this continuous supply of illegal goods and services the usury business, usually called loan-sharking, is increasingly gaining in importance.[17a] In all these spheres the use or threat of violence ensures for them an improvement or the monopolisation of their profit prospects.[18]

Crime for these people and their families became a vehicle of social advancement. The newly-immigrated young ruffians—provided they survived their fierce rivalries—turned into conservatively dressed businessmen with smooth manners, living in quiet suburbs, the typical residential areas of the upper middle class and sending their children to good schools. Many others, it is true, differ from the *vecchio mafioso* in that they prominently display their new wealth; conspicuous consumption is typical of them:

> ... They wear the same rich clothes, the diamond ring, the jewelled watch, the strong sickly sweet(=smelling) perfume.[19]

The investigation showed that Mickey Cohen had paid 275 dollars for his silver-embroidered pyjamas as well as 25,000 dollars for a bullet-proof car specially built for him, and that he owned 300 suits, 1,500 pairs of socks and 60 pairs of shoes.[20]

Thus Capone, Luciano and many others in their outward appearance are more like the bandit who conspicuously displays his newly-won fame. But there is no uniform personality type of the modern gangster. These men simply adjust to the spectrum of American success ideals—from the show-business star to the successful businessman who does not conceal his success —just as the Sicilian *mafioso* had endeavoured to become a dignified, revered *gentiluomo*.

But there is one other feature which distinguishes the gangster even more clearly from the *mafioso*: he lacks the sense of the needfulness and legitimacy of his action, the knowledge of being an *uomo d'ordine,* which has been shown to be a characteristic of the *mafioso*.[20a] And since in fact he has no necessary protective or mediatory function to fulfil within the social system he also possesses no legitimacy in popular morality, i.e. he is no longer a *mafioso* but a criminal. True, until the forties the Italo-American gangster still enjoyed a certain respect within the sub-culture of the immigrants, mainly because he was seen as a symbol of the social advancement of the ethnic group, but he has been losing that respect as this sub-culture has dissolved and the Sicilians have become Americans.

The Palermo gangster of the fifties and sixties similarly lacks this kind of prestige and legitimation in popular morality. It is this fact that makes him a new type far more than all external changes in his technical equipment—the motor car, the sub-machine gun and the plastic bomb.

The emergence of this new type is due to changes in the economic and social structure of Sicily and to cultural contacts with the USA.

His field of activity is no longer the agrarian society in which the *vecchio mafioso* controlled, above all, the land and its products, but the industrialised big city and here chiefly the consumer field. He tries to grab for himself favourable monopoly positions in the graet markets of Palermo, the Mercato Ortofrutticolo and the Mercato Ittico (the fruit and vegetable market and the fish market)[21] or to extort payment from building contractors for fictitious protection.[22] The vital contacts with Italo-Americans, which opened to the Palermo gangsters new sources of profit especially through cigarette and drug smuggling, came about in three ways—through the contact which many of the emigrants continued to maintain with their old country, through the American occupation of Sicily, and through the forcible repatriation or voluntary re-emigration of certain important *nuovi mafiosi* (Luciano, Gentile, Genovese, Coppola, Bonanno, Collura and others).

The *partito* relationships of the modern gangster are not nearly so manifold as those of the *vecchio mafioso*; they stem, as for the Americans, chiefly from financial participation in electoral campaigns.[23] His activities are virtually reduced to being functions only for the individual gangster himself. He is far from being an *uomo di rispetto,* a sought-after mediator in many small transactions. He grants no audiences and nobody calls on him. He is a specialist in a certain field, personally known only to the men within his own line of business, to the general public an anonymous big-city criminal, with no resemblance to the universally known and respected *mafioso* of the Sicilian village. To end this chapter an attempt will be made to juxtapose the main characteristics of the *vecchio* and the *nuovo mafioso,* or rather: the *mafioso* and the gangster:

Mafioso	*Gangster*
Marked sub-culture	Dissolving sub-culture
Weak State	Well-functioning State organs
Self-help system of law, e.g. real protection	Crime, e.g. fictitious protection
Legitimation by sub-cultural popular morality	Not legitimated
Agrarian society	Industrial and consumer society
Village, face-to-face group	Big city
Partito relationships through control of electors	*Partito* relationships through financial support of candidate or through bribery
Mafioso behaviour aimed at improving profit prospects in a legal occupation	Legal occupation only as camouflage
Gentiluomo, desiring legitimation and the rôle of respected benefactor, general recognition necessary for the discharge of his functions	For the general public only a kind of anonymous fame, similar to show-business stars
Concealment of power, simple exterior, status confirmed by show of respect from villagers	Status must be demonstrated to an anonymous surrounding public by conspicuous consumption

Notes

1 Nick Gentile: *Vita di capomafia,* Rome 1963
2 Letter of the Reale Prefettura della Provincia di Girgenti to the Prefect

of Palermo (27 September 1883) in ASP 1885, busta 85, cat. 20, fasc. 133

[3] Gentile 1963, p.46

[4] Ibid., p.73

[4a] On careers cf. also Salerno/Tompkins 1969, pp. 96–107

[5] Gentile 1963, p. 44

[6] Reckless calls this relationship a 'lord–serf arrangement' and 'feudal in character'; cf. Reckless 1950, p. 154

[7] Gentile 1963, p. 105

[8] Ibid., p. 91

[9] From the material published by the McClellan Committee of the US Senate (Select Committee on Improper Activities in the Labor and Management Fields) in 1958, dealing among others with the part played by gangsters in employer–employee relations, Frederic Sondern excerpted the following names of Italo-American defendants and, by including their wives, compiled a list of their kinships. Cf. Sondern 1959, pp. 211–212:

1.	Angelo Meli	
	Vincenza Di Mercurio	
2.	Frank Meli	Brother of 1
	Grace Panzica	
3.	Vincent H. Meli	Son of 1
	Pauline Perrone	Daughter of Santo Perrone
4.	Salvatore Meli	Son of 1
	Dolores Livorsi	Daughter of Frank Livorsi, sister of 16 and 17
5.	William Bufalino	Son of Charles Bufalino Sr.
	Marie A. Meli	Daughter of 2
6.	Charles Bufalino Jr.	Brother of 5
	Tina Volpe	Daughter of Santo Volpe
7.	Russell Bufalino	Cousin of 5 and 6
	Josephine Sciandra	Cousin of Angelo Sciandra
8.	Salvatore Falcone Jr.	Son of Salvatore Falcone Sr.
	Emmanuela Bufalino	Sister of 5 and 6, cousin of 7
9.	William Tocco	Father of 10 and 15 and 12
	Rosalie Zerilli	Sister of 11
10.	Jack Tocco	Son of 9
	Antoinette Meli	Daughter of 1
11.	Joseph Zerilli	Brother of 9
	Josephine Finazzo	
12.	Paul Joseph Tocco	Son of 9
	Josephine Zerilli	Daughter of 11
13.	Anthony Zerilli	Son of 11, brother of 12
	Josephine Profaci	Daughter of 14

14.	Joseph Profaci	Father of 13 and 15
	Nintfa Magliocco	Sister of Joseph Magliocco
15.	Anthony J. Tocco	Son of 9
	Carmella Profaci	Daughter of 14
16.	Thomas Dioguardia	Brother of John Dioguardia
	Rose M. Livorsi	Sister of 4 and 17
17.	Tom Ormento	Son of John Ormento
	Patricia Livorsi	Sister of 4 and 16

Ritual kinship continues to play an important part: I acknowledge and confirm that Chiapetta is my godchild's father, that I held his daughter over the font at the time I was in Pittsburgh. (Gentile 1963, p. 77.) Cf. also Salerno/Tompkins 1969, pp. 106 ss.

[10] Gentile 1963, pp. 150–1

[10a] Cf. Kefauver 1951, McClellan 1963, Kefauver Committee 1951, McClellan Committee 1963 and Task Force Report 1967

[10a] Cf. chiefly Hawkin's article 1969, also Albini 1971, pp. 1–8 and 221–61

[11] Gentile 1963, p. 21

[11a] Cf. Albini 1971, pp. 67–77, Cressey 1969, pp. 248–89, Salerno/Tompkins 1969, pp. 239–68

[12] Chiefly the Irish Democrats William O'Dwyer Mayor of New York City and later Ambassador to Mexico, who had immigrated to the USA as a young man and started his career as a simple policeman, and Michael Kennedy, Member of Congress and Democratic Party leader of New York. Also the Italo-American Judge Savarese. Cf. Romano 1966, pp. 279–80.

Romano has this to say about three leading Illinois politicians: Dan Seritella, for 12 years Senator from Illinois, maintained friendly and business relations with the gangsters who had financed his election—something that also happened elsewhere with other public figures. It turned out that Senator Roland Libonati, a Democrat, and James Aducci, the Representative for Illinois, were personal friends of numerous gangsters.

[13] Bell 1953, p. 148

[14] Gentile 1963, p. 81

[15] Ibid., p. 131

[15a] Cf. Albini 1971, pp. 75ff, Cressey 1969, pp. 248–89.

[16] This was revealed in particular by the investigations of the McClelland Committee. Robert F. Kennedy, formerly the parliamentary attorney of that Committee, has described the role of the gangster in the American trades unions in his book *The Enemy Within,* Harper and Row, New York 1960

Cf. ibid., p. 75:

Almost as soon as the Committee began to develop the evidence on Hoffa and his friends during the August 1957 hearings, it became apparent that the inner circle—of the Teamsters Union hierarchy has no counterpart in the United States today. We listened to testimony from the dregs of society. We saw and questioned some of the nation's most notorious gangsters and racketeers. But there was no group that better fits the prototype of the old Al Capone syndicate than Jimmy Hoffa and some of his chief lieutenants in and out of the union. ... They have criminal records to compare with those of the old Capone mob.

Ibid., p.p. 80–1:

Antonio Corallo, alias Antonio Freno, alias Mr. Zelzo, an underworld figure of great influence ... whose police arrest list includes drug and robbery charges ... had managed to muscle into the Teamsters movement in New York and had absolute control of five different locals.

Ibid., p. 82:

Johnny Dio (John Ignazio Dioguardi)] had brought into the union movement about forty hoodlums with 178 arrests and 77 convictions between them.

Ibid., p. 263:

A number of major ... companies have gangsters on their payroll to handle their labor problems.

On p. 239 Kennedy reports that of the 58 men arrested at Joseph Barbara's house in Appalachin, New York, in November 1957 (including Genovese, Russell Bufalino and the Falcone brothers) 'twenty-two were involved in labor or labor–management relations'

[17] Cf. Kennedy 1960, pp. 18, 71, 104–5, 107, 110–11, 132, 156–8, 255

[17a] Cf., especially for loan-sharking, the excellent detailed account in Cressey 1969, pp. 77–91

[18] It should be pointed out that the American gangsters are by no means all Sicilians but have included individuals from other ethnic groups in a similar situation of social advancement—e.g. men from Calabria (Costello), Neapolitans (Al Capone), Irishmen and Jews (Lepke alias Buchalter, Adelstein, Abner Zwillman, Meyer Lansky, Siegel, Diamond, Weinberg, Cohen, Goldstein). It is not some feature of their national psyche but their particular position in the social structure that turns them into criminals.

It would appear that the gangster described here was typical mainly of the first half of this century. The changing situation of immigrant groups will result also in different types of criminals. The two largest intact subcultures, the negroes and Puerto Ricans, have not so far produced anything analogous. Cf. on this point Salerno/Tompkins 1969, pp. 365–71

[19] Kennedy 1967, p. 75

[20] Ibid., p. 263

[20a] Faint echoes, as encountered, for instance, in Mario Puzzo's *The Godfather,* are no more than an ideological gilding. Although this was somewhat true also in Sicily, there it was only part of the truth. Today the necessary socio-cultural prerequisites are lacking

[21] Cf. *Relazione della Commissione Antimafia sui mercati di Palermo (Relazione Gatto, Adamoli e Biaggio)* in *L'Ora* of 26, 27 and 29 September and 1, 4 and 7 October 1966

The investigation revealed that 38 of the concessionaires and six of the wholesalers of the Mercato Ortofrutticolo had previous convictions, some of them serious. For the rivalry struggles of the various gangs cf. also Chilanti and Farinella 1964, pp. 83–95, and Poma and Perrone 1964, pp. 103–33

[22] The best-known names in this field are the Salvatore brothers and Angelo La Barbera; for their career cf. Poma and Perrone 1964, pp. 135–42, and Chilanti and Farinella 1964, pp. 125–45

[23] Cf. Dolci 1966, pp. 90–100 for Coppola's financial participation in the election campaigns of a certain politician

8 Conclusion

The *mafioso* type can now be characterised as follows:

(1) In certain regularly repeated social relationships (landowner–sharecropper, vendor–buyer, owner–thief, etc.) an agent, i.e. one of the parties or a mediator, uses physical violence or threatens physical violence. His power based upon this enables him arbitrarily to decide any conflict or to enforce the sub-cultural norms valid for it. Because of its weakness the State is not in a position to enforce its own norms applicable to the situation.

(2) In this manner the *mafioso* assures himself not only of a personal material or prestige gain but also discharges certain functions within the sub-cultural system by entering the service of others. His position is strengthened through the continuous repetition of his performance of such functions. Within the face-to-face group of a village he becomes known as competent for certain tasks.

(3) His behaviour is regarded as illegitimate by the codified law of the superimposed State but conforms with the sub-cultural norms and enjoys legitimation by public morality.

(4) The *mafioso* maintains a network of relationships, based upon reciprocal services, with the holders of formal and institutionalised, i.e. State, power and in this manner ensures that his actions escape the sanctions threatened by the codified law.

(5) Historically the type must be seen against a very definite background—the collapse of the feudal order on the one hand and the failure of the bureaucratic State to enforce its monopoly of legitimate physical coercion on the other. In this situation the rôle of the *mafioso* is that of a self-help institution. Only at a time when the feudal order has lost its legitimacy and the modern State cannot (yet) enforce its own norms is it possible to speak of self-help—and only in this situation of a dual morality, one claimed by the State and the other, the sub-cultural one, actually existing. In Sicily during the past 150 years these historical conditions applied. But in principle the concept can be applied to any power phenomena functioning analogously in other cultures.

If the term *mafioso* is used in this sense only—and in any more general sense it loses its specific meaning—it can be clearly differentiated from others, such as 'bandito', 'ladro' or 'gangster', and confusion can be avoided. Emphasis on the element of violence also prevents confusion—still all too common—between mere corruption and *mafioso* behaviour.

The area over which the *mafiosi* practised their particular form of rule is very difficult to delineate accurately. The records generally name the western provinces of Sicily: Palermo, Caltanissetta, Girgenti (now Agrigento) and Trapani. More detailed data can be found, above all, in two sources—the replies of Pretors and Mayors to a circular of the Parliamentary Commission of 1885 concerning 'condizioni morali' within their municipalities, collected and published in 'Atti della Giunta per la Inchiesta Agraria e sulle condizioni della classe agricola'[1] and a map attached by Antonino Cutrera to his book *La Mafia ed i mafiosi* in 1900. This reveals that *mafioso* behaviour is also known in the eastern provinces, but in each case in their western regions, the ones furthest inland, i.e. in the zone of the great estates.[2]

There is no doubt that, if one wishes to explain variations in geographical incidence, one of the principal criteria is the repeatedly emphasised connection between *mafia* and latifundia. Latifundia imply absenteeism of the weakened ruling class, a powerful intermediary rôle of the *gabellotto*, the use of *campieri* as protective organs against *banditismo*, widespread in the thinly populated countryside, and very poor communication facilities for the security organs of the State.[3] Originating in the latifundia zone, the *mafioso* type also establishes itself in the Conca d'Oro and in Palermo. This circumstance has been explained by some authors by the existence of numerous *bravi* whom the aristocrats had brought with them to Palermo for their protection. From these elements the *guardiani* and *fontanieri* of the intensive cultivation zone had then emerged.[4] More important, however, for the spread of the *mafia* is another factor: throughout Western Sicily the sub-cultural norm system of *omertà* with all its nuances is far more strongly developed than in the east; resistance against a governmental system imposed from outside has always been concentrated on Palermo and its hinterland. Ever since the days of the fugitive Arab-Berber groups hatred and mistrust of institutionalised power have been downright norms of popular morality. Revolutions and rebellions can be seen as their open eruptions, while behaviour according to the rules of *omertà* are their ever-present simmering reflections.

The moral, social, economic and geographical conditions of Western Sicily, combined with the decisive political factor of a weak central power situated outside Sicily, thus led to the emergence and continued existence of a *mafioso* self-help which stepped into a power vacuum and discharged functions whose performance the State had arrogated to itself since it was associated with the application of force.

Details of this have been given in Chapter 3; here we merely want to rein-

170

force the argument with historically more recent events. After all, the conclusion must be that *mafioso* behaviour would be rendered impossible as soon as the State fulfilled its economy-regulating and security functions and vigorously moved against all forms of private use of force.

Such measures against the *mafiosi* had always been urged by practical men (administration and police officials): 'The *mafia* must be dealt really radical blows, and in an unusual manner. ...'[5] Greater caution was demanded in the issuing of gun licences, there was a call for the abolition of private and for the reinforcement of State-employed field guards, for a more rigorous handling of *ammonizione* and the punishment of *domicilio coatto,* for all kinds of special laws, for a centralisation of security organs and for a greater freedom of action for the police. The cry went up for 'officials who will not allow themselves to be either influenced or intimidated in the discharge of their duties',[6] i.e. for a strengthening of the specific public servant ethic, a stricter observance of official secrets and other measures against *partito* relationships. These men unanimously opposed any form of local or regional autonomy and called for a strong central government:

> Certainly what the new national Government has been pursuing for a number of years is a risky and terrible experiment—trying to govern such people, which display the above-mentioned despicable forms of behaviour, by means of laws or institutions in the British or Belgian manner, institutions which presuppose an educated and moral people such as exist there or, possibly, in the northern part of the [Italian] Peninsula.[7]

> Everybody nowadays is forever talking about decentralisation but few risk the adventure or have a practical organic idea suited to our historical climate. People praise British self-government and forget that in England this is the living, spontaneous, historical result of public awareness and not something imported, some kind of 'let there be' decree, something implanted on an unprepared society.[8]

The importance of the school, i.e. the importance of educating the children in the spirit of the State norms, has also long been emphasised:

> In order to limit and diminish the effects from which society suffers through the existence of such dangerous men it is advisable, in my opinion, to resort to four means: spread of general education, but in the sense that the State schools should educate not only the minds but also the hearts of the young people. ...[9]

At the beginning of the Fascist era Francesco Ramistella summed up the necessary measures in a newspaper article. He listed four points: settlement of the latifundia and better education of the rural population; intensified police measures; restrictions on the right of landowners freely to choose their personnel. i.e. control of private protective bodies; tougher penalties for all kinds of 'favoreggiamenti', including complicity in criminal offences— still excused by Alongi because of its being generally done under pressure.[10] The last two points were entirely novel proposals, indispensable to the assertion of the State's authority. They were reflected in Mori's activities when he was Prefect of Palermo.

In 1925 the powers of the Prefect of Palermo were extended by the authority to co-ordinate all police and administrative measures against banditry and *mafia* throughout the island. In close co-operation with the judicial organs numerous trials, dropped in the past for lack of evidence or as a result of influential intervention, were resumed and thousands of persons were arrested and sentenced in show trials.

On 5 January 1925 a decree was issued in Palermo, designed to guarantee public safety in the countryside. It included the following ponts:

(1) Every *guardiano, curatolo, vetturale, campiere* or *soprastante* in order to discharge his function must possess a special licence from the appropriate *delegato di P.S.*

(2) It is his duty, moreover, instantly to report to the State security organs all thefts or other offences. At least every two months he must make a report on his work to the competent *delegato di P.S.*

(3) On the slightest suspicion of incorrect behaviour the *campiere* or *guardiano* shall have his licence withdrawn. He will then also be forbidden to remain (e.g. as *gabellotto*) on the property previously guarded by him.

(4) Any *campiere, curatolo, guardiano* or *soprastante* who refuses to take over the pos tof another, deprived of his licence, i.e. from fear of reprisals of the dismissed person, shall likewise have his job licence withdrawn.

(5) Payments of dues for protection through organs other than those of the State or those licensed by the State will be punishable.

(6)Goatherds and shepherds must possess a 'certificato di iscrizione' listing the number of animals guarded by them, the owner or owners, the grazing area and the route taken each day by the herd. In the event of irregularities or 'pascolo abusivo' (the use of someone else's pastures) the certificate will be instantly withdrawn.

(7)   Shepherds are forbidden to carry arms. They are furthermore forbidden, while performing their duties, to assemble in groups of more than three.

(8)   All landowners must report all caves on their land.

(9)   The parents of fugitives are placed under surveillance. They are obliged to account for the origin of any money or property.

(10)   A stricter general control of personal documents is hereby decreed.[11]

All *campieri,* moreover, had to swear a solemn oath of submission to the judicial and security organs of the State. The oath had the following text:

I swear that I will be faithful to the King and his Royal successors, loyally observe the statutes and laws of the State, discharge my functions as a man of honour and conscience, and defend the goods and people placed under my protection with all my might in accordance with the law, justice and morality, with absolute steadfastness, rectitude and solidarity with my comrades and in strict obedience towards the authorities appointed for the protection of public security.[12]

The oath was taken at an elaborate open-air ceremony which, among other things, also included a Mass. The same oath had to be taken by the 300 *guardiani* in the Conca d'Oro. These were placed under an even more rigid State control than were the *campieri:* they were organised on a military pattern and had to wear identification badges.

It is clear from all the measures taken by Mori that one of his aims was to break *omertà.* He himself wrote:

The struggle must not be a police campaign on a more or less grand style, but a rebellion of the conscience, a revolt of the spirit, an action of the people.[13]

The following illustrates his procedure:

In the course of a drive against the bandits of the Madonie many of them had fled to Gangi. Mori occupied the place and gave the bandits 12 hours to come out of their hideouts and surrender.

'It was my firm intention not to grant the bandits the honour of an armed clash. I did not want the underworld to surround itself once more, by fighting the State power, with a halo of prestige, courage and possibly even martyrdom. I wanted not only to win, i.e. to hand over the bandits to the judiciary, but I also wanted to give the population a visible proof of the underworld's cowardice.'

In order to ridicule the bandits he ordered the cattle found in their houses to be slaughtered and sold off very cheaply in the market place. This measure was a great success: 'They not only suffered damage but also disgrace.' Within a short time they all surrendered without any attempt at defence.

'The swiftness of the action and the truly inglorious end of banditry in the Madonie, which had previously possessed so much terrifying prestige and had been surrounded by so many legends, had immediate and profound repercussions throughout the island.'[14]

The attacks on the myth of banditry naturally also had their repercussions on the myth of the *mafiosi*. Mori realised clearly that attempts to break *omertà* must begin at school, that social identification in the sense of the State morality was one of the principal tasks. He believed that the *mafioso* regarded the school as his principal enemy:

> He fears prison less than he does school ... He is less afraid of the judge than he is of the teacher.[15]

Francis Guertio wrote in 1938:

> Since 1926 the Sicilian teachers have been co-operating with the Opera Nazionale Balilla by teaching that *omertà* is not a manly virtue, that the laws of the State are above private revenge, in short, that the traditions of the *mafia* run counter to the ideals of Mussolini and the new Italy and that they are totally unworthy of them.[16]

The Fascist State also deprived the *mafiosi* of their vital *partito* relationships by abolishing parliamentary and municipal elections. The old-style political parties and parliamentary deputies disappeared and the elected *sindaco* was replaced by the *podestà* appointed from above.

These measures very soon broke the power of the *mafiosi,* who were not only persecuted but had also become superfluous. The State vigorously embarked on its economy-regulating and security functions. We may recall the earlier-mentioned successes in the revision of sale and tenancy contracts which eliminated extortion in this field. The picture may be rounded off by two tables from Mori's book. In spite of a few reservations they are quite revealing. The first shows the decline in the number of gun licences issued, which was one measure in the struggle against the private use of force. The second reflects the success of this struggle: of particular importance here is the year 1926, when Mori's special powers began to show results.

Year	Licences for rifles	Licences for hand firearms
1922	25,459	18,215
1923	11,570	7,012
1924	13,467	8,039
1925	15,115	9,658
1926	12,596	6,760
1927	9,781	5,317
1928	6,224	3,839

Source: Cesare Mori: Con la mafia ai ferri corti.
Verona 1932, pp. 370–1.

Year	Murders	Robbery with violence	Extortions	Major cattle thefts
1922	223	246	56	51
1923	224	312	56	65
1924	278	283	64	46
1925	268	298	79	45
1926	77	46	28	7
1927	37	42	10	8
1928	25	14	6	6
Jan.-Apr. 1929	1	1	–	–

Source: Cesare Mori: Con la mafia ai ferri corti.
Verona 1932, pp. 370–1.

We are not concerned here with the historical facts of Fascist rule in Sicily nor with the great number of victims it claimed from the Sicilian people. We are even less concerned with Mori's person or the style of his book. We are merely concerned with proving once again the thesis of self-help. We want to show how the State vigorously asserted its monopoly to the use of physical force, how it attracted to itself the protective functions of the *mafiosi*, deprived them of their mediatory functions, brought the protective organs which did not belong to the State under its own control and bureaucratised them, tried to demolish the sub-cultural norm system of *omertà* and convert the population to identification with the State's morality. These measures played a part in diminishing the importance of the *mafioso* in the Sicilian social system.

The degree to which the State's administrative and coercive organs are mobilised naturally depends on the character of the stratum which uses the State as its instrument of government. If this stratum is conservatively oriented and derives its strength and assurance from the status quo, it can and will—within the framework of a conservative authoritarian or a liberal-democratic pattern of government—conclude compromises and alliances with the local powers from which it has largely risen. A new ruling stratum, on the other hand, one whose position is still threatened, will tend, in a totalitarian manner of government, to use all opportunities offered by the institutionalised government machinery, once it has seized it, and try to use this instrument for the elimination of independent and often rival local powers. It should have become clear that *mafioso* actions are possible only in a political system of the first kind.

Notes

[1] Cf. XIII, vol. II *(Relazione Damiani)* 1885, pp. 521–41

[2] On the geographical differences in agricultural ownership structure at the time cf. *Inchiesta Parlamentare sulle condizioni dei contadini delle province meridionali,* vol. vii *(Inchiesta Lorenzoni)* 1909, pp. 355–62: *Concentrazione reale della proprietà ben maggiore*

[3] Cf. Franchetti 1925, pp. 155–6, Novacco 1963, pp. 47–54, Sereni 1947, p. 292, and Francesco Brancato: *Genesi e psicologia della mafia* in *Nuovi quaderni del meridione,* vol. ii, no. 5, March 1964, pp. 8 and 11

[4] Cf. Franchetti 1925, p. 119, Novacco 1963, p.52, Salvatore Costanza: *Una inchiesta poco nota sulla mafia* in *Nuovi quaderni del meridione*, vol. ii no. 5, March 1964, p. 56

In referring to the *mafiosi* of Palermo one is not in fact referring to an urban phenomenon at all but to the numerous little communities which belong to the city of Palermo but represent independent agrarian settlements, E. G. Settecannoli, Mondello, Sferracavallo, Tomaso Natale, Boccadifalco, Mezzomorreale, Partanna, Pallavicino, Torrelunga

[5] Letter of the *delegato di P.S.* of Gangi to the Sotto-Prefetto of Corleone 19 July 1885) in ASP 1885, busta 85, cat. 20, fasc. 91

[6] Letter of the Prefect of Trapani to the Minister of Interior (16 May 1874) in Russo (ed.) 1964, p. 19

[7] Letter of the Prefect of Caltanissetta to the Minister of Interior (24 April 1875), ibid., p. 26

[8] Alongi 1887, p. 158

[9] Letter of the Prefect of Trapani to the Minister of Interior (16 May 1874) in Russo (ed.) 1964, p. 19

[10] Francesco Ramistella: *Mafia ed abiegato in Sicilia. Appunti e considerazioni di un ex funzionario di P.S.,* newspaper cutting in the Biblioteca Comunale of Palermo, no date. Although there is reference to the 'Governo Nazionale Fascista' it appears from the contents that Mori's measures had not yet been put into effect.

[11] Cf. the text in Mori 1932, pp. 282–91

[12] Ibid., p. 333

[13] Ibid., p. 242

[14] Ibid., p. 296

[15] Ibid., p. 92

[16] Quoted in Palazzolo 1958, pp. 43–4

Appendix

1 Etymological note

⁴ Il mafioso è semplicemente un uomo coraggioso e valente, che non porta mosca sul naso.

2 Brigantaggio—Ladrismo—Mafia

⁴ La legenda del brigante benefico passa di generazione in generazione, e non v'ha capo banda di vaglia che non colga qualche occasione di dotare una ragazza povera, o di pagare il debito a un contadino, o di remprovirare pubblicamente un suo sottoposto per aver svaligiato un povero mulattiere, e condannarlo alla restituzione.

⁴ᵃ I quartieri d'inverno delle bande armate sono sempre presi a questo modo: Il capo banda da licenza ai gregari, i quali si sbandono ciascheduno per la sua contrada e pel suo nido. Il capo banda non annunzia ad alcuno il luogo del duo ritiro e distribuisce l'onore della sua prezensa, una alla volta alle sue belle di Alia, di Ciminna e di Montemaggiore.

¹⁵ Esso divenne sinonimo di brigantaggio, di camorra, di malandrinaggio, senza essere nessuna delle tre cose o stato di cose, poichè il brigantaggio è una lotta aperta con le leggi sociali, la camorra un guadagno illecito sulle transazioni econimiche, il malandrinaggio è specie di gente volgare e comunissima, rotta al vizio e che agisce sopra gente di poca levatura.

¹⁷ La mafia è la coscienza del proprio essere, l'esagerato concetto della forza individuale, unica e sola arbitra di ogni contrasto, di ogni urto d'interesse di idee, donde la insofferenza della superiorità e, peggio acora, della prepotenza altrui. Il mafioso vuol essere rispettato e rispetta quasi sempre. Se è offeso, non ricorre alla Giustizia, non si rimette alla Legge; se lo facesse, darebbe prova di debolezza, e offenderebbe l'omertà, che ritiene schifiusu o'nfami chi per aver ragione si richiama al magistrato.

¹⁸ La maffia è la solidarietà istintiva, brutale, interessata, che unisce a danno dello Stato, delle leggi e degli organismi regolari, tutti quegli individui e quegli strati sociali che amano trarre l'esistenza e gli agi, non già dal lavoro, ma dalla violenza, dall'inganno e dalla intimidazione.

[19] Egli sa farsi ragione personalmente da sè e quando non ne ha la forza (nun si fida) lo fa sol mezzo di altri di medesimi pensamenti, del medesimo sentire di lui.

[20] Nei casi in cui quest'individuo ha avuto bisogno dell'aiuto di altri, non potendosi rivolgere alla legge, sia per far rispettare un suo diritto, o un preteso diritto, o di sciogliere qualche controversia, si rivolse all'autorità di persone note per la loro influenza e prepotenza o che per l'agire energico e violento avesse potuto rendere rispettato il suo giudizio.

[21] Dallo spirito di mafia prendevano vita non un'associazione, che non è mai esistita, ma piccoli gruppi, più o meno organizzati, di malfattori, obbedienti a capi locali. Il loro insieme costituiva quello che normalmente è indicato col nome di mafia.

[22] ... colla stessa parola (mafia) vien indicato in Sicilia non uno speciale sodalizio, ma il complesso di tante piccole associazioni che si propongono scopi vari, i quali però quasi sempre sono tali da fare rasentare ai membri dell'associazione stessa il codice penale e qualche volta sono veramente delittuosi.

3 Characteristics of the Sicilian social structure

[8] Sia però vietato il dar ricovero a' delinquenti o debitori nella Chiesa, e case adiacenti della medesima, anchorchè dessi fossero de'Singoli della Maestranza.

[17] Il Corpo dei militi a cavallo è stato sciolto con un semplice decreto reale e un centinaio dei suoi membri sono stati mandati senz'altro a domicilio coatto.

[18] In Sicilia le quote di delinquenza vanno elevandosi—causa prima il malessere economico—e il brigantaggio si rafferma sempre più, con quanto danno per il normale sviluppo delle forze produttrici, ognuno lo sa e purtroppo lo vede.

R. Delegazione di P. S. di Monreale all'Ill.mo Sign. Prefetto della Provincia di Palermo   5 qmbre 1893
... mi prego di segnalare alla S. V. Ill.ma che le Guardie Campestri di questo Comune ... per nulla si prestano a coadiuvare le Autorità governative nella tutela della sicurezza pubblica.

Esse, quando succede un reato, fanno momentaneo atto di presenza; ma poi si sottragono, con grande abilità ed astuzia, dal compiere a qualsiasi indagine, e non si può dalle stesse sperare la continuazione di alcun servizio nell'interesse della pubblica sicurezza. Non forniscono alcun indizio, alcun elemento che possa illuminare la giustizia, come non si può ottenere alcuna opera preventiva ed alcuna vigilanza sugli ammoniti, sui vigilati speciali, sull altre persone pregiudicate, e sugli esercizii pubblici. Non prestano alcun servizio di pattuglia ...

A deposizione poi di quest'Ufficio, è addetta una sola Guardia Campestre, la quale si presenta la mattina alle ore nove, va via a mezzogiorno, e comparisce la sera alle sei, per portare soltanto la posta. E non si è potuto ottenere di meglio.

Con perfetta osservanza
Il delegato di P. S.

R. Delegazione di P. S. di Piana dei Greci 6. Nov. 93
... le Guardie camprestri di questa giurisdizione, qualora venissero richieste per qualche servizio, sarebbero di volta in volta messe a disposione di questo Ufficio. Esse però hanno dimostrato che mal volentieri si prestano a coadiuvare l'Autorità Governativa nella tutela dell'ordine e nella sicurezza pubblica, riuscendo cosi inutile e talvolta anche forze nocive per questo Uffivio.

R. Delagazione di P. S.   Villabate, 5. Nov 1893

In risposta della lettera di V. S. Ill.ma controdistinta mi affretto farle conoscere che in questo comune non vi sono guardie campestri.
Con ogni riguardo ...

Municipio di Bolognetta   4 qmbre 1893
Le Guardie Campestri di questo Comune sono in numero di 8, oltre il capo; nessuno di esse a cavallo, incloso il capo; non hanno stipendio, eccetto del capo, e sono privatamente retribuite dai proprietari, a ragione della terra che possiedono. Non hanno altri emolumenti.

[19] ... Il vecchio sistema di mafia prevalse in tutte le contingenze, e il difetto assoluto di disciplina allontano sempre più alcune guardie dal sentimento del proproi dovere e da quello spirito di corpo, che rende utili i più inetti al Servizio.

Da ciò ne consegui necessariamente la sfiducia e una demoralizzazione, che cercai d'arrestare con atti di rigore ... Però non calcolai, che a talun'assessore e a taluni consiglieri la restaurazione della disciplina e del Servizio poteva suonare una disdetta. Avenne, che gli ammonimenti e le misure speciali per la divisione del servizio vennero compresi come effetto di prevenzioni personali, e le Guardie lunghi dall'obbedire al loro capo, presero dai rispettivi loro protettori la parola d'ordine ...

[26] ... la difficoltà in altri paesi sta nel trovare chi conosca fatti che possano giovare alle recerche; in Sicilia invece la difficoltà sta nel trovare chi parli.

[27] Se i delinquenti rurali, poi, sono associati operano a preferenza nelle zone di confine di circondario o di provincia, ben sapendo che colà la vigilanza della forza è più debole, e, se v'è, è rara e saltuaria.

[29] ... la completa deficienza di strade, per cui la compagna non solo restava segregata dai centri abitati, ma prendeva un aspetto di strano isolamento.

[34] E' convinto e ripete che il Governo è usurpatore, scomunicato, protestante, e lo combatte, numeroso e tanace, con tutti i mezzi e con tutte le armi che la superstizione, il pergamo ed il confessionale gli offrono. Spesso anche oggi senti il prete repetere in publico (di contadini, s'intende): Ma come possono far del bene e della giustizia governanti che non credono alle anime del purgatoria ed all'Immacolata? Ed is contadino lo crede e sente crescere la propria diffidenza pel funzionario del Governo. Il prete l'autorizza a mentire con essi, a non aver per loro che un apparente reguardo, ma ad odiarli in fondo.

[35] La composizione che rende lectio l'atto è subordinata all'acquisto della bolla e all'elemosina, alla chiesa, di tari due, grana dodici e piccioli cinque per ogni tari 77 e grana 7 del valore del corpo del reato, rimanendo libero e perdonato in foro coscientiae e tenendosi il denaro come sua cosa propria e giustamente guadagnata e acquistata.

[36] ... la legge è un patto convenzionale, una imposizione a danno del popolo; il governo un gran mostro personificato, dallo usciere fino a quell'essere privilegiato che si chiama Re. Esso assorbisce tutto, ruba a man franca, dispone degli averi e delle persone a beneficio di pochi perchè appoggiato dalla sbirraglia e dalle baionette.

[37] ... coi picciotti di Sant'Anna e di Coppolo che hanno raggiunti i volontari a Salemi; quattrocento conquanta uomini press'a poco. (S. 69) ... soltanto a quei primi colpi una parte dei picciotti scompare. Centocinquanta circa resistono. (S. 70) ... abbandonati dai picciotti che essi vedono fuggire attraverso la strada, i carabinieri furono costretti a ritirarsi sulle cime delle montagne. (S. 84)

[38] Emanuele Amoroso: Lo giuri dunque sulla anima del padre, se io non fui in casa sua.

Pubblico Ministero: Lo si può fare giurare.

avv. Marinuzzi: Ma giurare nel modo che ha detto l'imputato.

Presidente: Qui non vi è che un solo giuramento, quello prescritto dalla legge.

avv. Marinuzzi: Quello non va per il caso.

Presidente: Oh perchè?

avv. Marinuzzi: Perchè il volgo non vi crede.

Presidente: Anzi il volgo vi crede.

Si stabilisce, dopo altri discorsi, che il teste giuri sull'anima del suo padre.

Presidente: Giuseppe Amoroso, lo giurate?

Giuseppe Amoroso: Si.

[39] D'altra parte però, la magistratura non è sempre all'altezza del proprio ufficio.

[42] ... le difficoltà della pubblica sicurezza siano piuttosto questione di persone che di leggi.

[43] Fra gli uffici die pubblica sicurezza, gli stessi uffici giudiziari da un lato e il pubblico dall'altro, v'ha una corrente di relazioni continue e misteriose.. Persone designate per esser colpite da arresto, sono avvertite prima ancora che si firmi il relativo mandato, e la forza che viene per prenderli li trova partiti da tre o quattro giorni o più.

[44] Indifferente in politica, con tendenze però a principi spinti. Condotta morale pessimo. Scaltro ed intelligente in ufficio ma solo negli interessi del partito e più della mafia. I processi nelle sue mani vanno svolti secondo le protezioni e gl'intrighi, riducendo la carica an un mestiere qualunque. Come privato cittadino la pubblica opinione lo addita un camorrista, un capo-mafia, uno speculatore negli abigeati. L'anno scorso fu colto in fallo di un furto di animali, ne fu elevato analogo verbale processuale, dal cui esito non si ne seppe più nulla. Come pubblico funzionario è indiscutibilmente disonesto e sfiduciatissimo.

[45] A tutto ciò bisogna aggiungere che questi influenti signori, allorchè si arresta o si denunzia qualcuno per un reato qualsiasi, si vengono a conoscenza, come per incanto, delle più piccole circostanze del relativo processo, di guisa che riesce loro molto agevole preparare la discolpa dell'imputato.

[49] ... veniva naturalmente che l'instinto della conservazione portasse ognuno as assicurarsi l'aiuto di uno dei forti, giacchè la forza sociale nel fatto

non esisteva, laonde la forza che assumeva la società era quella della clientela. Per modo chel a società siciliana, immediatamente dopo l'abolizione della feudalità, aveva tutti i caratteri di quelle dei rimanenti paesi d'Europa nel Medio Evo.

50 ... si rende necessario, direi quasi indispensabile, il bisogno di aderire, cordialmente o per timore, ad una clientela, o, come qui si dice, ad un partito. Non si comprende la vita privata e pubblica esclusivamente nel domino delle leggi, ma sempre dentro un partito, perchè l'uomo onesto, anche ricco, ma isolato, è esposto alle prepotenze ed alle vessazioni del primo venuto, mentre un volgare mascalzone trova nel partito aiuti, difensori e riguardi anche di fronte ai gruppi rivali.

54 Hai mai partecipato a qualche organizzazione, di qualsiasi tipo? Non ti è mai venuta voglia di iscriverti in un partito? und Non to è mai venuta voglia di partecipare a un gruppo religioso? ist die Antwort stets eine Variation von No, mai. Fragt der Interviewer jedoch: Si può dire che il partito è la tua famiglia?, so erhält er eine andere Antwort. Sie lautet: Esatto, questo.

57 ... una o due famiglie baronali, ducali o quasi; un clero più o meno numeroso; un cinquanta famiglie borghesi; altretante o poco più di operai, ed infine la grande massa dei contadini.

58 ... pervertiti dall'orgoglio soddisfatto di essere usciti dalla massa dei contadini, si attaccno al ceto dei galantuomini a coppeddi.

61 ... mentre questi (die Piemontesen) abitano per la più in campagna, in casa poste nei loro stessi poderi, vestono come i contadini agiati, e, se pure tengono ai loro servizi qualche bracciante, non disdegnano di vangare essi stessi le loro terre, il galantuomo siciliano, che pure discende ordinariamente da un contadino, il quale, tre o quattro generazioni fa, potè, mercè l'intelligenza svegliata, il lavoro tenace, il risparmio rigoroso e qualche volta aiutandosi anche con l'usura, accumulare un discreto patrimonio, considera la vita in modo profondamente diverso. Egli quindi la consuma in uno sforzo continuo, tenace e spesso disperato, diretto a conservare l'abito, il rango e tutte le apparenze della persona civile, del borghese che non vive di lavoro manuale ...

74 C., un ex feudo di salme 120, sito in territorio di S. M., dava a noi un utile annuo di L. 4000 e ciò per più di un trentennio. Dopo la venuta di V. E. e la magnifica offensiva ai reprobi dell'altra sponda, lo abbiamo dato in affitto per L. 60000 annue anticipate.

75 In breve tempo nella sola provincia di Palermo 320 fondi vennero liberati dalla mafia e 28 000 ettari di terreno, sui quali la mafia aveva imposti affitti di estorsione, ripresero il loro valore. La differenza tra tali affitti e quelli nuovi fu di ben 18 milioni.

4 The Mafioso

1 ... i capi mafia sono sempre fra gabellotti e proprietari, cioè persone, che relativamente agli altri, a secondo della condizione sociale a cui apparten-gono, sono sempre in migliori condizioni economiche. Mentre il povero contadino, la vera vittima del latifondo e dell'attuale condizione economica sociale, raremente è un mafioso.

5 Fra i tanti pericolosi e occulti aderenti all'alta mafia annoverasi il perverso Filippo Battaglia da Alia il quale da semplice manovale di cretaglie seppe in un ventennio elevarsi ad una condizione sociale in apparenza individiabile, acquistando terre, case, fabbricando ne delle nuove, sostenendo un lusso smudato ... e quel che più sostenendo financo in Napoli il figlio Angelo agli studi per alcuni anni pel quale ebbe ad erogare non poche somme.

7 Voi, curatolo del Barone Occhipinti, con il lavoro vostro, rischiando spesso la vita, vi siete fatta una posizione economica e nelle Madonie avete un nome. Voi siete curatolo e soprastante della tenuta ... Mio padre diceva che cominciaste pascolando le pecore, conducendo le vache.

8 Spesse volte il campiere gode fama di avere uno o due cuio al sole, il che vuol dire che egli ha già comesso uno o due assassini. Circondato da quest'aureola, la sua cariera è fatta, egli diventa una persona temibile, cioè chi duna suggizioni, che da soggezione; necessaria, e perciò meglio ricom-pensata.

9 ... tutto il suo prestigio nasce dal suo passato e giovanile delitto, dalla potenzialità sua alla violenza, consacrata dalla sua giovanile impresa: è uno che può uccidere senz'altro, perchè ha già ucciso.

13 Li Destri Antonino di Antonio d'anni 35, possidente da Gangi, è ritenuto ed è maffioso, prepotente e manutengolo di latitanti di ogni importanza. Esso siccome è ritenuto in questo paese per un valente tiratore di spada, crede imporre timore a tutti ...

14 da dilettante, ossia per assistere semplicemente ai misfatti senza parteci-pare al bottino di cui non avea bisogno.

[16] Il Valenza in una al Murò Francesco, già cascesato, ed al Murò Salvatore fratello, prese parte personale nei mancati assassini di Fucurino Sebastiana e Macaluso Vincenzo avvennuto nel Settembre 1882.

[17] Il mafioso io lo vede dalla sua azione di mafia, quale può essere; e la mafia io penso che sia, in tutti i rami, usare un sopruso sopra un'altra persona.

[18] Per questo fatto fu arrestato, e subi tre anni di carcere preventivo; poi venne rimesso in libertà per insufficienza di prove.

[19] 1868 La Corte d'assise di Palermo lo assolvette dalla sud. imputazione, e fu voce generale che tale risultato egli ottene per intrighi di mafia e colla sborsa di più migliaia d'onze.

[20] 1877 Con un anonimo diretto alla R. Prefettura di Palermo nel Marzo fu denunziato come principale manutengolo della sud. Banda Capraro e Di Pasquale e come organizzatore del sequestro Mancuso Francesco da Palazzo Adriano.

1877 (Giugno) Il Pretore di Prizzi lo ammonì in contumacia essendosi dato alla latitanza rifugiandosi a Roma sotto la protezione di persona autorevolissima altolocata.
1877 (Agosto) Il Delegato di Prizzi lo denunziò come contravventore all'ammonizione essendo ancora latitante.
1877 (Agosto) Il Tribunale di Palermo lo assolvette dall'accennata imputazione di contravvenzione all'ammonizione.
1878 (Aprile) Il Pretore di Prizzi revocò la inflittagli ammonizione.

[21] Questura di Palermo
all'Ill.mo Sig. Prefetto di Palermo
Palermo 12 novembre 1885
Ogetto: Causa contro Valenza Giuseppe da Prizzi
Oggi alla Corte d'assise si discusse la causa del noto Valenza Giuseppe, imputato d'assassinio per mandato in parsona d'Alzardi Nicolò, e dietro verdetto negativo dei Giurati venne assolto, e messo in libertà.
Agevolò molto il compiuto della difesa, sostenuta dagli avvocati onorevoli Crispi e Cuccia, la deposizione del delegato Favini, che sconfessò i suoi precedenti rapporti, dicendo d'essere stato allora tratto in inganno ed affermando essere il Valenza una persona dabbene.
Ciò inverno non mi sorprende, avendo ritenuto sempre i Favini un Impiegato poco fedele.
Di tanto informo la S. V. Ill. ma per la superiore di Lei intelligenza.
Con osservanza
Il Questore

[22] Mafioso non è chi sente mafioso, ma chi è considerato come tale. Il pubblico fa il mafioso.

[24] La faccenda è che la gente sono vigliacchi in questo paese.

[25] Abbiamo riservatezza per la paura, perchè ci preoccupiamo che possono fare male a noi e alle nostre famiglie.

[26] Se siamo timidi tanti giovani e non parliamo, io direi che non è timidezza questa, perchè qui ce ne sono tanti che voglion parlare, ma sarà soltanto paura, perchè domani, stasera, quando vanno in campagna a lavorore, qualcuno pensa che una fucilata di lupara lo può fulminare.

[27] La maffia oggettivamente si può definire il senso misterioso della paura che l'uomo famoso per delitti o per forza brutale fa sentire ai deboli, ai pusillanimi, ai quietisti.

[29] E' strano che in questi paesi caldi ed immaginosi, ove il linguaggio ordinario è tanto mellifluo, iperbolico e figurato, quello dei maffiosi è breve, sobrio, reciso.

[30] Il mafioso vero, il mafioso autentico si mostra quasi sempre umile, parla ed ascolta con aria dimessa, ostenta una grande longanimità; se offeso in presenza di molte persone, non reagisce, ma più tardi uccide.

[31] Dopo l'arresto del controscritto in seguito a mandato di cattura, lo spirito pubblico si è un poco rialzato, e molti acquistano certezze e coraggio per parlare finalmente su certi fatti rimasti sino ad oggi mistero. Vero però che ancora tutto sta nei limiti di riservatissime confidenze, inquanto che molti di coloro che potrebbero fornire prove convincenti sui fatti stessi, si tengono ancora perplessi e retrivi nella tema che il Valenza colle molte influenze che gode, possa ben presto liberarsi dai lacci della Giustizia.

[32] Attraverso una certa vita le cose vengono dietro, una dietro l'altra. Quando c'è venuto e gli ho fatto un favore, quando è venuto un altro e gli ho fatto un favore, poi è venuto avanti cosi, una specie d'abitudine. Cosi s'è allargata la cerchia del nome mio.

[42] E' sempre a contatto coi preti, i preti vanno da lui, lui va alla banca, che è sempre capeggiata dai preti, che il direttore della banca è un prete, la banca è sempre stata dei preti. A stare con quella gente, si è evoluto, gli porta tanto di rispetto la polizia, lo salutano, gli danno tanti di quegli ossequi. Oggi è più ben vestito, il maresciallo gli va incontro, gli da la mano: Caraliese... —A fine

maggio, in occasione della campagna elettorale, lui, il ministro Zacagnini e l'onorevole Lanza sono stati a cena assieme e poi sono usciti a braccetto assieme.

[44] Questi che chiamate mafiosi e prottettori della mafia, birbone d'un Don Beppe Virgilio, son quelli che han tolto via dalla macchia ben diciotto malfattori in men che due anni ...

[45] ...io mi permetto accenarLe i servizi prestati dal Mazzarese alla P. S. sin da parecchi anni che lo conosco ... Sin dal 1866 nell'occasione della rivolta dei sette giorni di Settembre, il Mazzarese si cooperò a far presentare agli ufficiali dei Bersaglieri spediti da Palermo a Campofelice di Fitalia, a nome Sig.ri Ristori e Sivio, non pochi latitanti che furono causa di quei movimenti sanguinosi. I succennati ufficiali possono attestare della condotta del Mazzaese.

Circa sei anni addietro il Mazzarese indicò ai compagni d'armi di Lercara Friddi che in Campofelice si era ricoverato il brigante inteso Tredici, dopo quale indicazione la forza pubblica lo pedinò e finalmente to arrestò a Mezzojuso ...

Aggiungo oltre a ciò che il Mazzarese fu colui che indicò all'ex Brigadiere dei RR. CC. a nome Scópeci, circa quattro anni or sono, la domora del brigante La Bussa, e si mediò poi di farlo scoprire ed uccidere ...

Non voglio tediarLa ancora con i dettagli dei tanti piccoli servizi prestati dal detto Mazzarese alle autorità locali, mettendo in rischio la sua vita ed i suoi averi.

[46] Presidente: Il signor Cannizzo nella persecuzione di Nobile, spiegava un interesse personale, o facea ciò nell'interesse pubblico?
Ambrasi: La premura dell'arresto di Nobile era nell'interesse suo personale e del suo partito.
Presidente: Ella mi parla di partiti, dia delle spiegazioni.
Ambrasi: Cannizzo e i Cernigliaro stavano da una parte, e i La Franca e gli Scala dall'altra.
Presidente: Di talchè, se pel primo partito ci era interesse a perdere Nobile, pel secondo non ve n'era?
Ambrasi: Era interesse di arrestare Nobile perchè avea attentato alla vita di Cernigliaro.

[47] Adesso non ha bisogno di fare la voce grossa perchè già comanda, o ci manda gli altri. Non ha più bisogno di schiacciare per ottenere ...

[48] Dire, infatti, oggi, di una persona, in Sicilia, che è uomo ha un significato onorevole, dire che è mafioso ha significato ben diverso.

⁴⁹ Io era solo, combatteva la mafia in guanti gialli e quella colla carabina ...

⁵⁰ Il vero uomo è anzitutto il suo silenzio, la segreta presenza di un potere occulto e di vie lunghe e nascoste, l'essere e il farsi ritenere al centro di altri uomini, che come lui operano nell'ombra.

⁵³ Vestivano tutti di panno azzurro o di velluto, stivali alla scudiera, berretto rosso la più parte: portavano quasi tutti orologio d'argento a remontoir e un anello al dito, con la lettera iniziale R.

⁵⁴ Antonino Leone ridestavasi più che mai baldanzoso, e facea sapere per le bocche della fama, che egli viaggiava periodicamente in ferrovia da Termini a Palermo e che degnavasi assistere, quando gliene veniva la voglia, alle rappresentazioni del Politeama.

⁵⁵ Una fotografia a mia!? E picchi? Nenti sugnu iu. Un cittadino qualunqui sugnu ... E' curioso! ... La gente crede che sia per discrezione che io parlo poco. No. Parlo poco perchè poco so. Abito in un villaggio, vengo a Palermo solo di rado, conosco poca gente ... eppoi mi sono fatto grandetto ormai, ho più di settant' anni ...

⁵⁶ Sono l'ultimo degli uomini, qui riuniti, sono un povero agricultore; ma credo che posso parlare per tutti.

⁵⁷ Per la festa dell'otto settembre, della madonna Maria Santissima dei Miracoli, piglia il coppo e fa la raccolta dei soldi. Si mette in un punto, vicino al campanile, e chi ci da cinquecento lire, chi cinquanta, chi mille, chi dieci, a seconda della persona. Raccoglie lui solo centocinquantamila lire, li versa alla commissione della festa, ogni anno.

⁵⁹ Sono natto cosi. Senza scopi mi muovo. Chiunque mi domanda un favore io penso di farglielo perchè la natura mi comanda cosi ...
Viene uno e dice:—Ho la questione col Tizio, vede se può accordare la cosa—. Chiamo la persona interessata, o vado a trovarlo io, a seconda dei rapporti, e li accordo. Ma io non vorrei che si pensasse che le dico queste cose per farmi grande. Non voglio assolutamente che paia che io le dica queste cose per farmi grande: le dico queste cose per cortesia, perchè ha fatto tutta questa strada. Io non ci sono né vanitoso, né ambizioso. La gente chiedono come votare perchè sentono il dovere di consigliarsi per mostrare un senso di gratitudine, di riconoscenza, si sentono all'oscuro e vogliono adattarsi alle persone che gli hanno fatto bene.
Domani, per esempio, devo lasciare trebbia, animali, tutte le mie cose per correre a Agrigento a raccomandare uno perchè lo possino agli esami.

⁶⁰ Sapete, dico, quando si occupa un posto come il vostro ...

Che posto?

Voglio dire nell'opinione della gente.

Ah (Pausa)

Il fatto è, risponde dopo un poco, che in ogni società ci deve essere una categoria di persone che aggiustano le situazioni, quando si fanno complicate.

⁶⁴ Un cittadino qualsiasi, anche forestiero, che avesse bisogno di un favore, non deve fare altro che rivolgersi ad uno dei cosi detti capi-mafia. Egli è sicuro che la sua domanda sarà accolta con vero favore. Infatti il mafioso spiega tutto l'impegno possibile per servire l'amico novello, senza pretendere alcuna ricompensa, e disinteressatamente.

Egli sa che il suo lavoro non è mai improficuo, perche oltre ad essersi accresciuta la sua reputazione, si è anche accresciuto il numero delle persone che gli sono devote.

⁶⁵ Ambizioso di dominare e di venire a capo di questa Commune, e per ciò riuscire nella prossima elezione, di unito al suo indivisibile amico Milletari Alessandro di Michelangelo, Avvocato da qui, è dietro a formare una nuova Società Agricola, la quale sino ad oggi conta, per come si rileva dalla voce pubblica, circa 400 soci, per essere nominato Consigliere e poscià Sindaco, e quindi abbattere il partito dominante Mocciaro.

⁶⁶ Non è l'interesse di migliorare la condizione delle classi inferiori della società che ha spinto i suddetti signori ... sinnene il fine di farsi acclamare protettori della povera gente, e nello stesso tempo per sopraffare i loro avversari amministrativi e personali e avvantaggiare maggiormente la loro posizione finanziaria.

⁶⁹ La gente ci ha ammirazione per chi è più forte, chi è conosciuto, è logico.

⁷⁰ Se tu ti metti con la legge, sai quanto perdi?—perchè non avendo denaro non puoi rispondere al verbale, alla querela, agli avvocati. Invece con l'intermediatore s'accordano spendendo memo tutti. Ci hanno fiducia in lui benissimo, perchè è un uomo capace a poter accordare le faccende.

⁷¹ Stanno in obbligo. Quando uno fa da intermediatore, accorda la partita e stanno in obligo a chi l'accorda...

Pensa la popolazione:—Ci do il voto perchè lo merita, perchè ci ha fatto del bene—. Lui consiglia, pùo vedere meglio come appoggiare la popolazione per fare del bene. Lui è un uomo che per la gente si gira, per stare affiancato alla popolazione. Parecchia gente che sono oscuri, che sono oscuri della vita e dei partiti, lui ci consiglia:—Guardate che il partito Tizo non può andare avanti.

CALOGERO VIZZINI
con l'abilità di un genio
innalzò le sorti del distinto casato
sagace dinamico mai stanco
diede benessere agli operai della terra e delle zolfare
operando sempre il bene
e si un nome assai apprezzato
in Italia e fuori
grande nelle persecuzioni
assai più grande nelle disdette
rimase sempre sorridente
ed oggi
con la pace di Cristo
ricomposto nella maestà della morte
da tutti gli amici dagli stessi avversari
riceve l'attestato più bello
fu un galantuomo

5 The structure of mafioso groupings

1 Ogni gruppo di mafiosi è rappresentato allegoricamente da un carciofo, il cui torso rappresenta il capo, e le foglie gli aderenti. Infatti è volgare ed usuale in Sicilia chiamare lu trunzu ri l'omini (il torso degli uomini) chi è creduto un personaggio che vale molto.

3 Vi ha in molti paesi delle unioni o fratellanze ... senza colore o scopo politico, senza riunioni, senza altro legame che quello della dipendenza da un capo ...

6 Tutti e tre poi agivano per mandato ricevuto da Giuseppe Valenza che aveva già sborsato agli stessi la somma di L. 200 per cadauno riservandosi di dare maggiore compenso se il reato veniva puntualmente consumato.
Essendo lo Sparacio rimasto soltando ferito, il Valenza non volle dare agli esecutori il maggior compenso promesso.

7 ...ci dichiarò che da noi desideravano un favore avendo delle persone nemiche, che doveano morire.

8 Per esempio se c'è un pastore che ha trenta, quaranta pecore in mezzo la strada e non può mantenerle, ci dice:—Non ho dove pascolare gli animali, —lui ci dice:—Vattene tu con tutte pecore nelle mie mandre—. E sta un mese,

due mesi, e se vuole andare poi lo lascia libero, pur se gli animali hanno mangiato sul suo pascolo. Scemi, vagabondi, tutti vanno a mangiare da lui.

9 Più il malfattore sarà pericoloso e conosciuto, più sarà grande il rischio che corre di essere arrestato o condannato, maggiore sarà la smania nel signore di affermare la sua potenza, proteggendolo o salvandolo anche quando non vi abbia nessun interesse materiale. Naturalmente, il malfattore cosi salvato diventa l'uomo del suo protettore nel senso feudale della parola; ha in certo modo ricevuto da lui in feudo la vita, e, d'allora in poi, è pronto ai suoi servizi.

10 L'alta mafia...quando la sicurezza scopre e colpisce, si affretta allora a montar le difese, ad ammannire alibi e testimonianza, e falsare l'opinione pubblica della piazza, ad intrigare nelle carceri, nelle Cancellerie, a protestare contro la forza pubblica e contro gli stessi funzionari.—Se non riesce sempre allo scopo dell'ottenere la impunità ai malcapitati, riesce sempre allo scopo di affermarsi meglio in paese per protezione spiegata, per fermezza di propositi, per potenza di mezzi, per tendenza a rivincite.

E cosi fa nei reati di sangue consumati della canaglia del partito, siano essi reati appendici delle grassazioni o dei furti qualificati, siano essi premedite vendette contro le spie o conseguenza rabbiosa di fallito ricatto.

11 Il braccio destro di Vincenzo Lauria era come professione un fallito, stava sempre accanto al mafioso.

Sembrava solo. In realtà, senza perderlo mai di vista e senza mai scambiare una parola né fra loro né con nessum altro, lo seguivano a qualche passo di distanza due giovanotti in giacca di velluto e con la coppola in testa.

15 Antico amico del famoso brigante Valvo...come mai—nessuna famiglia si azzarda attualmente portarsi in campagna a fare delle baldorie mentre egli vi si reca spessissimo senza alcuna tema coll'intera famiglia?

16 4 persone armato di fucili a due canne, e che vestivano di stoffa scura, avevano in testa berette, non parlavano il dialetto di queste contrade, tutte di mezzana statura, e dell'apparente età di anni 30 circa.

...avvertendo non essere improbabile, che si tratti di un fatto simulato per secondi fini delle persone, che sono impiegate nell'ex feudo San Giorgio.

...debbo sometterla che poco nulla credo la comparsa dei 4 arnati, e che invece dubito molto che le persone ai servizi del Sig. Mancuso nell'ex feudo Tiberio, ritenuti autori di un altro incendio della casa di campagna in detto ex feudo. Ora essi temendo e per come sono stati minacciati dal detto conte di

192

essere sottoposti ad un processo e per lo meno mandati al domicilio coatto, suppongo, che i medesimi, abbiano combinato la lettera in parola per discaricarsi tanto della prima, quanto per l'incendio e forse per altre cattive mire, ossia vendetta che vorrebbero consumare a danno del Sig. Conte Mancuso, ed hanno fatto comparire—d'accordo col Mitra—i quattro individui, che per me non esistono affatto.

[19] Fu difatti Palizzolo che organizzava a forze elettorali delle squadre di malviventi.

[21] Egli si dà da fare per il padrone, si occupa molto di elezioni.

[22] come maffioso, sospetto per assassini, sequestri, grassazioni e manutengolismo ai più famigerati briganti...

[23] Egregio signor Questore,
Ho comprato un fondo a due Km. tra Monreale e San Martino, ai piedi del Castellaccio, detto Trifirò. Dovendo tenervi uva mia persona di fiducia ho scelto Salvatore Pesco, uno dei due Caccamesi che attualmente trovansi nell'altra mia proprietà in Bellolampo, contrada S. Croce.
    Vorebbe la S. V. autorizzarmi un tal mutamento? Nella speranza che micontenterà ne la ringrazio sentitamente.
            Dev. mo suo
            R. Palizzolo

[24] Egregio signor Cavaliere,
Il mio castaldo è stato posto in libertà, ed io mi affretto a renderle sentiti ringraziamenti per l'affettuosa premura, con cui degnossi di accogliere il mio reclamo.
    Intanto il detto mio uomo mi riferisce che ora dalla Questura gli si vorebbe contrastare il ritorno a S. Croce, ove ho di bisogno dei suoi servizi. Se Ella, come sempre, volesse farmi cosa grata, dovrebbe togliere queste difficoltà, che non credo troppo giuste. Mi creda con tutto rispetto
            Dev. mo R. Palizzolo

[25] A un certo Rini da più e più anni ammonito e non so con quanta ragione, domiciliato in Caccamo a norma delle leggi in vigore, veniva imposto di ritornare al comune natio. Credendo questa una disposizione superiore, di cui Ella non era che semplice esecutore, mi sono rivolto al sotto-prefetto, perchè si fosse degnato sospendere e revocare un ordine, che indirettamente apportavami pure delle noie, avendo di già dato in gabella ed a mezzadria non poche mie terre al Rini, che, partendo lui, non saprei più a chi meglio ac-

cordare, tanto più che sono chiamato dal Prefetto a Palermo, onde prender parte ai lavori della Deputazione Provinciale di caui sono Deputato.

Una lettera gentile del sotto-prefetto, or ora pervenutami, mi fa conoscere che la mia preghiera è stata accolta, tanto più che verificatisi gli atti riguardanti il Rini da quel degno rappresentante del governo, si è riconosciuto esser troppa durezza ridurre alla disperazione un padre di numerosa famiglia, che poi non ha i maggiori torti di questo mondo, come posso in mille modi addimostrarle.

Dopo ciò son sicuro che Ella non insisterà in quegli ordini che al Rini sono dati, ed io ne la ringrazio di cuore, mentre, come le ho già scritto, anch'io ne fruirò non lievo vantaggio.

Le restituisco il romanzo di Ponson du Terrail che ho letto, e nel quale le confesso, che senza alcuna soddisfazione ho vista campeggiare tanti di quegli episodi inverosimili, di cui si fa bella scuola francese. Giunto a Palermo le manderò copia di un mio lavoro in siffatto genere a desidero, che e suo comodo me ne scriva le impressioni, che subirà in leggerlo.

Ed ora accetti una stretta di mano e mi creda tutto suo
    R. Palizzolo
9 febbraio '76

[26] Noi sottoscritti quali cittadini domiciliati e residenti in Mezzojuso, come pure dello Borgato di Fitalia, certifichiamo e dichiaramo che il Sig. Damiano Mazzarese fu Vincenzo domiciliato e residente in Campofelice di Fitalia a Mezzojuso è stato di commendevole ed irreprensibile condotto...

[27] Si certifica da me sottoscritto Eletto Delegato della Borgata di Fitalia suffraganio a Mezzojuso che Mazzarese Damiano del fu Vincenzo, possedente, domiciliato e residente in questo suddetto Borgato, ha menato regolarissimo condotto, sia politico che morale, non avendo dato mai disturbo a questo pubblico.

E per costare ne rilascio il presente da me firmato e suggellato.
Rilasciato in Fitalia oggi li 23 Novembre 1881
    L'Eletto Delegato
    Domenico Cirrincione

[28] ...tanto il Mazzarese che il Cirrincione... sono stati in relazioni con i briganti faccendolo da manutengoli e ricattatori e per la loro mafia s'impongono a tutti i cittadini, e mi si assicura che hanno preso parte morale e materiale in tutti i reati avvenuti nel territorio di Campofelice e dei comuni adiacenti. E'incredibile quanti reati gli si adebitano, ma nessuno vuol formalmente dichiarare per tema della vita; ed hanno avuto l'arte di atteggiarsi a coadiuvatori della forza pubblica mentre nel fatto sono stati i traditori...La

loro agiatezza proviene dal delitto, e non dal sudore della fatica, oppure dall'industria...

²⁹ Possiede una discreta proprietà sia libera che censita nel territorio di Campofelice della quale buona parte acquistata da potere dell'illustre Sig. Principe di Fitalia...

³⁰ Amministrazione
dei beni
del Principe di Fitalia
Ill. mo Sig.r Prefetto—

Palermo, 4 Gennaio 1882

Le restituisco la lettera confidenziale del delegato da P.S. di Mezzojuso, ringraziando La per la cortesia usatami nel famela leggere...

...posso assicurarLa che io conosco il Mazzarese da parecchi anni e mi è sembrato sempre un onesto padre di famiglia, tutto dedicato agli affari campestri per migliorare le condizioni della stessa sua famiglia, ed è stato finora creduto onesta dalle autorità che gli hanno accordato sempre il permesso d'armi...

La prego infine volermi scusare per questa lunga e noiosa lettera, ma ho creduto mio dovere esporLe tutto quanto conosco sul riguardo del Mazzarese sicuro che la S.V. nella sua saggezza saprà valutare i fatti succennati.

Gradisca sempre i sensi della mia più alta stima e considerazione

Aff. mo Dev. mo
Principe di Fitalia.

³¹ V.S. Ill.ma non ignora che da lungotempo (1848) Antonina Rappa, a causa di rivalità d'amore, assecondata dall'opportunità dei tempi e della sua posizione, uccideva tal Costa Erasmo, e come di rimando questo assassinio produsse quello di Salvatore Rappa. Da qui ire, rancori e vendette fra le due famiglie onde quell' infelice paese fu d'allora in poi funestato... Nella notte dell' 11 Novembre 1878, Franscesco Di Marco (cognato del Costa) venne fatto segno a colpi d'arma da fuoco, e tosto s'indicano colpevoli Rappa Antonio mandante, La Bue Nicolò mandatario, causa a delinquere gase di elezioni amministrative...

³² Il rancore che da tempo esiste fra il Sig. Greco Pietro e il Sindaco Cav. Scordato, non soldanto perchè di parte opposta nelle lotte municipali, essendosi schierato fra gli ultimi dissidenti, ma...perchè avendogli alcuni anni or sono cheisto in isposa la figlia, il Cav. Scordato credette rifiutargliene la mano.

³³ Allorquando il Giuseppe Valenza, unito alla banda del Pugliese partecipò

al furto Alessi in Cammarata era gli fido amico e compagno d'azione questo proprietario pure ricco, D'Angelo Luciano fu Pietro che consumato il fatto portò con se ed all'insaputo di molti componenti della banda, buona parte del bottino assicurando il Valenza che avrebbe fatto con lui, col Filippo Greco ed altro fido compagno la divisione. Ma non fu cosi dal perchè il D'Angelo ritiratosi col bottino in contrada Malfarina si rifiutò alla progetta divisione. Da qui nacque un odio implacabile tra il Valenza ed il D'Angelo, odio che ebbe triste conseguenze.

[35] L'avvocato Alongi per come si disse era legato in intima amicizia coi fratelli D'Angelo, e più specialmente col Luciano che avevalo favorito coll' improntargli il danaro occorrento per lo acquisto di un vasto vigneto.

Avvenuto l'attentato, cominciarono scissure tra l'Alongi ed i D'Angelo per ragioni d'interessi, scissure poi che terminarono in aperta lotta per la quale attualmente pende tra loro causa civile.

Quando però le scissure si mutarono in aperta lotta, tra i D'Angelo e 'l Alongi, in allora il Valenza andò scemando la generosa esibizione giungendo fino al punto di dire che erapronto solo a mettere una zarola che potesse servire come garanzia nel caso che l'Alongi abisognasse prendere somma a prestito per difinire la vertenza coi D'Angelo.

[37] Signore. Sono nelle mani della giustizia e persiò mi persuado a dire tutto potendo solo da Lei avere qualche agevolazione.

Qui in Termini esiste una associazione di malfattori. Scopo di questa associazione è l'abigeato. Capo in Termini vi è Leonardo Di Nuovo fu Cosimo campiere alla Torrazza. Le relazioni si tengono con quella di Mezzojuso e Corleone, cioè per la prima col Como Salvatore fu Antonio, per la seconda con Luca Patti fu Giuseppe campiere nell'ex feudo Pirrello (Corleone). Il denaro che si ricava dalla vendita degli animali viene diviso dal nostro capo, cioè una doppia parte prende esso e quegli che apparano if furto ed una parte gli altri. Gli animali che vengono depredati in questo territorio e nei limitrofi sono condotti prima a Mezzojuso dal Como, il quale da gli ordini ove si debbono condurre, ma ordinariamente si dirige al feudo Pirrello da Luca Patti.

Denaro noi all'atto della consegna non ne ritiriamo, ma riceviamo altretanti animali che condotti in Termini si nascondono in casa dei meno sospetti alla P.S. e ciò in attesa dei certificati che il Como si fa pervenire avendo esso relazioni in molti paesi.

[45] Ha un modo di vedere, di pensare e di vivere che è esattamente il rovescio di come vede, pensa e vive l'onesto cittadino...Il suo occhio non ha mai un lampo di bontà.

196

⁴⁶ Allora il problema è semplice, essendo stato identificato l'apparato: un pontefice massimo, quattro capi provinciali poichè quattro sono le provincie mafiose, un centinaio e mezzo di capi locali. Si sa chi sono: arrestiamoli, processiamoli, mandiamoli in galera e tutto è risolto. Perchè non s'è fatto? O, s'è fatto, perchè non ha dato frutto? Perchè, evidentemente, le cose non stanno cosi.

⁵⁰ Le paranze della città e delle carceri erano indipendenti tra di loro, padrona cioè ciascuna dei propri guadagni, della disciplina e della giurisdizione sui propri membri.

⁵¹ Il professore F.S. nel gennaio 1888 mi scriveva: Credo bene che bisognerebbe studiare la camorra non solo nei delinquenti, ma anche in coloro che sfuggono alle sanzioni del codice penale; cosi per esempio nelle cmministrazioni locali, nei giornalisti e specialmente nel insegnamento. Nell'insegnamento secondario, per esempio, qui c'è organizzata una camorra vera e propria, di natura ignota alle altre città: coiè gli istituti pubblici governativi e municipali sono insufficienti a ricevere gli scolari, quindi una gran parte di essi sono obbligati a frequentare quelli privati…Il ministro domanda i locali al municipio per aprire nuove scuole secondarie, ma i direttori degli istititu privati sono tanto potenti da imporre al municipio di fare il sordo… L.C. infine mi assicura che un'altra specie di camorra si fa coi libri di testo.

⁵⁵ Domanda: Il vostro Dio chi è?
Risposta: Aremi.
Domanda: Il vostro scopo quale?
Risposta: Repubblica universale.
Domanda: Quando fecero a voi, chi ci era?
Risposta: Buona gente.
Domanda: Chi erano?
Risposta: N. 1 en. 2 en. 3 (indicare i nomi dei fratelli presenti alla ceremonia).

⁵⁶ Avi assai ca vi doli lu scagghiuni?
Dalla festa dell'Annunziata.
Cu c'era?
Bella gente.
Che gente?
Giuseppe Valentini, Francesco Polio e Pietro Puleo che mi hanno ricevuto fratuzzu.

⁵⁷ La testa.
Del tiranno.

Che pirù reca fra noi?
Eguaglianza, fratellanza, amor di patria.
Che ti è più sacro?
Libertè o morte.
Qual'è la vostra legge?
I dieci comandamenti di Dio.
Ditemeli.
Morte a tutti i tiranni, ai loro aderenti ed ai spergiuri...etc.

[61] I fratuzzi erano divisi in squadre, ogni squadra era composta di dieci persone, il preposto ad ogni sqadra era chiamato decimoprimo...

[63] Caratteristica specifica della quale, tra le altre—e per noi qui, particolarmente interessante—è appunto quella di sostituirsi al potere statale nei rapporti tra malvivenza e popolazione. Donde la conseguenza che, mentre dovunque i termini della lotta sul terreno della difesa sociale dalla criminalità sono tre: Stato, popolazione, malvivenza, in Sicilia divennero quattro: Stato, popolazione, mafia, malvivenza. (Mori 1932 S. 76)

Altro suo fine caratteristico è quello di sostituirsi al potere statale nei rapporti tra delinquenza comune e popolazione. Da ciò la conseguenza che, mentre nei paesi dove non esiste la mafia i termini della lotta sul terreno della difesa sociale dalla criminalità, nonchè su quello della repressione, sono tre: Stato, popolazione, delinquenza; invece, dove fiorisce la onorata società, i termini diventano quattro: stato, mafia, popolazione, delinquenza. (Montalbano 1953 S. 540)

[65] a) Obbligo tra gli associati di aiutarsi scambievolmente a vendicare col sangue le offese ricevute.
b) Obbligo di procurare e propugnare la difesa e la liberazione del socio caduto nelle mani della giustizia.
c) Diritto dei soci di partecipare alla distribuzione, secondo il prudente arbitrio dei capi, del prodotto dei ricatti, delle estorsioni, delle rapine, dei furti...e di altri delitti perpetrati per sorte comune sociale.
d) Obbligo di conservare il segreto, pena per i contravventori la morte, in seguito a decisione del competente organo giuriszidonale della mafia.

I quattro punti anzidette erano espressamente sanciti negli Statuti delle varie associazioni (vecchie e giovani) della mafla. Successivamente, però, quando si cominciarono a fare (sebbene timidamente) dei processi per associazione a delinquere, la mafia dovette rinunziare agli Staturi scritti, onde non fornire la prova documentale dell'associazione criminosa. Con gli Statuti scitti scomparvero pure, a poco alla volta, le formalità per entrare nelle associazioni della mafia, le cui norme sono divenute tradizionali, nel senso che vengono conservate e trasmesse dalla tradizione.

[66] ...quelle garanzie che in altri paesi dovrebbe cercare coll'unirsi con altri suoi simili e collo stabilire accuratamente con loro i reciproci doveri e diritti egli (der mafioso) le trova nei costumi della popolazione.

[70] ...la seguente favola è familiarizzata a tutti i Siciliani: Una volta molto tempo fa il Parlare ed il Mangiare interrogavano il re Salomone di decidere chi di loro poteva controllare la bocca, e Salomone decise che il Mangiare poteva controllare la bocca dell'uomo e non il Parlare, per timore che il Parlare sia la rovina dell'uomo, tanto che dall'ora in poi un uomo quanto meno parla meglio prospera.

[79] Il Pugliese, preso abruciapelo, appena abbe il primo colpo. cadde sul terreno e chiese aiuto, ma gli assassini avvicinatisi a lui, esplosero altro colpo di pistola ed indi se ne fuggirono.

Allora, visto che nessuno si era recato in suo aiuto, perchè la strada era deserta, da solo rusci a trascinarsi nella vicina casa di certo Tranfo, ove poi le Autorità locali lo rinvennero ferito gravemente.

[84] Un dovere di cittadino e non quello di spia mi spinge a dare schiarimenti alla Giustizia...

[89] Capisco, massaro, capisco: qua siete nato e qua—volete morire.

[92] La minaccia comune tra meridionali è in fatti: Ti taglio la faccia, ti guasto la mpigna (tomaio, per faccia); ...Lo sfregio si pratica anche contro le donne infedeli, o semplicemente sospettate tali.

[93] ...il caso di quel Caravotta che ha sibito, per vendetta, il taglio della mano destra ed ancor oggi tace!

Salemi Pace

perchè non vollero far attenere il porto d'armi a certi ex-manutengoli, ladri maffiosi da esso raccomandati...

Disgrazia per il paese e pel governo fu l'allontanamento del Mattiolo...perpetrato nella tenebra della maffia, sempre forte qui.

Ma egli tutto porre in opera per la sua riabilitazione, a ciò adoperandosi dell avv. Salemi Pace Giuseppe, fratello del Gaetano, domiciliato in Termini, avendo forte relazione alla Sottoprefettura.

Giuseppe Valenza

1874—Assunse al suo servizio certi Spallina Michele e Sciambra Giuseppe da Palazzu Adriano processati per delitti e crimini, pessimi sogetti, ed a mezzo dei medesimi favori la banda dei famigerati briganti Capraro e Di Pasquale.

Questo delegato capo ha oggi stesso spedito a codesto Sig. Procuratore del Re una dichiarazione testimoniale comprovante la pressione e le minacce che si fanno da Pietro e Giorgio fratello e figlio dell'arrestato Giuseppe Valenza da Prizzi verso i testimoni fiscali indotti nelle varie processure pendenti a carico di quest'ultimo.

Il Valenza ricco proprietario di Prizzi è ritenuto un soggetto pericoloso assai ...E' continuamente in giro nei vasti suoi possedimenti massime di notte e sempre disarmato, nulla avendo a temere dai malfattori e briganti, dei quali è amico e protettore.

...a mio parere dovrebbe costui esser colpito dalla legge almeno coll'ammonizione. Fino ad oggi però non sarebbe stato cosa agevole di raggiungere questo scopo, essendo prima necessario un cambiamento nel personale della Pretura di Prizzi. Io già segnali a codesto Centrale Ufficio la necessità d'un provvedimento sul Cancelliere Vizzinisi e più sull'Usciere Vajana che viene designato come cattivo soggetto. Ebbi anche a rappresentare che il Pretore Sig. Accarelli, quantunque brava ed onesta persona, era di caratere debole ed incapace di atti d'energia...

Canizzo—Cernigliaro—Scalia

Dopo la morte di suo figlio, il Notaro Cannizzo mi mandò a chiamare di sera. Io andai a trovarlo l'indomani alla banca e ci sedemmo nello stanzino di essa. Egli cominciò con l'amicizia antica tra lui e mio padre, che dicea voler continuare con me. Si parlò dell'assissinio di suo figlio; ed egli vantando autorevoli relazioni, disse che dovea vendicarne il sangue. Non si parlò d'altro; e quel colloquio durò più ore.

L'oodio comincia da un fatto ben antico. Un mio cognato, ora morto, Russo, offese la famiglia Cernigliaro; quell'atto riprovammo tutti, anche io, perchè offendeva anche mia sorella, moglie di Russo. Cernigliaro, a fin di vendetta, procurò di complicare mio cognato come mandante all'omicidio di tal Vutano. Mio cognato era innocente. Io cedento alle preghiere di mia sorella, m'interessai alla difesa di mio cognato che fu liberato. D'allora Cernigliaro fu mio nemico. Presidente: Ma con Cannizzo?

Scalia: Cannizzo cominciò dall'essere mio amico. Indi gli venne in mente che avessi potuto essere autore del taglio d'alberi nel suo fondo;—e propose querela contro me. Anche pria di questo fatto egli erasi da me allontanato. Si avvicinò ai Cernigliaro. Cosi cominciarono le disordine che divennero vivissime in seguito alle gare municipali.

Questo colpo fu attribuito a La Franca perchè egli aveva preteso una signora che fu sposata in seguito da Cernigliaro.

Indi più tradi l'alterco con mio fratello Benedetto per le terre alla Cambuca, e l'omicidio macato di mio fratello perchè il Cernigliaro gli vibrò un colpo di fucile.

In Partinico esisteva una società di molini, altri più tardi ne furono impiantati dai Cernigliaro, che recarono vantaggio al paese ma non alla società.

Le nimicizie poi divennero più, cordiali' per la elezione del Deputato.

Vidi tra gli altri candidati il Signor Gen. Alfonso Scalia, cugino di questi signori Scalia, uomo onesto ma che faceva parte della famiglia di cui io ero il bersaglio. Io mi chiusi in casa per non essere assassinato.

Si volle inoltre una persona rivestita di un'autorità che sospirasse pure al mio danno e fu trovato il pretore di Partinico che spiccò l'ordine di arresto...

Riguardo al Notar Cannizzo fu a suo carico spedito mandato di arresto. Tenutosi latitante, più tardi quel mandato che era stato rilasciato dal pretore locale, veniva rivocato dal Giudice Istruttore, essendo stato il Cannizzo eletto Deputato al Parlamento pel Collegio di Partinico.

Ci dichiarò che da noi desideravano un favore avendo delle persone nemiche, che doveano morire.

Grimaudo: Nel mese di luglio, il 20 o il 21, passando dalla fucina del fabbro ferraio Cammarata, vidi due individui ivi seduti, poscia un altro sconosciuto in compagnia di Giuseppe Reginella. Essendo quest'ultimo parente dei Cer-

nigliaro, dubitai qualche cosa a carico degli Scalia, onde andai ad avvertirli.
Presidente: Insomma in Partinico non vi sono che individui che sospirano o contro Scalia o contro Cernigliaro?
Grimaudo: Si dicea pubblicamente che gli Scalia correan pericolo.
Scalia: Surti dei gravi sospetti, con Benedetto Scalia mi recai sulla località, ove vidi quattro che si allontanavano.

Fu in tale convegno proposto di assassinare i fratelli Scalia con promessa di generosa mercede.

Il Cannizzo protesta che egli va inteso nel suo paese col proprio nome e cognome, e che l'aggiunta di Barabba è stata una invenzione, o meglio una ingiuria ritrovata dai suoi nemici.

Reginella Giuseppe fu uno di quelli che prese parte attivissima nelle lotte accanite che qui fervevano tra le note due famiglie Scalia e Cernigliaro. Fece prima parte di questo ultimo partito, ma poscià se ne distaccò, rimanendo in seguito aperto nemico dei Cernigliaro perchè questi fermi rimasero nel convincimento che il Luigi Cernigliaro, arrestato, lo fu in seguito a denunzia resa dal Reginella medesimo.

Il signor Cernigliaro si muove per un altro calcolo: Il di lui figlio Giuseppe intende sposare una figlia del signor Vincenzo Rosso che vi si oppone. Or la madre dell'accustato è parente della giovane pretesa perciò il Cernigliaro si serve della madre del giudicabile per notizie e per falicitare l'agognato matrimonio e quindi Cernigliaro ora in Palermo gli scelse l'avvocato...e in tutti altri modi che la S.V. Ill. ma ben comprende si adoperava a dritta ed a sinistra.
   L'imputato non avrebbe mezzi per due avvocati e per tutto altro: è il Cernigliaro che fa tutto...

Amoroso

Un tempo il Gregorio Turetta uomo di coraggio e capace di compiere qualunque colpo audace, era amico intimo del Salvatore Amoroso; ma poi nacque fra essi una forte scissura, ed il Turetta si unì col partito avversario.

Presidente: Il Lauriano, in che occasione lo conobbe?
Teste: Per le elezioni politiche.
Presidente: E della sua condotta che sa?
Teste: Non ebbi nulla a ridire allora.

202

Presidente: Quando?

Teste: Nel 79. Egli lavorò in mia casa a Salaparuta. Poi rammento che fu in prigione per un certo processo che ora non ho in mente.

Presidente: Per tutto il tempo che l'avvicinò in qual concetto la ebbe?

Teste: Era una persona sulla cui moralità non mi parve mai vi fossero degli appunti a fare.

avv. Figlia: Vorebbe sapere l'opinione che egli ha ora del Lauriano.

Teste: Ora non potrei rispondere con serenità di coscienza: in presenza di questo processo a me sembra che la opinione sul conto del Lauriano potrà corettamente formamela dopo il verdetto dei giurati.

Presidente: Conosce Di Paola?

Teste: Lo conobbi mi pare, quando conobbi il Lauriano, e lo tenevo per un buon giovane. Tanto che lo feci impiegare presso l'impresa Parisi.

Gaetano Amoroso: Vuol domandare al teste se mi conosce e se egli parlò per me affinchè non mi ammonissero.

Teste: Lo conosco e mi rammento di questo fatto—lo raccomandai insieme ad altri che formarono una lunga lista dei ammonendi, ciò avvenne appunto qualche tempo dopo la uccisione di un fratello dell'Amoroso: io invocai dall' autorità politica la sospensione del provvedimento che pareami non opportuno.

Gaetano Amoroso: Rammenta di avere chiesto il permesso d'armi per mio fratello Leonardo?

Teste: Lo rammento. Ma non so se poi il Questore glielo consese.

Io mi recai per avvicinare Badalamenti e quando fui quasi vicino al letto mi disse il direttore dell'Ospedale che nessuno poteva parlare col ferito, se non fosse stato visitato dai medici. Io vidi un signore con stivaloni alla scudiera e frustino in mano che parlava col ferito e me ne meravigliai. Anzi dissi al direttore: Se non posso avvicinare io al ferito, che sono Ispettore di P.S., si faccia allontanare anche quel signore. Anzi chiesichi fosse. Mi si disse: l'on. Valentino Caminecci.

Il conte Tasca dice di sapere il Lauriano per uomo onesto e che viveva del suo lavoro.

Teste: Conosco Lauriano da parecchi anni.

Presidente: In quale occasione?

Teste: Lauriano è fontaniere. Ho dovuto spesso adibirlo per l'acqua della mia villa di Malaspina. Egli contrariamente all'uso sei nostri fontanieri si mostrò sempre buono ed onesto. Intesi più tardi che fu diverse volte arrestato e processato—visto che tutte le volte la Sezione d'accusa lo rimandò con sentenza di non far luogo a procedimento e visto che era sempre monito di permesso legale di porto d'armi, pensai che egli non fosse altro che vittami di qualche persecuzione e ingiustament bersagliato.

6 The functions of mafioso behaviour

[1] Egli è sicuro che la sua domanda sarà accolta con vero favore. Infatti il mafioso spiega tutto l'impegno possibile per servire l'amico novello, senza pretendere alcuna ricompensa, e disinteressatamente.

[5] Signori Do Calogero Alongi
Noi venimo apregarlo che uni fano metto di bisogno una piccola somma se lei la credi noi sembre ni contentermo di quelli che manda basta che non si fara il cuore piccolo che avra portato altrimenti avra uni spergio sopra di lei e sopra della bestiame e dei fieghi.
La somma nonmeno di quattro cento onsi sapiamo certo che lei le puo dare abadassi che se e bona noi ne contentermo di questa somma altrimenti perseremo noi, la moneta deve essere arigento e garo o sia biglietti Liri due e di cinque e cci rriordarem. Si non darini passo alla giustizia, il due giorni franghe deve mandare le denare ali monte di Santuario di lato deve venire una persona con uno faccioletto biango intesta come ariva si deve fermare vicino delli ccombanaro.
Se lei vuoli spare chi e che cci domanda questa somma siamo le picciotti gangitane e altri colleghe
basta adio e lo pregamo sembre

[6] ...diecimila abitanti fanno una clamorosa dimostrazione dinanzi al municipio. Ero assordato dal pubblico clamore, tutti mi gridavano innanzi acqua. Dieci mila abitanti che dovevano abbeverarsi, cuocere il cibo, e nettarsi con cinque penne d'acqua. Imprecazioni, brighe, e causa de'disordini familiari, una lurida fonte ove occurreva tenervi una guardia, giacchè una libbra d'acqua era una quistione...L'acqua esisteva, la Comune aveva spesa 9000 ducati per portarla al paese, una mano rapace, e la inerzia amministrativa faceva commettere la più turpe delle frodi a carico di una popolazione, dell'ordine pubblico, della giustizia e decorosità del Governo e suo rappresentante. A due mila circa al luogo detto Pozzillo sin dal 1790 erasi costruito un condotto reale che riunendo in una cinta varie sorgive, e che per condotti diversi si portavano in Castellammare circa 30 penne d'acqua potabile, e per tanto effetuirsi la Comune aveva speso Ducati 9000. Il condotto reale passava per mezzo al fondo della famiglia Marcantonio che con impudenza senza pari ostruisce il condotto al di là della di lui casa di campagna, eseguisce un taglio nella parte superiore del condotto, e si serve delle acque per inaffia-

mento de' di lui giardini, formandovi in una delle bocche di luce un pozzo, e dal quale vendeva per un grano a cosi della quartara, e se ne aveva formata ancora un oggetto di specolazione, in modo che gli abitanti dovevano pagare l'animale da basto e l'acqua se non volevano perire.

7 ...i medesimi individui gli attribuiscono una pretotenza nel paese quand' egli facendo uso dei dritti nell'esercizio dei piati dominicali si richiama la proprietà che altri possiede—diritto neramente civile che i suoi titoli e la legge imperante gli permettono.

9 Nel 1881 io era agente di P.S. e il Di Chiara mi riferiva un giorno di avere un giardino di 15 tumuli e che cercava un agente di P.S. che avesse spogliato la divisa per adibirlo a guardia del fondo. Mi offersi io. Egli mi disse che Salvatore ed Emanuele Amoroso gli avevano rubato più di 10000 limoni. L'indomani venne il Salvatore che era stato prima di me guardiano e mi disse: che cosa fate qui?—Guardo il fondo—risposi. Egli brontolando se ne andò—e poi ritornò la dimane. Una notte intesi uno strepito: alla mattina un signore si presentò a mia moglie e le disse che lasciasse il luogo, se non voleva perdere la vita. Un giorno venne Salvatore e confabulò col Di Chiara, dopo di che costui mi licenziò con una scusa qualunque.

10 Presidente: Ma quando gli Amoroso erano custodi del giardino vi mancò qualche cosa?
Teste: Si, ma erano gente di fuori.
Presidente: E perchè prendeste un ex-questurino per guardinao?
Teste: Nessun'altro voleva venire. Per zappare si, ma per guardiani non ne trovavo mai.

13 Vincenzo Catanzaro prima era poverissimo, latitante, ora ha terra, una grossa mandria di vacche e di pecore, una casa nouva in cui s'incontra con brutte facce che vengono da ogni parte.

14 ...circa due miliardi... è stata poi valutata l'eredità lasciata da Nino Cottone da Villabate, ex garzone macellaio.

17 Questi malviventi per la loro arditezza e malvagita hanno generato tale timore nell'animo dei proprietari da fare occultare reati gravissimi che sono stati perpetrati a danno di quest'ultimi.
Per esempio, confidenzialmente son venuto a sapere che molte lettere di scrocco furono dirette a diversi signori di qui, ma nessuno volle denunziare il reato.

19 Questo delegato capo ha oggi stesso spedito a codesto Sig. Procuratore

del Re una dichiarazione testimoniale comprovante la pressione e le minacce che si fanno da Pietro e Giorgio fratello e figlio dell'arrestanto Guiseppe Valenza da Prizzi verso i testimoni fiscali indotti nelle varie processure pendenti a carico di quest' ultimo.

[20] Teste Cammarata: Nol rammento.
Presidente: Voi avete l'aria di chi ha poca voglia di dire la varità.

[26] Non siamo ribelli, come lei pensa, ma veri uomini d'ordine.

[27] Quando sarà vecchio, tanto vecchio, e massaro Turi, il capo-mafia, non sarà più, forse giudicherà meglio questo massaro e penserà che le sue leggi, non di Stato, erano leggi di natura ed egli le applicava in buona fede... Mi stringa la mano: sono un galantuomo!

[28] Il fatto è... che in ogni società ci deve essere una categoria di persone che aggiustano le situazioni, quando si fanno complicate.

[31] Il Questore di Caltanissetta, ricevendo nel giugno 1949 alcuni contadini e gli onorevoli La Marca e Colajanni, meravigliato delle proteste di costoro contro le violenze commesse dai mafiosi della zona nell'ex-feudo Pescazzo, ebbe a fare l'apologia della mafia (benemerita, secondo lui, dell'ordine pubblico e tutrice della pace sociale) esclamando: I mafiosi sono uomini di stato con quattro linee nel cervello.

[37] Corleone:
feudo Donna Beatrice di 32 salme, proprietari i fratelli Palazzo che sono stati più volte sequestrati, gabellotto Lo Bue Carmelo noto e pericoloso capo mafia di Corleone, già cacerato e confinato.
Feudo S. Ippolito di 415 ettari, proprietario il cavaliere Antonio Ferrara, soprastante, (ma forse qualche cosa di più del soprastante data la clandestinità dei rapporti e quindi la mancanza di informazioni precese sulla vera natura del contratto) Leggio Francesco, noto mafioso, attualmente confinato.
Feudo Rao di 50 salme, proprietaria la vedova Mangiameli, gabellotto Pennino Michele, il cui padre fu ucciso in circostanze drammatiche in America, noto mafioso, arrestato varie volte e latitante per lunghi periodi.
Feudo Chiatti, proprietario il signor Provenzano, gabellotto Sabella Mariano, pregiudicato e confinato.
Feudo Patria di 180 salme, proprietario il duca Papà di Pratameno, gabellotto Leggio Biagio, mafioso, cinque anni di confino scontati, attualmente detenuto.
Feudo Strasatto, proprietario il signor Pappalardo, gabellotto Liggio Luciano, noto mafioso latitante con mandato di cattura per molti reati.

Roccamena:

Feudo Caffarinni, di 170 ettari, proprietario il cavaliere Giambalvo, gabellotti Di Giovanni, Cliccia, fratelli Raimondi, Cirrincione, noti mafiosi pericolosi.

Feudo Gamberi di 159 ettari, proprietaria Sparacio Mirto Serafina, gabellotti Giornado Leonardo e Casato Gioacchino, attualmente confinati.

Feudo Galardo di 300 ettari, gabellotto Collura Vincenzo detto Criscione e il figlio di questi, mafiosi...

[38] ...come accadono i furti escono i mediatori ad offrire transazione pel ricuperamento degli oggetti involati. Il numero di tali accordi è infinito.

[39] ...mentre l'Autorità chiede al derubato di parlare (il che non è sempre igienico), la mafia gli chiede semplicemente di tacere (il che è indubbiamente più comodo e più utile)...

[40] Alquanto strana e misteriosa sembra sul momento la deplorata estorsione...Si chiedono L. 8000, se ne mandano invece L. 370 e si n'e contenti senz'altro...Il giorno convenuto nella lettera minatoria era il Giovedi 1 luglio e invece si mandò il danaro il Venerdi successivo, e i quattro che saranno dovuti trovarsi al luogo designato il Giovedi si trovano ancor li il seguente Venerdi...

Insomma è un insieme di circostanze che rende la cosa alquanto strana e misteriosa...

[41] Viene uno e dice:—Ho la questione col Tizio, vede se può accordare la cosa—. Chiamo la persona interessata, o vado a trovarlo io, a seconda dei rapporti, e li accordo.

[42] Se una persona ha bisogno di farsi rilasciare un documento, una carta, quasi sempre si rivolgono più a lui (Russo) che al Comune. Ci fa un biglietto e subito il sindaco...Per avere un certificato una donna deve aspettare sei mesi, certe volte mancano gli impiegati qui o là, e lui ci va e fanno tutto subito.

[43] Vidi tra gli altri candidati il signor Gen. Alfonso Scalia ...che faceva parte della famiglia di cui ero il bersaglio. Io mi chiusi in casa per non essere assassinato.

[44] Nella notte dell' 11 Novembre 1878, Francesco Ci Marco venne fatto segno a colpi d'arma da fuoco, e tosto s'indicanno colpevoli Rappa Antonio mandante, La Bue Nicolò mandatario, causa a delinquere gare di elezioni amministrative...

[47] Circa 200 schede...sono scritte in forme diverse e con titoli e qualificativi molteplici, intrecciati in modo che nessuna scheda è uguale all'altra! Cosi si legge: Saporito Ricca, Saporito Caimi, Saporito Gagliano, Commendatore, Deputato, ex Consigliere Provinciale, Barone, ex sottosegretario al tesoro, ecc. ecc. Cosi il segreto del voto fu totalmente evitato.

[51] Verso le ore 12 meridione del 19 Agosto p.p. il Maresciallo a piedi De Marchi Carlo, Comandante la Stazione di Montemaggiore, venne richiesto di Ufficio dal Signor Legrenzi Giuseppe, presidente di quel seggio elettorale, ad intervenire armato con due dipendenti nella sala delle elezioni amministrative, onde mantenervi l'ordine, alquanto turbato per quistioni di partito, dagli elettori Salemi Cav. Gaetano... farmacista, e Chianchiana Gaetano...proprietario, entrambi del luogo.

Appena la forza suddetta mise piedi nella sala, il presidente ordinò ad essa die fare allontanare da vicino al seggio i due accenati ellettori, i quali invitati perciò con modi urbani ad obbedire si rifiutarono, dicendo aver diritto di stare colà, e nel contempo vennero a parole col ripetuto presidente, il quale ne ordinò l'arresto...

[52] A Corleone ancora si parla degli elettori ciechi di Navarra; il giorno delle elezioni, centinaia(!) di uomini e donne sono diventati ciechi; fingevano di avere perduto la vista per dare modo ai mafiosi di Navarra di accompagnarli nella cabina elettorale e controllare il voto. (Pantaleone 1962 S. 140.)

[55] La gente chiedono come votare perchè sentono il dovere di consigliarsi per mostrare un senso di gratitudine, di riconoscenza, si sentono all'oscuro e vogliono adattarsi alle persone che gli hanno fatto bene.

[56] Per la campagna elettorale del '46, Bernardo Mattarella è arrivato nella mattinata a Salemi con cinque o sei macchine di persone di cui la maggioranza dell'Aspetto mafioso. Disceso in piazza Libertà, si è subito incontrato con alcuni che lo aspettavano: si è formato un gruppo in cui erano Mattarella, Santo Robino, capomafia di Salemi; Ignazio Salvo fu Alberto, notissimo pregiudicato; Vincenzo Mangogna, pericolossissimo mafioso irruente, condannato per assasinio; Luigi Salvo fu Alberto, ritornato dall'America; Foreddu Robino, che fu poi ucciso in America implicato nella droga; Alberto Agueci, mafioso che è stato poi assassinato in America, arrostito, sempre per la droga; Mariano Licari, grosso mafioso di Marsala, ora in carcere per sequestro di persona. Più lontani da Mattarella stavano mafiosi di mezzo calibro, curiosi, galoppini elettorali.

Mattarella e gli altri, dopo essersi salutati calorosamente, sono rimasti a parlare un po' di fronte agli occhi di tutta la popolazione e poi si sono avviati alla sede della democrazia cristiana...dopo un poco Matteralla è salito sul balcone del professor Favara a tenere il comizio. Erano sul balcone con lui Ignazio Salvo, qualche altro mafioso e il segretario della DC di quel tempo.

[57] A fine maggio, in occasione della campagna elettorale, lui (Genco Russo), il ministro Zaccagnini e l'onorevole Lanza sono stati a cena assieme e poi sono usciti a braccetto assieme.

[59] Mancino si presenta di giorno e si presenta anche di notte, per farsi meno vedere in certi casi; e certo di notte, se uno sente picchiare alla porta, e vede lì Mancino...chi può sapere le intenzioni di questa gente?

[60] Alia è un centro di mafia. I voti per Mattarella qui ad Alia sono saliti, sono quasi esattamente raddoppiati passando da 203 a 403, quando Ditta Vincenzo, capo-mafia amico intimo di Genco Russo, e Matteo Vallone, pure vecchio mafioso molto attivo negli abigeati e nel feudo con più di quindici anni tra carcere e confino, sono diventati i suoi capi elettori, cioè poco prima delle elezioni del '58. Mentre nel dopoguerra questi mafiosi, sol loro gruppo, sostenevano liberali e monarchici, per il '58 facevano distribuire e distribuivano loro stessi. andando casa per casa, facsimili dove era segnato il numero ed il nome di Mattarella...E molta gente diceva si, e molti impauriti, finivano per votare come dicevano loro. Andavano nelle case anche di notte, per intimorire di più.

7 Mafiosi and gangsters

[2] Egli aveva accettato lo incarico, a patto però che si versasse, come si versò in di lui mani, anticipatamente, la convenuta somma di 300 onze, pari a L. 3825. Se non che, venuto il momento di agire, drasi oltremodo soggezionato del Valenza, persona di ricco censo e temibilissimo per relazioni di mafia, cosichè, unite a detta somma altra 300 Lire, di cui lo Atoma disponeva, piuttosto che attentare alla vita del Valenza, si provvide di passaporto all'estero, e se ne fuggi in America.

Fatto ritorno in Italia, collo intendimento di spedire a Nuova York un carico di carrube e di legumi col denaro che gli rimaneva, ed aprire di tal guisa un traffico di simili generi coll'America, ove poscia avrebbe definitivamente emigrato...

[3] Un giorno Conti, del quale ero ospite, mi pregò di eliminare un tale, uomo pericoloso e senza scrupoli, che si era macchiato di tanti e gravi delitti.

[4] Tutti i capi sono feroci. Se non si è feroci non si diventa capi.

[5] Gentile: ...il potere era già nelle mie mani.
Chilanti: In che consisteva il suo potere?
Gentile: Avevo organizzato un gruppo di giovani per proteggere i siciliani. Quei giovani erano al mio comando.

[9] Risposi reaffermando che il Chiappetta era mio compare, al quale avevo battezzato una figlia nel periodo in cui mi trovavo a Pittsburgh. (Gentile 1963 S. 77).

[10] Informai Vincenzo Mangano che mi si presentava l'occasione per potermi associare negli affari a Charles La Gaipa, il quale avrebbe messo tutti i capitali necessari per l'acquisto della merce e mi avrebbe dato il 40% degli utili.— Lascio te arbitro di dividerli,—dissi,—fra te, Joe Biondo, Anastasia e me.

[12] Dan Seritella per dodici anni senatore dell'Illinois era in rapporti di amicizia e di affari con i gangster che avevano pagato le spese della sua elezione come del resto accadeva in altri luoghi e per altri personaggi. Il senatore Roland Libonati, democratico, e il deputato dell'Illinois James Adducci risultarono amici personali di numerosi gangster.

[14] In men che non si dica, non badando a spese, penetrai in tutti gli ambienti di Kansas City e mi guadagnai la stima della popolazione e l'amicizia del sindaco.
Per mezzo del suo segretario particolare, un giovane ebreo sveglio e attivo, proposi al sindaco un affare nel quale doveva diventare mio socio. Cosi, sotto l'egida della sua protezione, operavo sicuro.

[15] Il quartiere, malfamato, era continuamente sorvegliato da un forte gruppo di poliziotti, i quali venivano nel locale, bevevano un whisky e ricevevano la 'mazzetta'. Lo stesso aveniva per quelli che facevano la sorveglianza notturna. Inoltre vi era un altro gruppo di agenti, composto da 15 detectives della squadra omicidi, che ci assicuravano protezione. Al loro comandante venivano dati 500 dollari al mese.

8 Conclusion

[5] Alla mafia bisogna davvero dei colpi radicali, e darli in via eccezionale.

[6] funzionari che nell'esercizio del loro ministero non subiscano né influenze, né intimidazioni.

⁷ Certo un azzardoso e terribile esperimento è quello che da anni si sta facendo dal nuovo Governo nazionale, quello cioè di governare popoli come questi, e che hanno le deplorabili abitudini di sopra accennate, con leggi ed ordinamenti all'inglese o alla belga, che suppongono un popolo colto e morale come colà, o come almeno nella parte superiore della peninsola.

⁸ Tutti oggi ripetono decentramento, ma pochi per avventura se ne formano un criterio pratico, organico, adatto al nostro clima storico. Si inneggia al self-gevernment inglese e si dimentica che esso in Inghilterra è il prodotto vivo, spontaneo, storico, della coscienza pubblica e non l'importazione, il fiat d'una legge qualsiasi soprapponentesi ad una società impreperata.

⁹ A porre un freno ed a diminuire gli effetti che la società risente per l'esistenza d'uomini cosi pericolosi, amio avviso, giova ricorrere a quattro mezzi: alla diffusione del popolare insegnamento nel senso però che nelle pubbliche scuole non si coltivi soltanto la mente, ma eziandio il cuore dei giovani...

¹² Giuro di essere fedele al Re e ai suoi Reali successori, di osservare lealmente lo Statuto e le leggi dello Stato, di adempiere alle mie funzioni da uomo di onore e di coscienza e di difendere i beni e le persone affidate alla mia tutela con ogni mia forza a norma di legge, di diritto e di morale, con intransigenza assoluta, in leale solidarietà coi miei compagni e in rigorosa obbedienza alle Autorità preposte alla tutela della pubblica sicurezza.

¹³ La lotta non doveva essere campagna di polizia in più o meno grande stile, ma insurrenzione di coscienza, rivolta di spiriti, azione di popolo.

¹⁴ Era mio fermo proposito non dare ai banditi l'onore delle armi. Non volevo che ancora una volta la malvivenza si aureolasse di prestigio, di coraggio e magari di martirio, attraverso un combattimento con la forza pubblica. Non soltanto io intendevo vincere, cioè assicurare i banditi alla giustizia; ma volevo dare alle popolazioni la tangibile prova della viltà della malvivenza.

La misura era colma: oltre il danno, anche lo sfregio.

La rapidità dell'azione e la veramente ingloriosa fine del banditismo delle Madonie, già ricco di tanto pauroso prestigio e di tante leggende, ebbe immediata e profonda ripercussione in tutta l'Isola.

¹⁵ ...non teme il carcere quanto la scuola...non teme il giudice quanto il maestro.

¹⁶ Dal 1926 i maestri siciliani hanno cooperato con l'Opera Nazionale Balilla, insegnando che l'omertà non è una virtù dell'uomo, che le leggi del paese sono superiori alle vendette private, e, in breve, che le tradizioni della mafia erano retrograde e del tutto indegne degli ideali di Mussolini e della nuova Italia.

Bibliography

Agresti, Olivia Rossetti and Sellin, Thorsten, 'Mafia', in *Encyclopaedia Britannica*, Chicago-London-Toronto 1960, vol. xiv, pp. 619–20

Ajello, A., *Angelo Pugliesi ovvero Don Peppino il Lombardo*, Palermo 1868

Albini, Joseph L., *The American Mafia: Genesis of a Legend*, New York 1971

Alessi, Giuseppe *et al.*: Memoria Illustrativa per Galizia Luigi (Padre Carmelo), Jahma Antonio (Padre Agrippino), Morotto Liborio (Padre Venanzio). Corte Suprema di Cassazione. Sezione Prima Penale. Udienza del giorno 10 febbraio 1965

Alongi, Giuseppe, 'Mafia. Appunti di uno studio', in *Archivio di Psichiatria Scienze penali ed Antropologia criminale*, vol. vi, 1885, pp. 430–40 and vol. vii, 1886, pp. 131–50; *La Maffia nei suoi fattori e nelle sue manifestazioni. Studio sulle classi pericolose della Sicilia*, Turin 1887; *La camorra. Studio di Sociologia criminale*, Turin 1890; *L'abigeato in Sicilia. Studi di patologia sociale*, Marsala 1891; 'Le condizioni economiche e sociali della Sicilia', in *Archivio di Psichiatria...* vol. xv, 1894, pp. 229–55; *Polizia di sicurezza e polizia rurale*, Palermo 1899

Amari, Michele, *Storia dei musulmani in Sicilia*, Catania 1939, vol. iv

Anderson, Robert T., 'From Mafia to Cosa Nostra', in *American Journal of Sociology*, November 1965, pp. 302–10

Anonymous: *Il brigante calabrese in Sicilia Angelo Pugliese*, no date.

Anonymous: *La mafia*, no date. Manuscript in the Biblioteca della Società Siciliana per la Storia Patria in Palermo.

Arcoleo, Giuseppe, *Palermo e la cultura in Sicilia*, Milan 1907

Atti della Giunta per la Inchiesta Agraria e sulle condizioni della classe agricola, vol. xiii, book ii: *Condizioni morali e relazioni sociali dei contadini siciliani* (Relazione Damiani), Rome 1885

Avellone, G.B. and Morasca, S., *Mafia*, Rome 1911

Ballola, R. Carlo and Narzisi, G., *Il grano rosso. Vita e morte di Salvatore Carnevale*, Milan-Rome 1956

Banfield, Edward C., *The Moral Basis of a Backward Society*, Glencoe 1958

Barzini, Luigi, *The Italians*, Bantam edition, New York 1965

Bell, Daniel 'Crime as an American Way of Life', in *The Antioch Review* 13, 1953, pp. 131–54

Blok, Anton, 'Mafia and Peasant Rebellion as Contrasting Factors in Sicilian Latifundism', in *European Journal of Sociology*, vol. x (1969), pp. 95–116

Boissevain, Jeremy, *Poverty and Politics in a Sicilian Agro-Town*, unpublished manuscript 1964; 'Patronage in Sicily', in *Man*, vol. i no. i, March 1966

Briatico, Franco, 'Il problema storico della mafia', in *Terzo programma*, vol. i, 1963, Rome 1963

Bruno, Cesare, *La Sicilia e la mafia*, Rome 1900

Caizzi, Bruno (ed.), *Antologia della questione meridionale*, Milan 1950

Cammareri Scurti, Sebastiano, 'La lotta di classe nei proverbi siciliani', in *Critica sociale*, 1 August 1896; 'Crispismo e socialismo in Sicilia', in *Critica sociale*, 16 April 1898

Candida, Renato, *Questa mafia*, Caltanissetta-Rome 1960

Capuana, Luigi, *La Sicilia e il brigantaggio*, Rome 1902

Caso, Gemma, *Giambattista Falcone e la setta dei fratelli Pugnalatori*, Foggia 1908

Chilanti, Felice, 'Non c'è alibi che valga per il boss di Mussomeli', in *L'Ora* of 19 and 20 February 1964

Chilanti, Felice and Farinella, Mario, *Rapporto sulla mafia*, Palermo 1964

Ciasca, Raffaele, 'Mafia', in *Enciclopedia Italiana*, Rome 1934–42, vol xxi, p. 863

Colajanni, Napoleone, *La delinquenza in Sicilia e le sue cause*, Palermo 1885; 'La mafia' (Dai Borboni ai Sabaudi), in *Rivista Popolare*, Rome, 15 December 1899; 'Im Reiche der Mafia', in *Die Zeit*, nos. 275/77/79, Vienna, January-February 1900; 'Lo spirito della mafia', in *La propaganda*, Naples, 7 August 1902

Corso, Raffaele, 'Omertà', in *Enciclopedia Italiana*, Rome 1934–42, vol. xxv, p. 345

Cosentino, Giuseppe, *Nuovi documenti sulla inquisizione in Sicilia*, Palermo 1885

Costanza, Salvatore, 'Una inchiesta poco nota sulla mafia', in *Nuovi quaderni del meridione*, vol. ii, no. 5, March 1964, pp. 56ff; 'La rivolta contro i "Cutrara" a Castellammare del Golfo (1862)', in *Nuovi quaderni del meridione*, no. 16, Oct.-Dec. 1966, pp. 1–20

Cressey, Donald R., *Theft of the Nation: The structure and operations of organized crime in America*, New York, Evanston and London, 1969; 'The National and Local Structures of Organized Crime', in Cressey, Donald R., and Ward, David, *Delinquency, Crime, and Social Process*, New York, Evanston and London 1969, pp. 867–83; 'Delinquent and Criminal Structures', in Merton, Robert K., and Nisbet, Robert, *Contemporary Social Problems*, New York 1971, pp. 147–83; *Criminal Organization: Its Elementary Forms*, London 1972

Cutrera, Antonio, *La mafia ed i mafiosi. Origine e manifestazioni*, Studio di Sociologia Criminale, Palermo 1900; 'La mala vita di Palermo', *Contributo di Sociologia Criminale*, Palermo 1900; *Varsalona, il suo regno e le sue gesta delittuose*, Rome 1904

D'Alessandro, Enzo, *Brigantaggio e mafia in Sicilia*, Messina-Florence 1959

Davidson, Bill, 'How the Mob Controls Chicago', in *Saturday Evening Post*, 9 November 1963, pp. 22–5

Denti di Pirajno, Alberto, *Mara Lumera. Roman der Mafia*, Munich 1965

Di Menza, Giuseppe, *Cronache delle Assisi di Palermo*, vol. ii, Palermo 1878

Direzione Generale della Statistica, *Statistica Giudiziaria Penale per l'anno 1893*, Rome 1895

Dolci, Danilo, *Spreco. Documenti e inchieste su alcuni aspetti dello spreco nella Sicilia occidentale*, Turin 1960; *Umfrage in Palermo*, Berlin 1961; *Conversazioni*, Turin 1962; *Chi gioca solo*, Turin 1966

Dumas, Alessandro, *I Garibaldini. Scene, impressioni e ricordi della spedizione dei Mille*, Milan, no date

Duyzings, Martin W., *Mafia. Macht und Geheimnis der 'Schwarzen Hand'*, Frankfurt/M-Berlin 1964

Enciclopedia Universale Illustrata, article 'mafia', vol. xiii, p. 532, Milan 1954

Falcone, Giuseppe, *Mafia e omertà*, Conferenza tenuta il giorno 3 Febbraio 1895 nel Circolo Calabrese in Napoli, Avellino 1895

La Fiamma, *Organo settimanale dei nazionalisti siciliani*, Palermo, 11 March 1923

Fiumanò, A., and Villari, R., 'Politica e malavita', in *Cronache Meridionali*, no. 10, October 1955, pp. 653–63

Franchetti, Leopoldo, *Condizioni politiche e amministrative della Sicilia*, vol. i of Leopoldo Franchetti and Sidney Sonnino, *La Sicilia nel 1876*, Florence 1925

Frank, Stanley, 'The Rap Gangsters Fear Most', in *Saturday Evening Post*, 9 August 1958, pp. 26–8

Friedmann, Frederic G., *The Hoe and the Book*, Ithaca, New York 1960 'The World of la miseria', in *Partisan Review*, March-April 1963, pp. 220–32

Gaja, Filippo, *L'esercito della lupara*, Milan 1962

Garufi, C. A., *Contributo alla storia della inquisizione di Sicilia nei secoli XVI e XVII. Note ed appunti degli archivi di Espagna*, Palermo 1920

Gatto, Simone, 'Attualità di una inchiesta del 1876', in *Belfagor*, 1950, no. 2, pp. 229–33

Gentile, Nick, *Vita di capomafia*, Rome 1963

Giornale di Sicilia (Palermo daily newspaper) 21 October 1877 (Benedetto Scalia) and 10 September 1878 (Bandits Biagio, Di Carlo and Salpietra)

Guarinio, Crescenzo, 'Antologia della mafia', in *Nord e Sud*, no. 12, November 1955, pp. 63–84; 'Dai mafiosi ai camorristi', in *Nord e Sud*, no. 13, December 1955, pp. 76–106

Gullo, Stefano, *La mafia–ieri–oggi*, Palermo 1963

Hammer, Marius, *Probleme der sizilianischen Agrarstruktur*, Basel-Tübingen 1965

Hawkins, Gordon, 'God and the Mafia', in Knudten, Richard D., *Crime,*

Criminology, and Contemporary Society, Homewood, Ill. 1970, pp. 83–105
Hobsbawm, E. J., *Primitive Rebels. Studies in Archaic Forms of Social Movement in the 19th and 20th Centuries,* Manchester 1959; *Bandits,* London 1969
Hofstätter, Peter R., *Einführung in die Sozialpsychologie,* Stuttgart 1963
Ianni, Frances A. J. and Elizabeth, A., *Family Business,* Routledge & Kegan Paul, London 1972
Inchiesta Parlamentare sulle condizioni dei contadini delle province meridionali (Inchiesta Lorenzoni), Rome 1909, vol. vii
Kefauver, Estes, *Crime in America,* Garden City, New York 1951
(Kefauver Committee) Special Committee to Investigate Crime in Interstate Commerce, *Third Interim Report,* U.S. Senate Report No. 307, 82nd Congress, 1st session, 1951
Kennedy, Robert F., *The Enemy Within,* New York 1960
La mafia a Palermo. Memoriale della Federazione Communista di Palermo presentato alla Commissione Parlamentare d'Inchiesta sulla Mafia, Palermo 1963
La Mantia, Vito, *Origine e vicende dell'inquisizione in Sicilia,* Rome, Turin, Florence 1886; *L'inquisizione in Sicilia,* Palermo 1904
La Masa, Giuseppe, *Documenti della rivoluzione siciliana,* Turin 1850
Lepsius, M. Rainer, 'Immobilismus: das System der sozialen Stagnation in Süditalien', in *Jahrbücher für Nationalökonomik und Statistik,* vol. 177, no. 4, 1965
Lestingi, Giuseppe, 'L'associazione della fratellanza nella provincia di Girgenti', in *Archivio di Psichiatria,* vol. v, 1884, pp. 452–63
Lewis, Norman, *The Honoured Society. The Mafia Conspiracy Observed,* London 1964
Lionti, Ferdinando, *Antiche maestranze della città di Palermo,* Palermo 1886
Llaryora, Roberto, *Die sizilianische Mafia: Frühe Strukturen und soziale Dynamik in der Epoche der spanischen Herrschaft* (16. und 17. Jhdt.), forthcoming.
Lognone, Riccardo, 'Leggende e realtà della "ndraghita", I legami politici e sociali della mafia calabrese', in *L'Unità,* 8 September 1955, p. 2
Longo, Giuseppe, 'La nostra cara mafia', in *L'osservatore politico-letterario,* vol. iii, no. 4, April 1957, pp. 48–62
Loschiavo, Giuseppe Guido, 'Nel regno della mafia', in *Processi,* no. 5, January 1955; *Terra amara (La trilogia della siepe: Piccola Pretura, Condotta di paese, Gli inesorabili),* Rome 1956; *Piccola Pretura,* Rome 1962; 'La mafia della lupara e quella dei colletti bianchi', in *Nuovo quaderni del meridione,* no. 4, 1963; *100 anni di mafia,* Rome 1964
Maas, Peter, *The Valachi Papers,* New York 1968
Maggiorani, V., *Il sollevamento della plebe di Palermo nel 1866,* Palermo 1869

Marchesano, Giuseppe, *Corte di Assise di Bologna. Processo contro Raffaele Palizzolo e C.i, Arringa dell'Avv. G. Marchesano*, Resoconto Stenografico, Palermo 1902

Marino, Giuseppe C., *L'opposizione mafiosa (1870–1882). Baroni e mafia contro lo stato liberale*, Palermo 1964

Maxwell, Gavin, *Wer erschoss Salvatore Giuliano?*, Hamburg 1963

Mayer, Adrian C., 'The Significance of Quasi-Groups in the Study of Complex Societies', in Michael Banton (ed.), *The Social Anthropology of Complex Societies*, A.S.A. Monographs, Edinburgh 1966, pp. 97–122

McClellan, John L., *Crime Without Punishment*, New York 1963

(McClellan Committee) Hearings before the Permanent Subcommittee on Investigations of the Senate Committee on Government Operations, 88th Congress, 1st session, 1963

Mercadante Carrara, I., *La delinquenza in Sicilia nelle sue forme più gravi e specifiche*, Palermo 1911

Merlino, F. S., *Questa è l'Italia*, Milan 1953

Mischi, Archimede, *La Mafia, relativamente agli instituti di confino ed alle colonie agricolo-militari*, Palermo 1928

Montalbano, Giuseppe, 'La mafia e il banditismo', in *Rinascita*, no. 10, October 1953; 'La mafia a occhio nudo', in *Il Mondo*, 9 December 1958

Montanelli, Indro, *Pantheon minore*, Milan 1958

Mori, Cesare, *Con la mafia ai ferri corti*, Verona 1932

Mosca, Gaetano, 'Mafia', in *Encyclopedia of the Social Sciences*, vol. ix–x, pp. 36–8; *Partiti e sindicati nella crisi del sistema parlamentare*, Bari 1949

Mühlmann, Wilhelm Emil, *Homo Creator. Abhandlungen zur Soziologie, Anthropologie und Ethnologie*, Wiesbaden 1962; 'Zur Sozialpsychologie der Mafia', in *Kölner Ztschr. für Soziologie*, no. 21, 1969 pp. 289–303 and Müller, Ernst W. (ed.), *Kulturanthropologie*, Cologne 1966; and Roberto Llaryora, *Klientschaft, Klientel und Klientelsystem in einer sizilianischen Agrostadt*, Tübingen 1968

Nicotri, Gaspare, *Rivoluzioni e rivolte in Sicilia, Studio di Sociologia Storica*, Turin 1910

Notarbartolo, Leopoldo, *Memorie della vita di mio padre, Emanuele Notarbartolo di San Giovanni*, Pistoia 1949

Novacco, Domenico, 'La mafia nella struttura sociale siciliana', in *La terza sponda*, vol. i, no. 6, November 1955; 'Considerazioni sulla fortuna del termine "mafia"', in *Belfagor*, vol. xiv, Messina-Florence 1959, pp. 206–12; *Inchiesta sulla mafia*, Milan 1963

Nuovi quaderni del meridione, vol. ii, no. 5, Palermo, January-March 1964

Onufrio, E., 'La mafia in Sicilia', in *Nuova Antologia*, February 1877, pp. 361–71

L'Ora (Palermo daily newspaper) 13, 14, 16, 17 and 20 July 1962 (Monks of

Mazzarino), 26, 27, 29 September and 1, 4, 7 October 1966 (Relazione della Commissione Antimafia sui mercati di Palermo)

Orilia, Salvatore, *Mafia tra documento e letteratura*, Palermo 1965

Pace, Mario, *La mafia (a Cesare Mori)*, Palermo 1928

Pagano, Giacomo, *La Sicilia nel 1876–77*, Palermo 1877

Palazzolo, Salvatore, *La mafia delle coppole storte*, Florence 1958

Pantaleone, Michele, *Mafia e politica 1943–62. Le radici sociali della mafia e i suoi sviluppi più recenti*, Turin 1962

Petrai, Giuseppe, *Il romanzo di un bandito*, Milan 1900

Pitré, Giuseppe, *Usi e costumi, credenze e pregiudizi del popolo siciliano*, vol. ii, Palermo 1889; 'L'omertà', in *Archivio di Psichiatria...*, vol. x, 1889, pp. 1–7

Pitt-Rivers, Julian A., *The People of the Sierra*, Chicago and London 1961

Poma, Rosario and Perrone, Enzo, *Quelli della lupara. Rapporto sulla mafia di ieri e di oggi*, Florence 1964

Pontieri, Ernesto, *Il tramonto del baronaggio siciliano*, Florence 1943; *Il riformismo borbonico nella Sicilia del sette e dell'ottocento*, Rome 1945

Processo Catalfamo, Corte d'Assise Ordinaria, 6.–17. Aprile 1880, Tipografia del Giornale di Sicilia, Palermo 1880

Processo dei fratelli Amoroso e compagni. Resoconto del Giornale di Sicilia, Palermo 1883

Puzo, Mario, *The Godfather*, New York 1969

Ramistella, Francesco, 'Mafia ed abigeato in Sicilia. Appunti e considerazioni di un ex-funzionario di P. S.', undated newspaper cutting in the Biblioteca Comunale of Palermo

Reckless, Walter C., *The Crime Problem*, New York 1950 (esp. chapter 7: 'Organized Crime', pp. 142–160)

Redfield, Robert, 'The "Folk" Society', in *Human Nature and the Study of Society. The Papers of Robert Redfield*, vol. i, Chicago 1962, pp. 231–53.

Reid, Ed, *Mafia*, New York 1964

Renda, Francesco, 'Funzione e basi sociali della mafia', *Il movimento contadino nella società siciliana*, Palermo 1956, pp. 205–20

Romano, Salvatore F., *Storia della questione meridionale*, Palermo 1945; *Storia dei Fasci siciliani*, Bari 1959; *Storia della mafia* (edizione 'I Record'), Verona 1966

Rumpelt, Alexander, *Sicilien und die Sicilianer*, Berlin 1902

Russo, Nado (ed.), *Antologia della mafia. Documenti inediti, dibattiti parlamentari, inchieste, saggi, dai primi anni dell'unità ad oggi, su uno dei più gravi problemi ancora non risolti della società italiana*, Palermo 1964

Salerno, Ralph, and Tompkins, John S., *The Crime Confederation: Cosa Nostra and Allied Operations in Organized Crime*, New York 1969

Salvemini, Gaetano, *Il ministro della mala vito e altri scritti sull'Italia gio-littina*, Milan 1962

Sansone, V. and Ingrasci, G., *6 anni di banditismo in Sicilia*, Milan 1950

Scalici, Emanuele, *Cavalleria di Porta Montalto e la mafia siciliana*, Naples 1885

Scherma, Giuseppe, *Delle maestranze in Sicilia. Contributo allo studio della questione operaia*, Palermo 1896

Sciascia, Leonardo, 'La mafia', *Pirandello e la Sicilia*, pp. 163–80, Caltanissetta-Rome 1961; *Appunti su mafia e letteratura*, Palermo 1964; *Der Tag der Eule*, Freiburg im Breisgau 1964; *I mafiosi di Giuseppe Rizzotto, libero adattamento di Leonardo Sciascia*, stage manuscript of the Piccolo Teatro of Milan

Sereni, Emilio, *Il capitalismo nelle campagne 1860–1900*, Turin 1947

Smith, Denis Mack, *Storia d'Italia dal 1861 al 1958*, Bari 1959

Sondern, Frederic Jr., 'Brotherhood of Evil', *The Mafia*, Montreal 1959

Speciale, Giuseppe, *La mafia e l'opera del fascismo in Sicilia*, Trapani 1927

Steinmetz, Sebaldus R., 'Selbsthilfe', in Alfred Vierkandt (ed.), *Handwörterbuch der Soziologie*, Stuttgart 1931, pp. 518–22

Sutherland, Edwin H. and Cressey, Donald R., *Principles of Criminology*, Chicago-Philadelphia-New York 1960

Tambaro, Ignazio, 'I reati elettorali', in *Enciclopedia del diretto penale italiano*, vol. ii, Milan 1908, pp. 1001–69

Taormina, Francesco, 'Accuso la mafia', in *Eloquenza siciliana*, Palermo, March-June 1962, pp. 131–50

Task Force Report: Organized Crime, U.S. President's Commission on Law Enforcement and Administration of Justice, Washington 1967

Titone, Virgilio, *Considerazioni sulla mafia*, Palermo 1957; *Storia mafia e costume in Sicilia*, Milan 1964

Tocco, Matteo G., 'La mafia. Origine e carattere del fenomeno nel quadro politico e dell'ordine pubblico in Sicilia', *Quaderni Sala d'Ercole*, no. 10, Palermo March 1959

Tomasi di Lampedusa, Giuseppe, *Der Leopard*, Munich 1959 'Aufstieg eines Pächters', *Die Sirene und andere Erzählungen*, Munich 1963, pp. 45–67

Uccello, Antonino, *Carcere e mafia nei canti popolari siciliani*, Palermo 1965

Vaccaro, Angelo, 'La mafia', in *Rivista d'Italia*, anno II, vol. iii, Rome 1899, pp. 686–704

Vaina, Michele, *Popolarismo e Nasismo*, Florence 1911

Vierkandt, Alfred, *Gesellschaftslehre*, Stuttgart 1928

Villari, Pasquale, *Lettere meridionali*, Rome 1885

Weber, Max, *Wirtschaft und Gesellschaft. Grundriss der verstehenden Soziologie*, Cologne-Berlin 1964

Wermert, Georg, *Die Insel Sicilien in volkswirtschaftlicher, kultureller und sozialer Beziehung*, Berlin 1905

Archivio di Stato di Palermo, Gabinetto di Prefettura (ASP)

1839, without busta, cat. 20, fasc. 23 bis (Municipio of Collesano about campieri)

1874, busta 30, cat. 20, fasc. 20 (Sequestro nel territorio di Collesano del Barone Angelo Porcari)

1880, busta 55, cat. 20, fasc. 9 (Sulle propalazioni del detenuto Fazzino Giuseppe)

1880, busta 56, cat. 20, fasc. 15 (Estorsione in danno del Barone Callotti Antonio di Castelbuono)

1880, busta 56, cat. 20, fasc. 28 (Capi mafia di Montemaggiore con ramificazioni in altri comune persino con impiegati addetti alla Sotto-Prefettura di Termini Imerese)

1881, busta 63, cat. 20, fasc. 7 (Mancato assassinio di Rappa Antonino di Borgetto)

1881, busta 63, cat. 20, fasc. 15 (Lettere e documenti lasciati dal defunto Salvatore Marino-Rosario La Mantia)

1881, busta 63, cat. 20, fasc. 39 (Correspondence concerning Francesco Bonafede inteso Giorgiutano from Palermo on the Amoroso trial)

1881, busta 64, cat. 20, fasc. 62 (Tentata estorsione di L. 6000 in danno del Sig. Marchese Pietro Mancuso, Conte di Geraci)

1881, busta 64, cat. 20, fasc. 87 (Incendio nel Bosco Pomo a danno del Barone Oddo. Sambuca Zambut)

1881, busta 64, cat. 20, fasc. 146 (Misilmeri. Associazione di malfattori detta Palombella)

1882, busta 69, cat. 20, fasc. 20 (Ammonizione di Mazzarese Damiano e Cirrincione Giuseppe)

1882, busta 69, cat. 20, fasc. 121 (Disordini avvenuti in Montemaggiore in occasione delle elezioni amministrative)

1882, busta 69, cat. 20, fasc. 191 (Associazione di malfattori ad Altavilla)

1883, busta 72, cat. 20, fasc. 12 (Lettera anonima sul abigeato di Roccapalumba)

1983, busta 72, cat. 20, fasc. 98 (Lettera di scrocco al Barone Alongi Calogero di Petralia Soprana)

1884, busta 77, cat. 20, fasc. 20 (Borgetto. Guardie campestri)

1885, busta 83, cat. 20, fasc. 1 (Filippo Battaglia, manutengolo)

1885, busta 84, cat. 20, fasc. 55 (Biografie riferibli ai Signori Li Destri Antonino di Antonio e Milletari Alessandro di Michelangelo da Gangi)

1885, busta 85, cat. 20, fasc. 91 (Sullo stato della pubblica sicurezza di Gangi)

1885, busta 85, cat. 20, fasc. 107 (Termini. Associazione di malfattori)
1885, busta 85, cat. 20, fasc. 127 (Lettera anonima)
1885, busta 85, cat. 20, fasc. 133 (Giuseppe Valenza)
1885, busta 85, cat. 20, without fascicolo (Letter of the delegato di P.S. of Partinico to the Questor of Palermo, 30 May 1885, and letter from Giuseppe Reginella to the Questor of Palermo, 19 May 1885)
1887, busta 100, cat. 20, fasc. 25 (Antonino Li Destri)
1887, busta 100, cat. 20, fasc. 109 (Fratelli Mannino, gabellotti)
1887, busta 100, cat. 20, fasc. 116 (Bagheria. Associazione di malfattori)
1888, busta 106, cat. 20, fasc. 16 (Salvatore Gambino, zum Amoroso-Prozess)
1893, busta 134, cat. 20, fasc. 127 (San Giuseppe Jato. Guardie campestri)

ASP, Sentenze Corte Assise Ordinaria:
1894, busta 137, cat. 16, fasc. 21a (Marco Palazzolo aus Balestrate)
Sentence of 15 May 1878, Miceli Paolo fu Pietro, 39, Miceli Baldassare fu Pietro, 33, di Monreale
Sentence of 15 May 1878, Marino Salvatore di Rosario, contadino di Monreale (so-called Stoppaglieri trial)

ASP, Tribunale Civile e Penale di Palermo:
Fascicoli dei procedimenti di Corte di Assise, Anno 1887, no. 47: Processo Cannizzo

Archivio di Stato di Trapani (AST)
Corrispondenza Polizia, 1849. Collocazione provvisoria (Letter of the Commandant of Castellammare del Golfo to the Prince of Satriano, 23 September 1849)

Index of Names

Subject Index

SICILY

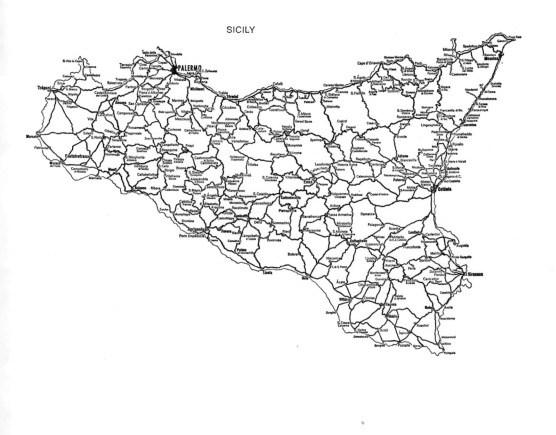